HARD IS THE JOU...

Caitlin Press Inc.
3375 Ponderosa Way
Qualicum Beach, BC V9K 2J8
www.caitlin-press.com

Text and cover design by Vici Johnstone
Front cover: Jung Ling, image 1797 and back cover funeral procession, image 4100 courtesy of the Revelstoke Museum and Archives
Edited by Catherine Edwards and Sarah Corsie
Printed in Canada

Caitlin Press Inc. acknowledges financial support from the Government of Canada and the Canada Council for the Arts, and the Province of British Columbia through the British Columbia Arts Council and the Book Publisher's Tax Credit.

Canada Council   Conseil des Arts   BRITISH COLUMBIA   Funded by the   Canada
for the Arts   du Canada   ARTS COUNCIL   Government
                                                              of Canada

Library and Archives Canada Cataloguing in Publication

Hard is the journey : stories of Chinese settlement in British Columbia's Kootenay / Lily Chow.
Names: Chow, Lily, 1931– author.
Identifiers: Canadiana 2021031690X | ISBN 9781773860749 (softcover)
Subjects: LCSH: Chinese—British Columbia—Kootenay Region—History. | LCSH: Immigrants—British Columbia—Kootenay Region—History. | LCSH: Racism— British Columbia—Kootenay Region—History. | LCSH: Kootenay Region (B.C.)— Ethnic relations. | LCSH: Kootenay Region (B.C.)—History.
Classification: LCC FC3850.C5 C554 2022 | DDC 971.1004/951—dc23

Hard Is the Journey

崎岖的旅途

Stories of Chinese Settlement
in British Columbia's Kootenay

Lily Chow

Caitlin Press 2022

To my children, Steve, Stephanie and Warren

Contents

Map

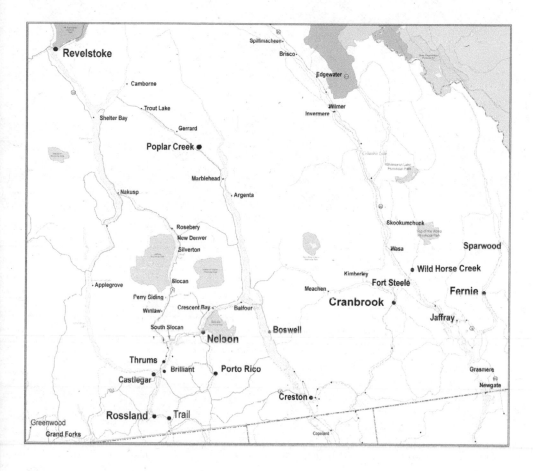

Introduction

In August 2001, I drove to the Kootenay with the intention of collecting information about Chinese immigration and settlements in the various towns and cities in the region. Nelson was the first city I visited. After finding and checking in to a motel, I drove downtown and parked my car in front of a Chinese restaurant. By then it was evening, so I went into the restaurant to have dinner. The restaurant was packed with diners, but a kind waiter found me a small table tucked in a corner of the dining room and waited on me. The service was good and the food delicious. After I finished my meal, I paid my bill and met the cashier at the till. The gentleman who received payment was Cameron Mah, an owner of the restaurant. He asked me if I was visiting friends or just touring the city. I told him I was doing neither and said that I was on my way to find out about the history of Chinese immigration in the Kootenay, that I had arrived in Nelson in the afternoon and planned to visit the museum and archives and the Chinese community in town. He smiled and gave me a thumbs-up. I could sense his interest and enthusiasm and ventured to ask him if he was a Chinese immigrant or a citizen of Canada. He said, "Both." Then he told me that he had immigrated to Canada in 1959 and became a citizen in the early 1960s.

Cameron Mah immigrated to Canada in 1959. He lived in Nelson, BC.

I asked him for the location of the museum and archives in town. Immediately, he offered to take me there the next day. I thanked him, and we made plans to go to the museum shortly after it opened at 10:00 a.m. After thanking him again for his assistance, I left the restaurant and returned to the motel for a good night's sleep.

The following day, Mah took me to Touchstones Nelson: Museum of Art and History and introduced me to Shawn Lamb, the curator and archivist at the museum. Lamb was delighted when she learned that I had come to Nelson to research the history of the Chinese in the Kootenay. Mah left us to return to the restaurant, and Lamb accompanied me to the archives. She allowed me to go through all the files that documented the lives of the many Chinese immigrants who had arrived in town, beginning with the earliest days of Nelson's history. I spent two days in the archives, recording the information and photocopying documents related to the Chinese immigrants who had lived in the area.

While I was in the archives, Lamb introduced me to Art Joyce, a journalist and historian who had written a series of articles about the Chinese immigrants to Nelson and the surrounding area. Joyce's stories had been published in the *Nelson Daily News*. Both Lamb and Joyce were very generous and knowledgeable. They shared with me many stories about the lives of Chinese immigrants in the area, and they showed me the location of the early Chinatown in Nelson on a map. Joyce generously gave me copies of his articles and permission to quote them in my writing. Lamb provided me with a record of the deceased Chinese individuals buried in the Nelson Memorial Park cemetery and also introduced me to Henry and Audrey Stevenson. This couple had volunteered to survey the cemetery for the British Columbia Genealogical Society, which needed the information for a book and CD it was compiling. The Stevensons took me to visit the section of the cemetery where the Chinese immigrants were buried.

When I returned to the museum and archives, Lamb suggested that I interview Cameron Mah, Lawrence Mar, and the chair of the Chee Kung Tong—also known as the Chinese Freemasons Society after this English name was adopted in 1921—in town. Mah was a pillar of the Chinese community; Mar had been president of the local chapter of the Guomindang (中国国民党), also known as the Chinese Nationalist League, and had been the chair of the Chinese Youth Association in 1955. After I had gathered the necessary information on the history of Chinese immigrants in the archives, I interviewed Mah and Mar, as well as the chair of the Nelson chapter of the Chinese Freemasons Society, who asked me not to state his name but allowed me to include the history of the organization in my writing. I thanked him and have honoured his request.

Before I left Nelson, Mah told me that he had a brother, Ronald Mah, who lived in Rossland, and suggested that I contact him, because he knew the history of the Chinese market gardeners who had lived there years ago. Mah said he would phone his brother and inform him that I would be visiting Rossland in the immediate future. This trip to Nelson was truly rewarding.

On my way to Rossland, I stopped in Trail, where I stayed in a youth hostel.

I assumed there was no Chinatown in this industrial town, because there were only a couple of Chinese restaurants, one Chinese laundry shop, and a grocery store operated by Chinese people. It never occurred to me to find out whether there was a museum in the city. But I knew there was a museum and archives in Rossland, so I travelled between Trail and Rossland daily.

In Rossland, I met and interviewed Ronald Mah, who informed me that "in the early days Rossland had about three hundred to five hundred Chinese people residing or in transit to this area. Most of the early Chinese were engaged in vegetable gardening, the laundry business and the grocery businesses. Some VIPs in Rossland employed Chinese [individuals] as cooks and servants or houseboys in their homes."[1] He took me to the site where the Chinese gardens had been located and told me a sad story about two Chinese gardeners. Their story—told in the chapter on Rossland—is significant, since it illustrates the trials and challenges the two Chinese gardeners faced. I also had an opportunity to meet and interview Lindsay Wong, a councillor in Rossland.

I then visited the Rossland Museum & Discovery Centre and met Joyce Austin, the curator and manager, who shared with me the *West Kootenay Chinese Heritage Society, Summary Report, 1995* and the *Historical Guide Map and Story of the City of Rossland, British Columbia*; the latter publication was compiled by the Rossland Historical Museum & Archives Association. After I returned home to Prince George, Joyce Austin sent me a few images of the gardens in Rossland. Unfortunately, the images were dark and unclear, so they could not be used to illustrate the Rossland chapter.

When I had completed my research in the museum and archives in Rossland, I ventured to Cranbrook where I stayed in the College of the Rockies residence. (In the summer, classes were not held, so visitors could rent a room and stay in the student dormitories.) While I was in town, I visited the Tamarack Centre shopping mall where I met the Rotarian Jim Chiu and his wife, Helen, who owned and operated a drug store in the mall. They were very friendly and invited me to dinner in their home. Unfortunately, Jim Chiu suffered from pancreatic cancer and he passed away in 2018. His friends and fellow Rotarians in Montana, Idaho and Washington State miss him, as do his other friends and associates in the Kootenay. I remain grateful to Jim's wife, Helen, for writing to me every now and then.

In Cranbrook, I visited and interviewed a few owners of Chinese restaurants, including a couple of Chinese immigrants who were scientists. These two scientists—Cai Yi Hai and Ma Zhong Lam—left Guangdong during the Cultural Revolution (a movement in China from 1966 to 1976). From them, I learned about Chu Ban Quan, a Chinese immigrant who arrived in BC in 1882 and migrated to the Kootenay a few years later. He established the Ban Quan Mining Company in the Wild Horse Creek district, and after accumulating wealth from mining, built the Tamarack Centre shopping mall in Cranbrook and established his business in the mall. I didn't realize that Chu had passed away, and my ignorance led me to knock at the door of a house marked "The Ban Quan Home." No one answered the door. Later, I learned from the vital statistics records in the Royal British Columbia Museum and Archives that Chu had passed away in 1947.

I continued my search for historical information and arrived at the Fort Steele Heritage Town, where I met Derryll White, the curator of the museum and archives. White showed me a printed image of a photograph of a Chinese altar in Fisherville, an early mining town near Fort Steele that no longer exists. While I was there, employees of the historic park were heading out to install signposts at the site on Wild Horse Creek that had once been a Chinatown. I left my car at the parking lot of the heritage town, hopped on the truck with the workers and visited the site of long-gone Fisherville on the bench above Wild Horse Creek. The trip gave me the opportunity to take a few photographs at the Chinatown site.

In the Wild Horse Creek district, I had the good fortune of meeting Ingrid Lum and Peter Ah Lum, a well-known miner and entrepreneur in the area. After visiting the Wild Horse area, I returned to the College of the Rockies residence in Cranbrook to rest for a day, eating, sleeping and doing nothing, to replenish my energy. I turned on the tape recorder and listened to music!

The following day I drove to Revelstoke, where I met Cathy English, manager and curator of the Revelstoke Museum & Archives. English allowed me to go through all the files in the archives that contained the history of the Chinese immigrants to the city. As well, she accompanied me to the cemetery where the deceased Chinese were buried. On the tombstones I noted the names of the Chinese villages in Guangdong Province from which the immigrants had come. While I was in the archives, Margaret McMahon, a historian, came in and gave me her book, *Pioneers of Revelstoke, British Columbia*, which included the history of the well-known Wong Kwong family. I am very thankful for her generosity.

English and I became good friends, remaining in contact for years. She helped me to connect with two descendants of the Wong Kwong family. In addition, she shared with me volumes of the *Revelstoke Review* that contained information about Chinese-Canadian history in the Kootenay.

Having completed my research in Revelstoke, I returned home to Prince George. I was exhausted and stressed physically and mentally. While I was carrying out research and interviews, I kept my findings on a couple of floppy disks, hoping that one fine day I would spend time organizing my findings and listening to and transcribing the interviews. At that time, I had no zeal or desire to begin writing. I just wrote notes and numbered some of the images related to the Chinese Canadians and immigrants who had lived and spent their lives in the Kootenay region. Procrastination set in, and I totally forgot about the findings in my files!

At the annual general meeting of the British Columbia Historical Federation held in June 2019, I received the very sad news that Cameron Mah had passed away. This alarming news motivated me to review my research on the Kootenay; it had become necessary to share my findings, especially the immigration history of Mah, with my children and readers. His deeds and contributions, strength and determination, and achievements and successes reflected the endeavours and convictions of the Chinese immigrants who called this land home.

To my dismay, I could not download the WordPerfect files from the floppy disks to my desktop computer. I cried out for help. Thank goodness my son Steven and good friend Susanna Ng were able to retrieve the information from the floppy disks and convert the files from WordPerfect to Word. Meanwhile, Susanna sent me a link to a database of old BC newspapers that enabled me to continue my research online. At the same time, Greg Nesteroff, another kind friend in Nelson, sent me information, including maps and images, to illustrate my writing. I am truly indebted to these two good friends and associates. Their assistance gave me the courage to contact Vici Johnstone, publisher of Caitlin Press, and to sign a contract for publishing this book.

While I was searching or looking at various online resources, I found two works about Chinese-Canadian history in Rossland: "The Chinese and Chinatown of Rossland: Fragments from Their Early History," a paper by Professor Ronald A. Shearer of the University of British Columbia; and "Placed on the Margins: The Idea of Chinatown in Rossland, British Columbia, 1890–1902," an article by Professor Michael Ripmeester of Brock University in Ontario. I asked Professor Shearer for permission to quote his writing, and he graciously gave me his consent. I particularly love Professor Ripmeester's article because it denounces racism.

Indeed, prejudice and discrimination against Chinese immigrants—as well as other immigrant groups and Indigenous peoples—is a part of Canadian history. In the case of the Chinese, several pieces of legislation demonstrate the resentment that the mainstream society felt for the Chinese newcomers. In 1885, once the Canadian Pacific Railway was complete and the Chinese labourers were no longer considered essential, the Chinese Immigration Act was passed, which imposed a Head Tax on new Chinese immigrants to Canada. The Head Tax was fifty dollars at first but was later raised to one hundred dollars and then again to five hundred dollars. In 1923, a second piece of discriminatory legislation was passed, which was known as the Chinese Exclusion Act. This act prohibited Chinese immigration, with just a few exceptions. It was not repealed until 1947. The province of British Columbia also enacted several pieces of discriminatory legislation, including an 1890s law prohibiting Chinese miners from working underground in the province's mines; in 1923, a law was passed forbidding Chinese employers, such as restaurant owners, from hiring white women—apparently due to a fear that white women and Chinese men might marry! Also demonstrating the discrimination and racism that Chinese immigrants faced was the derogatory language used when referring to them— terms such as "Celestials" and "chinks" appear often in the historical newspapers that provide information about these early immigrants to the Kootenay.

Each chapter in this book begins with an acknowledgement of the Indigenous peoples in the area of the Kootenay that the chapter describes. Then I briefly describe the locations of the major towns and cities in the region, followed by the size of the historical general population and the numbers of Chinese Canadians and immigrants that lived in the Chinese settlements commonly known as Chinatowns. I made an effort to find out the occupations of the early Chinese immigrants, how they lived in Canada, and how they supported their families who remained behind in Guangdong Province, China. In my search, I learned that Chinese immigrants were employed as houseboys, servants and cooks in almost every town and city in the Kootenay. I also researched the lives of Chinese families in Canada who were reunited after the repeal of the Chinese Exclusion Act in 1947.

In Rossland, there was a mysterious murder case. In 1900, Ernest Chenoweth, an eight-year-old boy, shot Mah Lin, a Chinese servant and cook, with a rifle. The Chinese Benevolent Association hired a detective to investigate the murder case. Chenoweth was arrested and tried. The details of the trial and the verdict in this case are included in the Rossland chapter.

The Chee Kung Tong (Chinese Freemasons Society) was found in cities throughout the Kootenay. This organization provided accommodations and found work for its members and other Chinese immigrants who arrived in town and needed employment. The chair and board members of this society tried to preserve Chinese culture and heritage. They held celebrations for their members and other Chinese immigrants during Spring Festival and honoured Chinese festival days according to the traditional Chinese lunar calendar. These included Qing Ming Jie, or Tomb-Sweeping Day, which occurs around Easter; Duan

Wu Jie, the Dragon Boat Festival, which takes place on the fifth day of the fifth moon; Yu Lan Jie, which takes place on the fifteenth day of the seventh moon; Zhongqiu Jie, or the Mid-Autumn Moon Festival, which takes place on the fifteenth day of the eighth moon; and Zhong Yang Jie, which takes place on the ninth day of the ninth moon in the Chinese calendar, and is another day on which the deceased Chinese are honoured in cemeteries.

The Guomindang, or as it was called in English, the Chinese Nationalist League, was a political organization affiliated with the Republic of China (currently located in Taiwan) that had a presence in Cranbrook, Nelson and Revelstoke. The late Wong Kwong of Revelstoke was the president of the Guomindang party there. Interestingly, the Chinese Empire Reform Association was found in Nelson and Rossland. This organization was established in mainland China when Emperor Guangxu was on the throne, but this movement lasted only one hundred days. The powerful Empress Dowager Cixi sent Guangxu to Yingtai, an island within the premises of the imperial palace in Beijing, where he was kept under house arrest. Both Guangxu and Cixi passed away in November 1909.

In 1911, under the leadership of Dr. Sun Yat-sen, the Chinese revolution succeeded in overthrowing the Qing regime and established the Republic of China. The governing party was the Guomindang. Many Chinese immigrants to BC and other Canadian provinces established Guomindang branches to support the Republic of China. But in 1927, the Guomindang and the Chinese Communist Party, led by Mao Zedong, came into conflict with each other and a Chinese civil war broke out. When the Japanese invaded China in 1937, the two parties reconciled and united to resist the Japanese invasion. After World War II, Chiang Kai-shek, called "the Generalissimo," initiated attacks against the communists. In 1949, the Chinese Communist Party defeated the Guomindang, and the latter relocated and formed a government in Taiwan. Following this, the Chinese Communist Party established the People's Republic of China on the mainland.

In 1947, when the infamous Chinese Exclusion Act was repealed in Canada, the country's Chinese immigrants could finally send for family members still in China to join them in Canada. After the arrival of their families, the Chinese men moved out of the boarding houses they had occupied, and lived with their families in apartments or houses. Gradually, many of the Chinese organizations dissolved—with the exception of the Chee Kung Tong—because they were no longer needed to house and take care of the original immigrants. As time went by, nearly all of the Chee Kung Tong's buildings in the Kootenay either burned down or were sold. In Nelson, the board members decided to sell their building because most of the members moved to the Lower Mainland after their families arrived, and the aging caretaker was no longer capable of taking care of the building. The organization sold the building, and used the funds realized from the sale to observe Qing Ming and celebrate Chinese New Year each year.

My research process in various towns and cities gave me the opportunity to meet curators and archivists who were very knowledgeable about their local history. They helped me find records and documentation related to Chinese immigration and settlements in their localities. Almost all of them allowed me to copy and print out information, and the fees were minimal. The research process took place over many years and some of the original source documents have been lost and, in some cases, individuals have passed away; still, every effort has been made to ensure the accuracy of the book. Although the process of research and writing required time and energy, nothing could be more rewarding than meeting historians and scholars and learning from them about the history of the Chinese in the Kootenay.

The Wild Horse Creek Gold Rush: Fisherville

The Wild Horse River—which was known as Wild Horse Creek at the time of the nineteenth-century gold rush—is a tributary of the Kootenay River in southeastern British Columbia. This is part of the traditional territory of the Ktunaxa/Kinbasket peoples. (The Kinbasket are a people who moved into Ktunaxa territory and were absorbed by the Ktunaxa.) The Ktunaxa have lived in this river valley, as well as in the adjacent watersheds of the Columbia and Kootenay Rivers and the area around the Arrow Lakes, for more than ten thousand years. Seven Ktunaxa First Nations live in this area today, which covers approximately seventy thousand square kilometres within the Kootenay region. Traditionally, the Ktunaxa territory also included part of Alberta adjacent to the Kootenay, as well as parts of Montana, Washington and Idaho in the United States. In the past, the Ktunaxa people followed a seasonal round within their territory, sourcing plant and animal foods when and where these were most readily available. The Ktunaxa language is unique, unrelated to any other language. The Ktunaxa people are today combining their traditional knowledge with modern technology to ensure that their language survives.[2]

Wild Horse Creek and its tributaries in the neighbourhood of Fort Steele in the East Kootenay, where the historical Fort Steele Heritage Town is located, were rich in deposits of gold, silver, copper, lead and zinc. Gold was first discovered in the Wild Horse Creek area in 1857.[3] Jack Fisher, the leader of a group of miners, struck the first claim on a small tributary of Wild Horse Creek in 1863, and a gold rush to the area ensued. This tributary became known as Fisher Creek, and the incoming miners established

Today, visitors can find this small sign indicating the original location of the once prosperous site of Fisherville, named after Jack Fisher, the leader of the group of miners who discovered gold in the small tributary of Wild Horse Creek. Lily Chow photo, 2001

The main street of Fort Steele in the 1920s. In 1961, Fort Steele was declared a Historic Park and the well-preserved townsite is now a popular tourist destination.
Image C-00778 courtesy of the Royal BC Museum and Archives

Fisherville, the first town in the East Kootenay, on its banks. Today this town no longer exists, but its site is located approximately 5.5 kilometres northeast of Fort Steele.

Fort Steele Heritage Town is located north of the Crowsnest Highway along Highways 93 and 95, approximately seventeen kilometres northeast of Cranbrook. Tourists and visitors from different parts of British Columbia and Alberta can drive to this historic town. Those who arrive in Cranbrook by plane or bus can rent a car or hire a taxi to visit this renowned heritage site.

A popular tourist attraction, Fort Steele Heritage Town is a well-preserved historical town with many buildings related to the history of the Kootenay. The town includes an excellent museum and archives. The artifacts and images displayed in the museum provide glimpses of the Kootenay's colourful past, particularly during the days of the Wild Horse Creek gold rush. Interpreters at the museum offer guided tours to visitors who are interested in learning about the history and significance of Wild Horse Creek. The town's attractions include lively musical comedy shows at the Wild Horse Theatre, steam train rides to a scenic viewpoint, horse-drawn wagon tours of the town, and blacksmith and tinsmith demonstrations of the production of horseshoes and other metal hardware. The shows feature actors playing the roles of old-time sheriffs, merchants, prospectors, miners and other fortune-seekers to bring the town's history to life. Other events include sheep herding and shearing and ice cream making, and Clydesdale horses are shown driving pioneer farm machinery.

The Discovery of Gold

In 1863, Finlay, an Indigenous man with some European ancestry, and some of his friends left Montana and travelled to the Kootenay region in search of gold. The men arrived at a creek where they discovered and took out about a thousand dollars' worth of gold. They named the creek Finlay Creek (today it is spelled Findlay Creek). They sold their gold to Linkletter, a clerk at the Hudson's Bay Company (HBC) at Tobacco Plains, a place in the traditional territory of the Ktunaxa people where they grew a kind of tobacco—hence the area's name. After selling their gold, Finlay and his companions spent the winter in Frenchtown, a settlement located at the confluence of French Creek and the Goldstream River in the Columbia River valley.

Once the HBC learned that gold had been found in the creek, the news quickly spread. Two prospectors, H.L. Amme and Chas. Elwood of the Gold Hill Mine, explored Boulder Creek, located near Wild Horse Creek. The two prospectors found a vein of gold-bearing quartz estimated at over one hundred tons (ninety tonnes). This mining company constructed a ledge about two hundred feet (sixty metres) wide that extended up the mountain in a series of steps that ran the entire length of its mining claim.[4]

Early in March 1864, Finlay and his companions returned to Finlay Creek and struck rich diggings again. Their strikes triggered a stampede of gold seekers to Wild Horse Creek. During the ensuing gold rush, the creek yielded close to forty-eight tons (forty-four tonnes) of gold.[5]

A party consisting of Pat Cuddy, Curly Carrol, James Smith, Lem Harris and Bob Dore entered the Wild Horse district. Cuddy, Carrol and Smith travelled to Finlay Creek, while Harris and Dore went up to Wild Horse Creek.[6]

In one day, Dore took out as much as $7,000 worth of gold from his claims, which he called the "Dore." He obtained an average of $3,500 in gold each day in the area surrounding Wild Horse Creek. In three years, he mined $521,750 worth of gold from the Dore.[7] He constructed ditches with a team of Chinese labourers to deliver water for his mining operations. The largest of these ditches was the Victoria Ditch, an almost five-kilometre ditch running from Victoria Creek in the northeast to Wild Horse Creek.[8] Other miners could use the water, but they had to pay Dore up to fourteen dollars a week for it.[9] At the beginning of the frosty season in the fall, the miners who had gone to Finlay Creek found their way to Wild Horse Creek to obtain better feed for their horses.[10]

When prospectors and miners learned about Bob Dore's success in finding gold, they converged on Wild Horse Creek to stake claims at various sites. "The rush to the diggings was a wild one," reported the *East Kootenay Miner*.[11] The gold was coarse and easy to recover with pans, small sluices and rockers.

Nuggets found at these sites were valued at anywhere from $2.50 to $78.00.[12] The prospectors' initial claims were quickly worked out, and they then staked new claims along the banks of Wild Horse Creek for a distance of three to five kilometres. The claims on the banks usually paid better than those in the creek. Some miners took out as many as forty or fifty ounces of gold a day—during the gold rush, gold was measured in troy ounces, which are about 10 per cent heavier than standard ounces. Many miners who arrived there in 1864 were well rewarded, commented the *Cariboo Sentinel*.[13] By the end of the year, approximately five thousand miners—mostly Americans, some Canadians, and a few other nationalities, including Chinese miners—had arrived in the Wild Horse Creek district, determined to make their fortunes.

The Dewdney Trail

The colonial authorities in New Westminster were concerned that the profits being made in the goldfields of BC's Interior were being diverted to Americans. They decided that a route contained wholly within British Columbia's territory would reduce or prevent this. The contract to construct the route was won by

Edgar Dewdney. He began construction in 1860, in partnership with Walter Moberly, and built a pack trail that extended from Hope, BC, to the Similkameen Valley mining camps. In 1865, after gold strikes were made in the Kootenay, Dewdney extended the trail as far as Wild Horse Creek, using a work force made up of Chinese labourers and First Nations packers. The extension of the trail to Wild Horse Creek was quickly completed, at a cost of $74,000. This trail became known as the Dewdney Trail and formed the principal east-west route across British Columbia for a number of years.[14]

Originally built as a pack trail, the Dewdney Trail, was completed in 1865, and was the first all-Canadian route and the principal east-west route across southern British Columbia. Much of the labour in building the trail was performed by Chinese and First Nations workers. Image A-03532 courtesy of the Royal BC Museum and Archives

Chinese Miners

About 250 Chinese miners arrived in the Wild Horse Creek district, where they staked and worked on claims. These Chinese miners were very meticulous in their mining. They swept the dirt from rocks and

Construction of the Dewdney Trail. Image C-08076 courtesy of the Royal BC Museum and Archives

boulders with a broom into a pan and washed the dirt to obtain tiny particles of gold and gold flakes that often gave them very good returns. However, many Chinese miners could only secure the right to work on ground previously exhausted by white miners. White miners seldom honoured Chinese claims, and they often "jumped" the Chinese claims—occupying them for themselves.[13] Those Chinese miners who could not stake a claim would work for other miners, including both Chinese and white mining companies.

After the Dewdney Trail—a 1.2-metre-wide mule trail at its eastern end—was completed, the Chinese labourers who had worked on the trail remained in the Wild Horse district where they engaged in gold mining or vegetable farming. The Chinese miners worked diligently on mining sites that white miners had abandoned. White miners often did not have the patience to sift through gold-bearing sediments looking for gold flakes and instead moved on to richer claims once the easy gold had been removed. By 1865, Chinese miners and labourers were living in all areas of the Wild Horse district. They had become dominant among the miners and had also established businesses that supported the miners; storekeepers, butchers, and bakers were among these businesses.[16]

On July 22, 1865, the *Cariboo Sentinel* reported that the creek and low benches along Wild Horse Creek paid well; three companies were able to mine as many as 100 ounces a day.[17] On June 1, 1866, the *Walla Walla Statesman* reported that two Chinese miners, See Yung and Doo Tne, had travelled to Wild Horse Creek. See and Doo evidently delivered a positive report on their diggings, since groups of Chinese miners then left Walla Walla, Washington, for the Wild Horse district.[18] In July 1866, Gold Commissioner Peter O'Reilly

Once white miners had gathered their fortunes in gold, they left their Fisherville mining claims to the Chinese, and by 1874, Chinese miners, living in cabins in the established Chinatown, outnumbered the white settlers in the area. Image D-06562 courtesy of the Royal BC Museum and Archives

visited the mining camp to settle disputes between the Chinese and white residents, because "there [was] a good deal of litigation arising from attempts to take advantage of the Chinese.... Parties coming from Kootenay informed us that Chinese had taken almost entire possession of that mining camp."[19]

That same year, 1866, the Nip and Tuck Hydraulic Company of Vancouver arrived in the area to mine its claims at Fisher Creek, a tributary of Wild Horse Creek. Next to this Vancouver company was a Chinese company consisting of four men. The Invicta Gold Mining Company of London, England, also arrived at Wild Horse Creek that year. In the following years, many other European and Chinese companies staked claims and mined in the Wild Horse district. Later arrivals included the International Placer Company, the Ban Quan Company, the Tit and Tat Company and several other smaller companies. All these companies employed hydraulic monitors—nozzles that used jets of water under pressure in the mining process.

Challenges in the Gold Rush Period

All supplies of provisions and goods to the goldfields had to be packed in on horses over six hundred kilometres from Walla Walla, and packers had to pay duty in addition to the fee of $1.50 for each animal on every trip they made.[20] For instance, in the spring of 1865, one pack train that brought supplies and goods to Fisherville had to pay $5,000 in duty to the BC government! Great dissatisfaction was expressed, and many American miners left the goldfields and returned south to the United States because they did not want to pay the costly tariffs to the BC government. The departure of American miners was alarming to O'Reilly, the BC gold commissioner, who noted that "the people at Kootenay... 'skedaddled' to the American mines, so that that [sic] there was danger of sufficient men not being left to work the claims on Wild Horse creek."[21]

In truth, it is impossible to tell how much gold was mined at Wild Horse Creek and its tributaries. The government had levied a tax of fifty cents an ounce on the gold, and records show that nine million dollars of the gold taken out of Wild Horse Creek was taxed. However, this monumental sum did not include the large amount of gold that had been smuggled across the boundary line to the United States. It has been estimated that no less than twelve million dollars in gold was taken out from the Wild Horse district. During just two years—1864 and 1865—some seventy quartz locations were located. Many large and rich veins carried gold, silver and copper. But only rough trails connected the gold mines to the ore processers. Therefore, prospectors and miners, merchants, and freighters—the individuals who transported goods and provisions to the goldfields—all urged the government to improve trails and construct roads to the Wild Horse district so that they could reach the mining sites faster and more safely. With proper facilities for transportation and a means to treat ore in Fort Steele, the district would "take a leading place among the best mining camps on the continent," said a local newspaper, the *Fort Steele Prospector*, in 1895.[22]

There were contradictory accounts about the wealth in the Wild Horse area. In 1864, many miners went south or to the Cariboo for the winter, but no miner returned to the area to sell out his claim when the mining season began in spring.[23] The "cream of the crop" had already been taken out, according to a packer and reliable correspondent of the *Cariboo Sentinel* identified only as H.W.S.[24] Writing from Lewiston, Idaho, this man reported in 1865 that he had just spent four weeks in Fisherville and noticed that "a distance of about two miles [three kilometres] comprises the whole of the paying mining district" along Wild Horse Creek. The correspondent thought it would be able to support about six hundred miners, "but many of the claims within those two miles [three kilometres] will not pay over wages." He added that "the reputation of the extent and richness of the Kootenay diggings has been greatly overrated."

The correspondent noticed that "many hard-working men were leaving [the Wild Horse district] every day, going to new excitements... and swearing never to prospect any where [sic] but on the American side." Furthermore, he told the *Cariboo Sentinel*, in summer it would be "a most disagreeable trip" to take. The mosquitoes were desperate, and he had been partially blinded for about two days due to the attacks of the insects. He stated that men were fortunate if they could go through "without losing a portion of their ears"![25]

Another correspondent from Victoria, BC, known as Mr. Weil reported that the inundation of the Kootenay River and fallen timber had caused the trail from Fort Shepherd to the goldfields to become quite impassable for animals, so no pack train from the Fraser region could possibly arrive in the Wild Horse district before fall. On his return trip from Wild Horse Creek to Victoria, he had no choice but to go around by Spokane and Colville, which added another three hundred miles (almost five hundred kilometres) to his journey. On his return to the Wild Horse district, he noticed that about seven or eight hundred men were on Wild Horse Creek, including about three hundred Chinese miners, who owned about two-thirds of all claims. Weil thought the white men's claims would be mostly worked out by fall.[26]

Transporting goods and supplies on rivers, streams and creeks was challenging. There were five gravel bars in the Kootenay River that obstructed navigation by steamboats. It was not easy for the vessels to sail through the river, especially when the water level was low. Consequently, a few merchants and suppliers charged enormous prices for the goods and provisions they brought to the mining camp at Fisherville.

After a long winter, the prospectors and miners in the Wild Horse district were seriously low on provisions and faced with the high cost of food items. An early settler and miner in the area, David Griffith, reported that the miners "had to pay good prices for what we got. Coffee was seventy-five cents per pound, so was beans, flour and everything of the kind. It was just a flat price, seventy-five cents a pound, no matter what the cost was at Walla Walla," the source of the supplies. By the spring of 1865, flour was sold for $1.25 a pound, and tobacco was $15 a pound. Some merchants would soak the tobacco in the creek overnight so that it would weigh more when they sold it to the miners and other customers.[27] Thus, the gold in the ground was not the only source of wealth in the Wild Horse district; supplying provisions brought good fortune to merchants and suppliers of goods.

Like the miners, the merchants and suppliers also had to pay duty to the BC government. It was reported by the tax collectors that the income derived from taxation during the year 1864 was $80,000.[28] Taxation on goods and food supplies contributed to price inflation for local miners and other residents.

Incidents at Fisherville

By the summer of 1864, a substantial mining town, Fisherville, had become established in the Wild Creek district. The town consisted of dance halls, four saloons, a number of gambling houses and brothels, six general stores, and some restaurants, which sold liquor, a brewery, a post office, a Hudson's Bay Company office, and about fifty residential buildings. According to early arrival David Griffith, "There was no court, no police, nothing but the men themselves to preserve order."[29]

In the early days of the Wild Creek gold rush, huge nuggets were found, with the biggest tipping the scale at thirty-six ounces. At its peak, miners working in and around Wild Horse Creek were earning about twenty to fifty dollars a day each. After one resident in Fisherville found a nugget the size of his fist under his house, the whole town was demolished, so the miners could dig underneath their properties for gold. They then moved the townsite higher up the bank of the creek.[30] Thus, the original town of Fisherville disappeared as quickly as it had appeared!

On the night of August 6, 1864, 27-year-old Thomas Walker was shot outside Charlie Fortier's Café in Fisherville. The café was filled with miners and prospectors at the time, relaxing with liquor and socializing with each other.

A conversation between Walker and William Burmeister, an American known as "Yeast Powder Bill," erupted into an argument! In a fury, Walker, a hot-tempered Irishman, pulled out his gun, pointed it at Burmeister, and fired. The shot missed anything vital, but Walker had managed to shoot off Burmeister's right thumb. In agony, Burmeister returned fire, and managed to shoot Walker through the heart, killing him instantly.

The other prospectors and miners in the café immediately took sides in the altercation, Walker's friends on one side and Burmeister's on the other. A shoot-out ensued between the two parties. Five men were seriously wounded in the gunfire, but Walker's was the only death. His friends buried Walker in Fisherville.[31]

One of the posters at the Fisherville historic site provided by the Fort Steele Heritage Town describes the robbery of a man known as Old Cuddy.

> One of the most popular ways to pass the time in the gold camps was gambling. One such gambler was an Irishman by the name of Old Cuddy. He ran a small store and held shares in a large placer mining company. Cuddy was not much of a gambler and owed money to many Fisherville residents, often refusing to pay his debts. However, as gambling was officially illegal, Cuddy's card-playing compatriots could hardly go to the authorities to remedy the situation.
>
> Cuddy had managed to acquire 1,000 ounces of gold dust, a small fortune which he planned to take with him when he left

Kootenay. He kept the gold in his store under the watchful eye of a trusty guard.

Late one evening, two men approached Cuddy's store and fired their revolvers. They let out a cry that someone had shot Old Cuddy. The guard ran from the store to a nearby saloon to save his friend, only to find Cuddy, playing poker, quite alive and well. When [the guard] ran back to the store, he found the two men were gone and Cuddy's gold along with them.

There were rumours that the whole episode had been a scheme concocted by Cuddy to get his gold past the Gold Commissioner and the 50 cent per ounce export duty. The robbery did prove genuine, but there was little sympathy in the camp for Old Cuddy because of his infamous reputation for reneging on his debts.[32]

These two episodes illustrate the wild and rowdy situations that could occur in a frontier settlement and the different kinds of people who resided there during the Wild Horse gold rush.

The Big Bend Gold Rush

In 1865, gold was found in the Big Bend of the Columbia River. Many prospectors and miners ventured there to find their fortune. The *Cariboo Sentinel* reported that while there was no big strike on the Big Bend of the Columbia River, the twelve to fifteen companies at work there were satisfied finding two to five ounces of gold per miner per day. The newspaper's report continued "On Rich Bar, at the Bend of the Columbia, a large number of Chinamen were at work, and reported to be making from three to five dollars to the hand per day. A great number of celestials [*sic*] were met on the way to the Columbia, where many made a good deal of money last year."[33]

The gold rush in the Big Bend was very short-lived. When the gold was depleted, the prospectors, miners, merchants and other entrepreneurs left their sites. Thus, the gold rush on the Columbia River became only a short page in the exciting history of the Kootenay.

Galbraith's Ferry and Fort Steele

In 1864 or 1865 (sources vary on the date), John Thompson Galbraith arrived in the Wild Horse district and established a ferry across the Kootenay River to transport miners to Wild Horse Creek; "this ferry was the only practical way to cross the river for the many miners making their way to the goldfields of Wild Horse Creek via the Dewdney Trail."[34] The crossing became known as Galbraith's

Ferry and a small community grew up there. The North-West Mounted Police arrived at the crossing in 1887. Colonel Sam Steele was in command of the troop and remained in the settlement for about a year. While there, he built an extensive barracks. The police force had been sent to investigate a conflict between members of the Ktunaxa Nation and a white settler. After investigating the incident, Steele judged that the Ktunaxa were innocent of any wrong-doing. In honour of the legendary Sam Steele, Galbraith's Ferry was re-named Fort Steele in 1888.[35]

The Arrival of Mining Companies

Although the first miners in the Wild Horse Creek area were individuals who staked claims, they were quickly followed by mining companies. For example, in the summer of 1866, the Invicta Gold Mining Company of London, England, and the Nip and Tuck Hydraulic Company of Vancouver, BC, arrived in the Wild Horse district and began hydraulic mining operations. Chinese companies such as the Hang Company and the Quong Yung Tong Company, as well as individual miners, also came to the area over the following decades.[36]

The Invicta Mining Company acquired water privileges between Boulder and Brewery Creeks. Chu Ban Quan, a well-known citizen of the Kootenay, later became the owner-operator of this company's Wild Horse mining operation. Its equipment consisted of four large hydraulic monitors, an electric light plant, and other apparatus. The company's mining property covered a mile and a quarter (1.6 kilometres) of hill diggings on the northwest and southeast side of Wild Horse Creek. The gold obtained from these properties was coarse, and nuggets worth eight and ten dollars were common. The largest piece taken out weighed eight and a half ounces. The Invicta mining syndicate in London announced that $75,000 would be set aside for improvements to the mining property in the upcoming season. In later years, the upper portion of the property was leased to a company of Chinese miners who were each able to obtain four or five dollars' worth of gold daily.[37]

The same year, 1866, the Nip and Tuck Hydraulic Company purchased a mining property from a Vancouver mining syndicate for a sum of two thousand dollars, reported the *Fort Steele Prospector*.[38] This company leased the property to Chinese miners who collectively paid a yearly rental of fifteen hundred dollars to this company. These Chinese miners did extensive work on the property before the commencement of the next mining season. They were reported to be doing well after they started mining.

In 1867, David Griffith, the owner of the Tit and Tat Company, had four claims in the Wild Horse Creek area. His mining property was located in an area of gold-bearing quartz, which had been evaluated to be worth $600,000.

Waterwheel at Wild Horse Creek. Here, a number of mining procedures were used, from simple panning to wing dams built of stone and hydraulic mining with heavy steel pipes. Image D-06806 courtesy of the Royal BC Museum and Archives

Different Methods of Gold Mining

Jack Lee panning for gold. Jack was one of the first Chinese miners to arrive at Wild Horse Creek, where he grew to be known as a cheerful character until his death in Cranbrook in May 1929. Image C-00752 courtesy of the Royal BC Museum and Archives

Because the greatest amount of gold was located along a stretch of about six kilometres between Boulder Creek and Brewery Creek in the Wild Horse district, different kinds of mining operations were used in those placer deposits. Mining operations included using a pan, a rocker, hydraulic monitors, building a wing dam on streams and creeks, and sinking shafts into the mining properties as well as constructing sluices and flumes in the mining claims.

Many individual Chinese miners used a pan to scoop up a small amount of gravel, which would be carefully washed with water in a rotating fashion so that gold flakes would not be spilled away. Miners had to hold the pan at an angle with both hands to remove surplus gravel, leaving sand, gold nuggets and flakes at the bottom of the pan. Gold nuggets could be simply picked up. In order to obtain the gold flakes, the procedure of rotating the pan with water had to be repeated until most of the sand was removed before the miner could gather the gold flakes. It was quite a tedious operation!

Quite a few Chinese miners at Wild Horse Creek used a rocker to mine gold. A rocker consists of two wooden boxes, the larger one with an open end and no top cover. On the surface of this box is a series of ridges. The open top of this box is fitted with a metal sieve. The smaller box, which has no top or bottom covers, is attached to the large

Jack Lee with a rocker. Royal BC Museum and Archives, C-00751

box and it has a handle. In the process of mining alluvial dirt, water is poured into the top box, and then the miner would take the handle to rock the top box like a cradle, and the sediments containing nuggets and gold flakes would be caught in the ridges of the bottom box. In order to obtain the gold flakes or tiny gold particles, the miners who used a rocker to mine gold, had to do panning after picking up coarse gold and removing rocks from the sediments.

Jack Lee was one of the first Chinese miners to arrive in the Wild Horse diggings and remained there until his death. He used pan, rocker and sluice boxes to mine for gold. Sometimes he found gold flakes and nuggets, other times he found no treasure—but he did not give up and continued mining. When he found gold pieces, he would keep them until such time that he felt his gold accumulation was worth trading to the merchants in Cranbrook. There he spent the money to purchase supplies and groceries, and to reward himself with a bottle of *lum*, a Chinese wine, before returning to his claim to find more gold.

On May 29, 1929, Jack Lee died in the Cranbrook hospital and was buried in the Cranbrook Cemetery. In his obituary, the *Cranbrook Courier* stated that Jack had remained cheerful during "both times of plenty and those of famine. His wants were few, and he never complained. Given a lot of rum, he would have exchanged it with no man. Such was the nature of the old Chinese man, who was brought into the hospital in Cranbrook at the end of February with a frozen foot. His death is deeply regretted by many who knew and liked the old fellow who was almost as much of a landmark of Wild Horse gulch as the mountains above his lonely cabin."[39]

A wing dam. Photo Lily Chow

Some Chinese miners constructed wing dams—stone structures that extended from the bank of a stream or creek where the flow of water was slower. A wing dam enabled miners to get down to the water and allowed them to see the gravel at the bottom of the creek within the enclosure of the stone structure and to pan there for gold. Some wing dams constructed by large mining companies in the Wild Horse district were huge and occupied almost their entire mining properties. Several Chinese mining companies constructed wing dams on the bed of Wild Horse Creek, and one Chinese company flumed the creek near the mouth of Brewery Creek at a cost of fifteen hundred dollars.[40]

At the mouth of Boulder Creek, a group of Chinese miners employed hydraulic mining. They used high-pressure jets of water to dislodge gold-bearing sediment from a slope and then directed the gold-bearing soil through sluice boxes. Gold nuggets and flakes, together with rocks and heavy sediment, would sink to the bottom of the sluice boxes. Afterwards the miners would stop the jets of water, pick up rocks from the sluice boxes and dig up the gold particles at the bottom of the sluice boxes. These Chinese miners were making good wages, according to the *Cranbrook Herald*.[41]

Hydraulic mining at Big Bend on the Columbia River in 1904. Though there was no long-lasting rush at Big Bend, gold was consistently found here, and many Chinese miners were guaranteed three to five dollars' worth of gold a day. Image A-03815 courtesy of the Royal BC Museum and Archives

In 1901, the Ban Quan Company, the International Placer Company, and the Tit and Tat Company were all employing hydraulic mining at their mining properties. The Ban Quan Company, consisting of twelve Chinese miners, worked on the east side of Wild Horse Creek. It employed five large hydraulic monitors in their mining.

Bob Dore was one of the partners of the International Placer Company of Chinese miners. After having worked with hydraulic mining for a good number of years and accumulating their wealth, the partners dissolved the company. Bob Dore, however, retained the ground. No work was done in the summer of 1901, reported the *Fort Steele Prospector*.

The Chinese Settlement: Chinatown

In September 1865, after the Dewdney Trail to the Wild Horse District was completed, the Chinese labourers who had constructed the trail were dismissed. Many of these labourers, as well as other Chinese miners from the Cariboo and the Similkameen migrated to the Wild Horse district and settled at the site of Fisherville, which had largely been abandoned by white miners after the initial gold rush, who had moved on when they felt their claims were exhausted This townsite became Chinatown. It consisted of numerous one- and two-storey houses, a butcher shop, a blacksmith shop, general stores and gambling establishments—although gambling was illegal in Canada at this time, it formed one of the major amusements among the miners; in particular, the Chinese had an ancient tradition of gambling expressed in such games as fan tan.[42]

By 1870, it was estimated that about 250 Chinese individuals lived in Chinatown. Many of them continued mining in the district, while others cultivated vegetable gardens near their homes and at other sites adjacent to the St. Eugene Mission at Cherry Creek, Skookumchuck, Wardner and Windermere. The gardeners dug miles of ditches to ensure a water supply for the vegetables they cultivated.

Since Chinatown was located on a slope, several of the Chinese vegetable gardens were terraced. Despite the mountainous terrain, these vegetable gardens proved successful.

Wild Horse Creek gave profitable employment to about five thousand white miners

Lum Kim, gardener and miner near Wild Horse Creek. Royal BC Museum and Archives E-01808

for several years. After they had harvested millions of dollars' worth of gold from the ground, they abandoned the mining claims to the Chinese and left the district. Thus the population of white miners began to decline. By 1874, Honourable A.C. Elliott, the minister of mines in British Columbia, reported that the Chinese miners outnumbered white miners in the Wild Horse district. This statement indicates that some of the Chinese in Chinatown continued mining and that they were successful. The expected yield in a year was estimated to be $50,000.[43]

In 1887, Chinese labourers were brought in to dig a canal between the Kootenay River and Columbia Lake, located along today's Highways 93 and 95. A brigade of two hundred men formed themselves into a conveyor. The canal was "just over a mile long, 45 feet wide and from 8 to 10 feet deep."[44]

Chinese New Year

In February 1896, the Chinese residents in Chinatown celebrated Chinese New Year in their own "peculiar" way, reported the *Fort Steele Prospector*. On Chinese New Year's Eve, all the Chinese stopped work, put on their best clothes and celebrated the beginning of the new year. They held a fireworks display, exploded firecrackers and drank *sam suie*, "the Chinese whiskey." They gave presents wrapped in red paper to guests, called on their friends, paid off their debts, took baths, and "enjoyed themselves to the greatest possible degree…. Red the most brilliant and gorgeous red possible was over everything." Little red signs, figures and symbols were pasted on their doors. They even coloured hard-boiled eggs red to offer as gifts to their gods. At night, the air was red with the fire from burning crackers intended to scare away the devils of misfortune and bad luck for the coming year. The Chinese sat up all night, and watched the sunrise on New Year's morning, which they believed would give them long life. "The grand finale [was] a tremendous, and sudden burst of fireworks, a large decoction of *sam suie* and a prolonged sitting at fan tan."[45]

Robbery and Other Incidents

Six successful Chinese miners wanted to return home to China. James Rogers, who had been freighting for the Galbraith family, agreed to take them to leave the country. These miners carried with them a large sum of money in gold dust taken out of Wild Horse Creek. On October 10, 1893, Rogers and the Chinese miners reached and camped at Wolf Creek, eighteen miles (twenty-nine kilometres) from Fort Steele. After fixing up the camp for the night, the party retired. At midnight, Rogers was aroused in his tent by a masked man who told him that two other masked men found and took away about $2,500 in gold dust and bills from the Chinese men. Three of the Chinese, who were sleeping in the wagons, escaped and hid in the bush. One unfortunate man who refused to submit was badly beaten on his face and head. Then the masked man left Rogers.

Early the next morning, when Rogers and the six Chinese miners arrived at Fort Steele, the injured Chinese was promptly attended to by Dr. McLean, and the police were informed about the robbery. S.M. Cummins dispatched special constables to hunt for the robbers but the constables failed to arrest them, since the robbers had already ridden off in the direction of Tobacco Plains. The robbers were described as two tall men wearing white masks and long black coats, and a third man who was much smaller. The robbery was well planned and carefully carried out.[46]

On December 15, 1894, Moloch, a Chinese man, was riding on horseback to Moyie. When he was near Fisherville, the horse galloped and he fell, landed on a rock, and died instantly. He had with him a tin of opium, which a man named Choo Chee Woo claimed was his. A government agent then took Choo to county court for selling opium without a licence—although at this time opium use was legal in Canada, it was an industry regulated by licensing. Choo ended up paying a fine of seventy-five dollars and court costs.[47]

Since English was a foreign language to many early Chinese immigrants, they required an interpreter to translate their messages or defence whenever they were brought to court. Tai Yee, a Chinese immigrant, was always called upon to serve as an interpreter in court at Fort Steele. As he wished to remain neutral, he announced his position in the *Fort Steele Prospector* as follows:

> I the undersigned Tai Yee, who have acted sometimes as Chinese Interpreter in court at Fort Steele, wish to make it public that while I am always willing to act in friendly cases, I do not want to act when the case is likely to make enemies for me among my own people. I came to Fort Steele some years ago and I have no relations here; I am all alone. Some Chinamen make trouble and want to take me to court but I will not go, for I am not concerned in their trouble and do not want to make enemies. I want to take care of myself in my business.
> Tai Yee
> Fort Steele, Dec. 7, 1897[48]

The census taken in 1901 showed that there were only sixty-seven Chinese men left in the Wild Horse district. They worked on claims that were leased to them by white miners. No one knew the amount of their earnings.

When payments for their leases were due, they weighed out and paid with gold nuggets.[49] A lot of gold had been taken out of Wild Horse Creek by Chinese miners in the previous few years. In 1902, nine Chinese miners returned to China. Not one of them took back less than fifteen thousand dollars, according to the *Cranbrook Herald*.[50]

The Lum and the Ban Quan Families

In 1846, Chin Lum (陈霖 – 译音) was born in Guangdong. During the Fraser Gold Rush (1858–1860), he immigrated to Canada, arrived in Rock Creek and worked as a helper to a Secwépemc man who operated a packing outfit moving goods between Hope and Rock Creek. Lum married Lucy Williams, a young girl of 16, who was the daughter of the packer at Hope. Then he set up a grocery and dry goods store in Rock Creek to supply miners and settlers in the area. He and Lucy had four boys—Dick, George, Peter and Jim—and three girls—Lillian, Maggie and Caroline. All of their children were born in Rock Creek and attended school there.

In 1907, Chin moved with his older children to Cranbrook. There he opened a Chinese grocery store. Lucy Lum arrived later with her younger sons, Peter and Jimmy. After the arrival of his family, Chin moved to Fort Steele where he opened a butcher shop. Peter and Jim then attended school in Fort Steele.

Lillian Lum married Chu Ban Quan, the owner-operator of the Invicta Mine on Wild Horse Creek. Maggie married Hop Yuen, a market gardener, and Caroline worked as a cook at the Invicta camp. In 1910, Caroline Lum married Jim Buckman, a blacksmith in Fort Steele. Buckman had come to Canada from California and made a good living as a blacksmith. He was a rawhide expert, and made custom leather goods for Great West Saddlery in Calgary.

George Lum worked with Al Doyle, a livery-man at Fort Steele. Dick Lum found work on a ranch in southern Alberta.

In 1920, Chin "felt his end was near. He burned his shops [*sic*] records to indicate he forgave his debtors, then sailed for China, escorted by son George."[51] Six months later Chin died in his village in Guangdong. George arranged his father's burial, then returned to Fort Steele. Lucy Lum lived in Fort Steele, caring for foster children and her family, until she died in 1951 at the age of 97.

In 1931, George "married an English girl who was working at Chateau Lake Louise. They worked at Lake Louise during ensuing summers but made their home at Fort Steele."[52] This couple had seven children.

Peter Lum worked at many trades over the course of his life. While still a teenager, he helped Astor William Drayton install penstocks—sluices controlling the flow of water—feeding a length of heavy steel pipe used in hydraulic mining up the Wild Horse Creek. The next summer, he operated the hydraulic monitor used to flush gravel down specially constructed sluice boxes.

At 17, Peter finished school. As Naomi Miller wrote,

> he and a classmate rolled up their blankets, purchased cork boots on credit and walked sixteen miles [twenty-six kilometres] to Bull River to seek work driving logs. They were taken on and told to walk to the upper camp fourteen miles [twenty-two kilometres] upstream. The log drive lasted almost two months. The boys were paid $8 per day plus board. Later that year (1915) Pete was recruited to help a young man develop a claim up the Skookumchuck River.... In the fall he assisted big game guide Arthur Nichol, on pack outings with rich hunters. He then spent several winters logging on Bull River. In 1921 when fire wiped out logging operations on the river, Pete found work where he could. Peter married Matilda Samson, [a] native from Washington State in 1925.[53]

Unfortunately, Matilda died in 1931, leaving Peter with their son. One major accomplishment Peter achieved was cutting and clearing a ten-mile (sixteen-kilometre) trail from Wild Horse Creek to the Kootenay King mine. An early bulldozer operator was hired to turn the trail into a road, then to transport supplies in a truck. Peter was then assigned to assist a geologist's survey.

Peter Lum operating a hydraulic monitor. Image C-05516 courtesy the Royal BC Museum and Archives

Between 1929 and 1939 the Lums catered to tourists at Lake Louise with a pony stand and trail rides. Pete and George Lum had twenty-five horses; Dick Lum and son Ira had a separate stand with eighteen horses. The family and their summer employees lived in tents near their horse corral. The journey from Fort Steele to Lake Louise took six or seven days, following the Banff-Radium highway to near the summit where there was a trail to their destination. The summer of 1939 was their last because Brewsters had opened competition, and war in Europe curtailed the number of tourists.

Pete's home in the meadows across the river from Fort Steele was flooded in 1948. He took his horses to much higher ground near Premier Lake. This new home was an ideal headquarters for hunters, and pack trips to big game areas. Pete was a licenced guide and trapper until 1977 when he reluctantly sold his horses and stayed home with his dogs.[54]

Chu Ban Quan (朱炳坤 –译音) arrived in San Francisco from Guangdong in the late 1860s, came through Bonners Ferry, and gradually worked his way to the Kootenay. In 1882, he arrived at Wild Horse Creek to pan for gold, and there he became a prosperous prospector and miner. In 1896, the *Fort Steele Prospector* reported that Charles Edwards was called upon to perform a wedding ceremony for Chu and Jennie Quong, a girl from the "flowery kingdom," that is, China. The bride was given away by David Griffith, another well-known prospector and miner in the Wild Horse district.[55] No records following up on that marriage could be found. Perhaps Quong had passed on or the marriage had fallen apart. In any event, in 1907, Chu married Lillian Lum, the daughter of Chin Lum. At that time, Chu was the owner-operator of the Invicta Mine on Wild Horse Creek. He had a crew of twelve Chinese men working the first hydraulic operation on the west side of the creek.

Indigenous people in Kootenay hunted or fished in the Wild Horse district, and observed miners working their claims. White men were intolerant of any Indigenous people who came near their camps, but Chu "treated them graciously and won their friendship." At Christmas one year, many Indigenous people visited Chu. To show his hospitality, Chu "opened a big box of soda crackers and gave one to each visitor. By the end of the day he had emptied four boxes of crackers. Other miners were occasionally harassed [by the Indigenous people] when travelling between towns and claims, but Ban Quan went unobstructed."[56]

In 1912, Chu moved to Fort Steele, where his son Joe was born. "In 1913, he opened a billiard room in Cranbrook, but moved away from there in 1915 because his patrons had joined the army for service in World War I. Ban Quan and Lily rented five acres from the priests at St. Eugene Mission to establish a market garden. The Ban Quan children attended school at the Indian boarding school at the Mission, girls in the morning, boys in the afternoon." In later years, Chu moved his family to Cranbrook, where he acquired a large piece of land to cultivate vegetables and where he hired Indigenous people to work for him. (That piece of land is the current site of the Tamarack Centre in Cranbrook.) His son Joe recalled "travelling in a horse drawn Bennett buggy to sell a load of produce in Marysville, staying there overnight with a friend, and driving home the following day."

Chu died in 1947 and is buried in the Westlawn Cemetery at Cobham Avenue and Borden Road West, Cranbrook. Lillian "continued to run the market garden with the assistance of her sons Charlie and Joe until her death in 1966."[57]

The Chinese Gravesite at Wild Horse Creek

A short walk uphill from the grave of Thomas Walker is a small area where a number of equidistant coffin-sized depressions can be seen. This area once served as a gravesite for Chinese individuals who passed away in Fisherville and its vicinity during the Wild Horse gold rush and later. For example, in May 1898, Gon Up, an aged Chinese placer miner, died in Palmer's Bar but his body was taken to this gravesite in Fisherville for burial.[58]

These depressions indicate that the remains of the deceased Chinese in the burial ground were exhumed and returned to China for burial, a tradition that was practised by early Chinese immigrants. Peter Lum, a well-known miner and packer in the Wild Horse Creek area, stated that the deceased Chinese who passed on in the Wild Horse district were buried in this Chinese gravesite, and that each burial had about forty-five centimetres of soil above the coffin. The shallow burials were intended so the exhumation of the deceased could easily take place, and the remains could be returned to China for burial in the deceased's home village.[59] During exhumation, the bones of the deceased would be cleaned with alcohol, left to dry on a piece of white cloth, and then arranged and kept in a jar, waiting to be sent back to their home villages in Guangdong, China, for reburial in the deceased person's family plot.[60] There are no longer any bodies in this cemetery.

Indeed, many of the early Chinese immigrants who ventured overseas to find a better life for themselves and their families were sojourners—temporary residents of another country. They had no intention of spending their entire lives in a foreign land. Many hoped to return home after they had made their fortune in a foreign country. They wanted to earn enough money so that they could buy a piece of land in China where they could cultivate food and vegetables, and build a house in their home villages so they could enjoy living with their families, especially in their sunset years. Unfortunately, many early Chinese sojourners were not able to realize these hopes and dreams and remained in Canada for the rest of their lives.

Due to prejudice and discrimination, many Chinese immigrants could only find jobs as houseboys, gardeners tending flower beds and yards, as cooks for families in white communities, or as kitchen helpers doing such menial tasks as peeling potatoes, washing dishes and cleaning floors in restaurants. These jobs did not allow them to save enough money to go home; thus, many of the early Chinese immigrants remained poor and died and were buried in a foreign country. Friends and relatives or clan associations and the Chee Kung Tong (Chinese Freemasons Society) in various towns and cities overseas, however, helped fulfill the wishes of deceased members: after the deceased had been buried for seven years or so, their remains were exhumed and sent back to the villages of Guangdong for reburial.[61]

The jars containing the remains of the deceased were kept in tin containers before they were shipped home to Guangdong villages via the Tung Wah Hospital, (东华医院又名东华三院– 译音) in Hong Kong. Due to the second Sino-Japanese war in China (1937–1945), and for hygienic reasons, exhumation in BC was not allowed after 1939, and those jars that had yet to be shipped back to China were buried at Harling Point, the Chinese cemetery in Victoria, BC.

All the Chinese remains in the Wild Horse Chinese gravesite had already been exhumed prior to 1939, leaving the above-mentioned depressions in the burial ground. However, an image showing the Chinese altar is kept in the Fort Steele Museum and Archives. This altar served as a place where meals were offered to the deceased, said Peter Lum.[62] Due to the passage of time and erosion, this altar no longer exists at Wild Horse Creek.

There are three Chinese festivals—Qing Ming Jie (清明节), Yu Lan Jie (孟栏节) and Chong Yang Jie (重阳节)—at which Chinese Canadians venerate deceased family members, relatives and friends. The early Chinese immigrants would have been familiar with these traditional festivals. Qing Ming Jie, also known as the Tomb Sweeping festival, usually occurs between the second or third moon in the Chinese lunar calendar, around Easter. During the Qing Ming festival, members of the traditional Chinese community and Chinese-Canadian families go to cemeteries to clean the tombs of their relatives and friends, as well as those of the single men who died without families or loved ones and were buried in cemeteries in foreign countries such as Canada. The Chinese Canadians who sweep the tombs and clear grass and weeds near them, usually light joss sticks (incense) and offer flowers to the deceased. The relatives and friends as well as some Chinese-Canadian organizations such the Chee Kung Tong (the Chinese Freemasons Society), the Chinese Benevolent Association, and clan associations in various towns and cities in Canada, usually offer a feast to the departed souls and spirits in the cemeteries. The feast usually consists of roast pork, steamed chicken and rice, vegetables and fruits. After the ritual of honouring the departed souls is completed, they consume the food and fruits in the cemeteries. Many members of the younger generations, especially teenagers, often refer to the Qing Ming festival as a picnic in the cemetery.

Yu Lan Jie occurs on the fifteenth day of the seventh moon of the Chinese calendar. Chinese Canadians usually do not go to the cemetery during this festival, but instead honour the deceased on the family altar. At sunset on this day, traditional Chinese-Canadian families offer a feast in the backyards of their homes or in quiet lanes to console the wandering souls/spirits who died without families in foreign lands. The feast usually consists of steamed rice, bean curd or tofu, vegetables and fruits. In addition, they light joss sticks and burn paper money for the lonely departed souls.

Chong Yang Jie falls on the ninth day of the ninth moon in the Chinese calendar or around the beginning of October. The ritual of honouring the deceased is similar to Qing Ming but less elaborate, as the feast consists of less meat and fruit but would include flowers. There is seldom any picnic in the cemeteries during this festival. The Chinese people in the Wild Horse district would likely have observed at least Qing Ming among these traditional Chinese festivals, honouring their relatives and friends.

Application for Recognition

In 1958, the East Kootenay Historical Society successfully nominated Wild Horse Creek as a historic site. It was designated a heritage site by the province of BC in 1996. The Statement of Significance available at Canada's Historical Places states that

> [the site] is the former gold rush town located on a forested bench on the northwest side of the Wildhorse River, approximately 5.5 km northeast of Fort Steele and northeast of Cranbrook in the Kootenay Land District, British Columbia. The historic place consists of the remains of the original town of Fisherville, including building remains, cemetery, Chinese burial ground and

apple orchard, along with traces of the final section of the Dewdney Trail. There are numerous landscape scars and manipulations from previous mining activity. Site features are connected by an interpretive trail. The site is bounded by the Wildhorse River, the Wildhorse River Forest Service Road and private property.

Wildhorse Creek Historic Site is of historical, cultural, scientific, spiritual, and social significance, particularly for its connection to gold mining in the East Kootenay region, its association with Chinese settlement and as the eastern terminus of the Dewdney Trail, the first all-Canadian route across southern British Columbia, completed in 1865 to access the goldfields on the Wildhorse River. Remnants of the Trail are still perceptible on site.

Wildhorse Creek Historic Site has historical importance as the site of the first gold rush in the East Kootenay region. While gold was discovered in the Wildhorse Creek area in 1857, the gold rush did not begin until the spring of 1864. With a population of almost 5,000 in 1865, the substantial mining town of Fisherville offered services including a post office, the Gold Commissioner's office, general stores, saloons, brewery, restaurants and miners' dwellings. The various remaining features of the site, such as building remains, cemetery, Chinese burial ground and orchard reflect the extent and activities of the original town.

The site is significant as a good example of the history of Chinese settlement across the province and particularly in the West Kootenay region. The Chinese arrived, possibly after working on the Dewdney Trail, after the initial gold rush waned, establishing a Chinatown within the original townsite.

The Chinese burial grounds at Wildhorse Creek Historic Site are valued because of their contribution to an understanding of Chinese overseas burial practices including the siting of the burial ground on a slope above the river, fengshui principles, and interred and non-interred grave sites.[63]

The content of this application records the essence of the Wild Horse Creek history, including the contributions of the first Chinese immigrants to come to the East Kootenay. The great effort made to recognize the significance of Wild Horse Creek not only reflects the early involvement of the East Kootenay Historical Society but has also been appreciated by many scholars and students of archaeology and history, curators and archivists in numerous museums and archives in BC, and journalists, researchers and authors across Canada.

Chinese prospectors sluicing on Wild Horse Creek. Frank Swannell photo. Royal BC Museum and Archives I-33947

Nowadays, the Wild Horse Creek gold-mining area is an interpretative site managed by the Fort Steele Museum and Archives. The staff of the museum have installed informational posters at various sites in the former town as well as at locations nearby, describing their historical importance.

The story of the Wild Horse Creek gold rush is a page of colourful and important history that records the endeavours of the early Chinese immigrants to Wild Horse Creek and its vicinity in the East Kootenay. The collective work and efforts of the East Kootenay Historical Society as well as that of the management and staff of the Fort Steele Museum and Archives have documented a piece of significant history in the Kootenay for all Canadians from various ethnic groups; for scholars, researchers and lovers of history; and for all visitors and tourists to Fort Steele and the Kootenay district.

The Key City: Cranbrook

Cranbrook is located near the western edge of the Rocky Mountain Trench, on the Crowsnest Pass Road in southeast Kootenay, British Columbia, the traditional territory of the Ktunaxa Nation.[64] Five First Nations bands, four of them Ktunaxa and one Secwepemc (known as Kinbasket), and the Métis have traditionally lived in this region. In the past, the Indigenous people and the earliest European settlers called this area Joseph's Prairie in honour of Chief Joseph Isadore.[65]

Cranbrook can be reached from BC's Lower Mainland via Highway 95 and from Calgary, Alberta, via Highway 93. Highway 95 also connects Cranbrook to the Fort Steele Heritage Town. Cranbrook has an international airport where airlines can refuel and load and unload goods and passengers.

The Origins of Cranbrook

John Thompson Galbraith and his wife, Sarah, were the first settlers in what became Cranbrook. Galbraith had previously operated a ferry across the Kootenay River, taking miners to the Wild Horse Creek mining district. In 1873, he pre-empted a plot of land (lot 4) and bought the adjacent lots 5 and 24 where Cranbrook would emerge. He then built a sawmill and combination residence/store on the property.[66]

In 1886, Galbraith sold this property to Colonel James Baker, who had arrived with his family from England.[67] Colonel Baker picked the name "Cranbrook" for the property, likely naming it after the town in Kent, England, situated near his birthplace. He built a fence around this property that kept the Ktunaxa out of their traditional territory where their cattle had grazed. The fence created tension between the Ktunaxa people and the emerging settler society, which by then included miners, ranchers and merchants. In 1887, when the North-West Mounted Police arrived in the area, talks were held between the Ktunaxa and Colonel Baker as well as with others with an interest in the area. A settlement was reached between the parties in which the Ktunaxa grazing land was replaced, and under the leadership of Chief Isadore, the Ktunaxa were compensated for the development of a townsite.[68]

Colonel Baker gifted half the townsite to the Canadian Pacific Railway (CPR), ensuring that the railway would pass through Cranbrook rather than

In 1886, Colonel James Baker purchased property from John Galbraith, which he named Cranbrook after a parish near his hometown of Kent in England. Image A-01977 courtesy of the Royal BC Museum and Archives

Fort Steele, and contributing to its eventual status as the most important community in the area. Between 1897 and 1898, the CPR built the Crowsnest Pass Railway to enable access to the coal deposits in the Elk River Valley. This railway ran from Lethbridge, Alberta, to Kootenay Landing, BC.[69] The CPR established its divisional headquarters in Cranbrook.

In 1886, Baker was elected to the Legislative Assembly of British Columbia.[70] As the Member of the Legislative Assembly (MLA) representing the Kootenay, Colonel Baker was often confronted with the so-called "Chinese problem." At that time, many within European settler society wanted to exclude Chinese immigrants from many professions and businesses, and even to stop Chinese immigration altogether. Baker's position regarding the Chinese was coloured by the fact that many of his allies and supporters managed industrial and other large construction projects. These individuals often reaped a substantial benefit to their businesses from a steady supply of cheap Chinese labourers. In response to this dilemma, Baker preferred levying a head tax on the Chinese rather than excluding them altogether.[71]

Colonel Baker retired from politics in 1900 after having served in the BC legislature for fourteen years. While in office, he had served as the provincial secretary and as minister of Education, Immigration, and Mines at different periods. He returned to England after his retirement, but unfortunately he passed away shortly after he arrived home.

By 1897, the townsite of Cranbrook had been almost completely surveyed, and plans had been laid out for streets and avenues to be graded and sidewalks constructed. The planners anticipated that houses, stores, hotels and warehouses would soon come to line these streets. The plan for the townsite also included "a proper system of sanitation,..., a good drainage scheme and a proper water supply," according to a report published in the *East Kootenay Miner*.[72]

By 1900, the development of Cranbrook's townsite was complete, building lots had been sold, people from all walks of life were gradually moving in, and the *Cranbrook Herald* newspaper advertised that Cranbrook was a growing town.[73] In 1905, Cranbrook was incorporated as a city.

Mining Near Cranbrook

The southeast Kootenay was rich in gold, silver, copper, lead, coal and oil. Therefore, numerous mines were established in the neighbourhood of Cranbrook. In 1897, a report stated that "the North Star and Sullivan groups of mines [are located] 25 miles [40 kilometres] to the north of Cranbrook; the famous Moyie mines including the celebrated St. Eugene lie 23 miles [37 kilometres] to the south; on its west side are the noted Perry Creek mines, which are about 20 miles [32 kilometres] distant; on its east side are the famed Dibble group of mines in about the same distance away."[74]

The locations of these mines confirmed Cranbrook as a mining centre. When investors, prospectors and miners came to look for mining properties, they would first visit Cranbrook before they staked their claims. Since the town

The townsite of Cranbrook from Baker Hill in 1910. Image B-07539 courtesy of the Royal BC Museum and Archives

was sitting on the main wagon road with trails leading to different parts of the East Kootenay, its infrastructure, together with the Crowsnest Pass Railway, provided channels through which mineral ores could be sent to assay offices and smelters, and provisions and machinery transported to the various mining camps. The following villages and towns in the mining district were connected to Cranbrook.[75]

Fort Steele	12 miles [17.5 km]
Wasa	21 miles [35.7 km]
Mission	6 miles [9.65 km]
Wild Horse	18 miles [30 km]
North Star	23 miles [37 km]
Swansea	11 miles [18 km]
Moyie City	22 miles [35.4 km]
Kootenay Lake	80 miles [129 km]

When coal and coke were discovered and mined, they replaced wood as the fuel used to create the steam that powered trains. Large quantities of coal and coke, however, were exported to other provinces or to the United States. In 1897, the total output of coal was 892,205 tons.[76] The minister of mines reported that the collieries of BC employed 1,717 white miners, 534 Chinese and 80 Japanese miners, and 151 teenaged boys. The average daily wages in 1898 for white miners were $2.50–$3.00; for Chinese miners, $1.00–$1.25; and for boys, $1.00–$2.00.[77]

In 1898, BC's Supreme Court decided that the section of the Coal Lands Regulation Act that prohibited Chinese labourers from working underground in the coal mines was constitutional.[78] This clause prompted a ruling in London declaring that the section of the mining act prohibiting the Chinese from working underground was unconstitutional. The province responded spitefully: "Since the privy council decided in favour of the Chinese working under ground, the province has issued a special order to the effect that all men employed in this way after August 1 must be able to read the mining regulations in English."[79] This special order caused the editor of the *Cranbrook Herald* to predict that "the new scheme adopted by the provincial government to shut out Chinese from working in the mines [will] prove abortive. An educational condition would act as strongly against a vast number of foreigners besides Chinamen, and if enforced would create no end of difficulty for the coal mines of the Province...."[80] In truth, not only Chinese, but also Japanese, Doukhobors, French, Italians, Hungarians and other Europeans worked in the coal mines, and many of them would have had just as much difficulty reading the English mining regulations as the Chinese would have. As the *Cranbrook Herald* reported, "one day last week within an hour's time, the *Herald* men heard people conversing in English, French, Chinese, Japanese, German, Swede, Italian, and Indian [First Nations] languages."[81] The *Cranbrook Herald* further showed its resentment against employing Italians as well as the Chinese in the coal mines in Kootenay. An editorial stated:

> The mine owners of West Kootenay over-reached themselves when they imported a lot of Italians from the United States to work in the mines. British Columbia has no need of Italians to work in her mines. The merchant, the manufacturer, the artisan, the laborer, the capitalist, all have reason to oppose such a move. The future of British Columbia depends upon her masses. If all labor is to come down to the basis of Chinese and Italian wages, the days of prosperity in British Columbia will soon be over. Good wages means good times and more rapid development of every resource of the country. The money earned by the Italian and Chinamen is sent away. It is never invested in homes and home improvements. Not a dollar of it is spent in public spirited enterprise. They are a class that absorb but never give up. The bare necessities of life keeps them, and very little of their money circulates in the legitimate channels of trade. One white man working at good wages is better for a community than ten Chinks or Dagoes [*sic*].[82]

In spite of the provincial regulations and the prejudice against them, some Chinese were employed in the major mines in the Cranbrook region. In addition, some Chinese men panned for gold in streams, creeks and rivers.

Other Chinese Occupations

Besides working at mining, many Chinese individuals were employed in other occupations. For example, Lee Ginn, a Chinese man, was hired as a wiper to clean windows on the Crowsnest line of the CPR—a wiper was responsible for cleaning the engine and other parts of the trains. Unfortunately, on March 4, 1911, Lee Ginn had a serious accident on site, and was taken to St. Eugene Hospital in Cranbrook. He died there on the morning of March 9, reported the *Cranbrook Herald*.[83] The CPR hired Chinese labourers for various jobs, such as cleaning cabooses, boxes and flat boards on its trains, sweeping away fallen leaves and other debris on the tracks and in the yards, and shovelling snow from the railway tracks during winter. Some lumber companies also hired Chinese workers to saw timber. For instance, E.L. Staples, a lumberman, employed some Chinese labourers.[84] Quite a few ranches hired Chinese men to tend and irrigate their fields. Mr. Bostock Hewitt, a rancher, businessman and politician, for example, employed three Chinese workers at his ranch: a cook, a gardener and a person whose job was to irrigate the grassland on his property.[85]

A good number of homeowners employed Chinese men as houseboys, cooks and gardeners. Ah Sing was a servant in the home of A. Leitch. One Sunday in October 1902, having hitched up his employer's ponies, Sing attempted to drive them around to the front door of the house. The ponies were spooked by something and started to gallop away. Sing became frightened and jumped out of the cart, breaking one of his legs just above the ankle. He was sent to St. Eugene Hospital to have his injuries attended to. The ponies stopped galloping just a few yards away from the house.[86]

Other Chinese people operated grocery stores, restaurants and laundries in the city. In 1900, for example, Kwong Chin Jane bought a hardware store on Armstrong Avenue from John Lee, a prominent Chinese merchant in Chinatown. He reduced the prices of all the items in the store.[87]

In 1907, Chu Ban Quan, who had previously mined for gold at Wild Horse Creek and was now also the manager of the Quong Yuen Company, posted a notice in the *Cranbrook Prospector* stating that Hop Yuen was no longer a partner in the company and that "said Company is not liable for debts incurred by said Hop Yuen." Furthermore, any debts owing to the company should be paid to it directly.[88] In 1914, Wah Sang, the tailor's shop owned and operated by Lee Li and Lee You, advertised in the *Chinese Times* (大汉公报), a Chinese newspaper in Vancouver.

The shop's mailing address was included—P.O. Box 642—but not its physical location. The advertisement claimed that the shop could produce fashionable and modern clothing for men and women at very reasonable prices, and would welcome customers from Cranbrook and other cities in the Kootenay.[89]

Also occurring in 1914 was an incident regarding the supply of poultry to Chinese restaurants and other merchants in Chinatown. It was brought to the attention of the Cranbrook Poultry Association that the Chinese were able to purchase chickens at a very low price from a number of young boys, who had stolen them. One director of the association actually caught a boy carrying a bag of birds over his shoulder! "So bold and insatiable" were these young thieves, according to the association, that a board of directors meeting was held to pass a resolution offering to assist those whose birds had been stolen. W.W. McGregor, the association's secretary-treasurer, had already obtained circumstantial evidence in the case, and required only one or two more pieces of evidence to build a conclusive case. His fellow board members included A.B. Smith, president of the association; E.H. Slater, vice-president; and T.S. Gill, C.R. Sheppard, W. Harvey and A.H. Pigott, directors.[90] It is not known what the impact of losing their supply of cheap chickens had on the Chinese restaurants.

Many of the Chinese in Canada owned and operated hand laundries. Laundries were easy to set up, required little in the way of equipment or space, did not require a great deal of skill, and cost little to operate. They were also low-status occupations and were therefore open to the Chinese, who were prevented from working in many occupations.[91] Two of the well-known Chinese laundries in Cranbrook were owned by Sing Lee and Ah Quai. On April 6, 1899, the Sing Lee Laundry advertised in the *Cranbrook Herald*, and the Ah Quai Laundry also advertised later on. Ah Quai, owner of the latter laundry, was quite a resourceful person. Besides operating his laundry, he would do any kind of job available, including house cleaning and cooking. In addition, two more laundry shops, Wing Lee and Ye Chung were found in Chinatown around the turn of the twentieth century.

In October 1900, an incident occurred in Ah Quai's laundry. A white man came into the shop to pick up his clean clothing. Ah Quai was not there, but some of his employees were. One of these clerks told the customer he didn't know where his clothes were. The customer said that he could recognize his own clothes, picked them out, and paid the fee to a clerk. But the clerk was uncomfortable letting him take the clothing away, perhaps because he was not sure that the customer had picked out the right clothing. The clerks together tried to prevent the customer from leaving the shop, but the customer's patience ran out and he began punching the clerks. The *Cranbrook Herald* reported that "in about ten seconds, Chinamen were lying in all sorts of places and positions, one with a table on top of him, another doubled up around a stove, and altogether it looked as though a cyclone had hit 'em." After this altercation, the Chinese clerks made no further objections, so the customer left the laundry shop with his laundry.[92]

Earlier, the editor of the *Cranbrook Herald* had commented that "the Herald office is getting so many Chinese laundry buildings around its place of business that we are considering the advisability of putting in a few Chinese fonts of type and starting a Celestial edition."[93] The existence of Chinese laundries in the neighbourhood annoyed the staff of the newspaper because they noticed the Chinese used their saliva to moisten dried clothes before ironing them, and they considered this method of dampening the clothing unsanitary. The newspaper reported in 1906 that another community nearby that looked upon Chinese laundries "as a menace to the city" had passed a bylaw requiring a licence fee of $100 from each Chinese laundry. The *Herald* maintained that it would be a good idea to pass a similar bylaw in Cranbrook, and suggested that such a high cost would force the Chinese to move their laundries outside the city, thereby improving the appearance of the neighbourhood.[94]

The staff of the *Herald* were also irritated when the Chinese laundry men played the *erhu*, a two-stringed fiddle. The editorial complained that:

> if something is not done by Constable Morris, Magistrate Leith or Magistrate Moffatt toward dispossessing the Chinese contingent in Cranbrook of a new musical instrument... there will be a revolution in the Herald office. The boys do not object to the howling of the coyotes, the whistling of numerous engines, the exhuberant [*sic*] jollification of those who have lingered too long over the flowing bowl, or the snarling and fighting of the too numerous canines in town, but they draw the line on a Chinese fiddle. Say, gentle reader, have you ever heard one? If not, you have no idea of hades, or any conception of mental torture that racks the soul and makes the heart grow weary.... It is played with a reckless disregard of harmony, and sounds like the wild dreams of a pipe fiend.... It screeches, it yells, it moans, it curses, it runs up to an ear splitting tone and drops down again like an empty wagon going over a frozen road. The man who made it ought to be quartered alive and boiled in oil, and the one who would play it should be taken to an insane asylum. The Herald force is praying for relief, and its prayers are long and loud.[95]

Indeed, it takes skill to play the *erhu* (二胡) and to produce a sweet melody. The tunes that most of these single Chinese men played were melancholy. They missed their loved ones and families in their home villages in Guangdong and their music revealed their loneliness and homesickness, and the hardships and destitution they experienced living in a foreign country.

Good business in Chinese laundries created envy as well as distaste among some white merchants. The *Cranbrook Herald* commented that "money paid to a Chinaman never does any good to a town. It is hoarded, and finally taken to the home country. Money paid to a white man is spent in a white man's country. It is time Cranbrook had a steam laundry operated by a member of Anglo-Saxon race. Leave your money at home."[96] The newspaper further stated that the white people who patronized Chinese businesses were the very ones most affected by Chinese and Japanese labour, since they were labourers themselves. And the only way to force the Chinamen out of business was to boycott them. Eventually, some merchants and the miner's union formed an anti-Chinese committee and printed signs that said "We Neither Patronize or Employ Chinese Here" that they distributed to every business in town. In most cases, the cards were requested by business owners. The *Cranbrook Herald* commented about the campaign that "the Chinese are acting glum and seem pretty well discouraged, and it is said that most of them are getting ready to move out. One thing is certain they are getting but little if any work to do."[97]

In 1911, Mr. C.T. Davis invested $10,000 to purchase a lot and construct a building for the Cranbrook Steam Laundry. He installed modern machinery in the building and hired three skilled white men and three white women to work there. The three white women were skilled ironers. Joe Bird was an engineer, the second man was an expert laundryman and the third man drove the delivery wagon. A *Cranbrook Herald* journalist visited the business and noticed that a steam boiler and an electric dynamo had been installed in the building. The dynamo generated electricity needed to operate several machines and irons, as well as to provide light inside the building. The laundry also had a special fireproof drying chamber. Davis told the journalist that he would hire more women when the laundry was fully operational. The residents of Cranbrook would recognize that they could get their laundry done under the most modern sanitary arrangements, reported the *Cranbrook Herald*. Eventually, twenty-five more workers would be steadily employed.[98] However, the Cranbrook Steam Laundry did not replace or stop the Chinese laundry men from carrying on their businesses, since many of the white families still preferred to have their clothes "picked up, laundered and delivered to them by the Chinese."[99]

The same year, the city of Cranbrook needed to hire a hundred men to install a sewer system in the townsite. The contract between the city council and Galt Engineering Works, which undertook the installation of the sewer system, stated in clause 6 that "the engineers shall not directly or indirectly employ Chinese, Japanese or any other Asiatic upon, about or in connection with the works, and in event of their so doing the city will not be responsible for payment of their wages or remuneration."[100] Anti-Chinese sentiment had become dominant in the white community.

Chinatown

As time went by, many Chinese immigrants arrived in Cranbrook, but they confined themselves to an area between Fifth and Seventh Avenues facing Van Horne Street (First Street), across from the railway station and not too far from the downtown business centre. This area became commonly known as China-town. From only a few residents in 1899, it grew to several hundred residents by 1907.[101] One 1905 estimate was that there were 413 Chinese individuals living in Chinatown. "That is far too many Chinamen for a town this size," declared the Cranbrook Herald.

The buildings in Chinatown consisted of residential houses, boarding houses, gambling houses, opium dens, restaurants, grocery stores, numerous laundries, a jewellery shop, a tailor's shop and a joss house—a building where the Chinese could offer respect to their deities and their ancestors. The buildings in Chinatown did not meet with the approval of the white community. In a 1906 editorial, the Cranbrook Herald referred to the buildings as "shacks" and an "eyesore" that did not provide an "inviting view for people going through town on the trains" and failed to contribute to the beautification of Cranbrook.[102]

However, the Cranbrook Herald also commented that "these people have always been a most interesting and extraordinary study with their noiseless, shadowy, mysterious ways.… As Bret Harte [an American writer] has said, 'For ways that are dark and for tricks that are vain the heathen Chinee is peculiar.' Their costumes are quaint, their music shadowy and elfin, and their art without perspective. The atmosphere in their houses is always brown with yellow lights playing on brown walls, and lurking shadows that silhouette carved figures of dragons and demons, wooden clogs, Chinaware covered with crimson butterflies and blue landscapes."[103]

On January 25, 1900, the Chinese community celebrated the Chinese New Year in Chinatown. The Cranbrook Herald stated that "the Oriental population of Cranbrook is preparing for a 'heap good time.' There are quite a number [of Chinese] here now, and most of them have made money the past year. A [C]hinaman may live on nothing for fifty-one weeks in the year, but New Year week everything goes, and expenses don't count. Fire crackers will be used in profusion to frighten away the devil, and great chunks of Chinese fun will be tossed about by the happy Mongolians."[104]

The celebration went on for a few days. On the night of New Year's Eve, an explosion of firecrackers awoke the town. The *Cranbrook Herald* declared that "the noise was kept up until a late hour Tuesday. It was a great day for the Chinks [*sic*]. They got out their best clothes and celebrated with enthusiasm. During the day they received callers and served refreshments, and had an all round good time." Among the refreshments were drinks and nuts, accompanied by cigars.[105] On February 8, the *Cranbrook Herald* declared that the Chinese New Year celebrations had finally come to an end, and the *Herald* staff was "feeling better. It is now possible to talk in that part of town without using a foghorn!"[106]

Since the office of the *Cranbrook Herald* was located in a neighbourhood with numerous Chinese laundries, the staff had many opportunities to notice Chinese practices and habits, and get to know about some of their traditions and beliefs. They learned, for example, that during the Chinese New Year festival, "every Chinaman is supposed to pay his creditors before New Years, but if he is unable to do so, the score is wiped out, he owes nothing and credit is extended to him for another year, as though he had always paid his debts.... Grievances are also settled during the New Year season.... Etiquette requires him to forgive and forget."[107]

One journalist described how the Chinese people ate rice with a pair of chopsticks:

> Nothing is more curious than to see them eat... with their famous chopsticks.... Everything is served them in bowls or saucers, and with the chopsticks they raise the pieces of meat or fish to the mouth with sufficient grace. Each one has a bowl of rice, which he holds near his lips, and with the aid of the chopsticks he pushed the contents into his mouth. It is curious to see them pick up with their chopsticks the grains of rice that had fallen on the ground. Their children are taught this art from their earliest years.[108]

The Chinese, especially the peasants, appreciated their staple food, rice, since they knew what a back-breaking task it was for farmers to cultivate rice in their fields.

Another reporter wrote about some of the traditional beliefs of the Chinese—which he characterized as superstition. He noted that the Chinese believed that when a baby took a nap in day time, his or her soul would leave the tiny body. If the baby took too long a nap, it was an indication that the young soul could not find its way back to his or her body; it meant that the baby might die eventually. Therefore, Chinese parents usually woke the baby up from his or her nap within a couple of hours. If they failed to do so, they would go out to the streets and call out the name of the baby again and again as though the spirit of the child was lost, said the *Cranbrook Herald*. They believed calling the baby's name would lead the soul back to the little body, thus saving the baby's life. Also, when the parents carried a sleeping baby from one place to another, they must call out his or her name aloud, so that the soul would not stray away.[109]

Interestingly, on June 1, 1907, the *Cranbrook Prospector* reported that "there is a little chink lad [who] arrived from China three months ago. He wears knee pants and has already learned how to play ball." Clearly, the white community approved of any signs of assimilation.[110]

The newspapers reported on another Chinese belief related to the punishment of a crime. If a Chinese man committed a crime, he had to face the consequences:

> If he chooses to escape justice by running away,… the remaining members of his immediate family are held and punished in lieu of the real culprit. This may seem a strange way of getting the real criminal back to the scene of his crime, but it appeals to the religious side of the man's superstitious nature. According to their religion, the man who forsakes his parents when in peril would find his soul sailing around through hades without chart or compass for all eternity.[111]

Many of the single Chinese men in Chinatown needed some kind of recreation so they could forget their isolation and misery. They often spent their leisure hours in gambling dens with the hope of winning a windfall. On one occasion,

> a bunch of Boxers rushed forth into the opening and made an attack upon a brother Celestial and apostate who had deserted the traditions of Confucius and dwelt entirely on the rules of poker and fantan. It was a desperate affair for about two minutes, and there was more talking than one could hear at a political conference. Epithets were used that were shocking to the sensitive, and many present were thankful that they could not understand Chinese and thus escaped the shock. After a time quiet was resumed, and when peace had been restored the allied powers (Constables Morris and Dow) appeared upon the scene and approved of the situation.[112]

A few Chinese residents, particularly those who had their families living with them, realized the evils that could come from gambling. Wong Fong, a Chinese merchant with a shop on Armstrong Avenue, was one of them. In December 1912, he went to the *Cranbrook Herald* office pleading for help. He said that the gambling houses in Chinatown were operating every day, with games beginning at 12 noon, 6:00 p.m. and 9:00 p.m. with breaks in between to "possibly put outsiders off their track." Wong and his wife were dismayed to see some of their relatives having lost so much money. Wong asked the staff of the *Herald* whether they could forward his concerns to the city council so that a bylaw could be passed to stop the gambling in Chinatown.

The *Herald* told him to report the gambling to the police instead, since gambling was already illegal and no new bylaw was needed. Wong claimed that he had reported the situation to the police but the officers only laughed at him and brushed him aside. While he was narrating his experience with the police, an officer passed by. " 'See that man,' he said, as one of the City Police passed the door. 'I have told that man 10 or 12 times [about the evil of gambling] and he has done nothing. Police no good. Who must I see? What must I do?' "

The staff of the *Herald* empathized with Wong and forwarded the matter to the justice of the peace. Later, they learned that Wong had drafted a petition to stop gambling in Chinatown and gone around the city asking people to sign their names. Then he found someone to forward the signed petition through proper channels.

Wong's cry for assistance motivated a journalist from the *Cranbrook Herald* to visit a gambling den. He found that there were eight tables in the gambling den on which poker, dominoes and fan-tan were played. Some white people were among the Chinese gamblers playing the games. Having learned about the situation in the gambling den, the editor of the *Cranbrook Herald* suggested that orders should be given at once to remove the tables, thereby eliminating the temptation to those so weak they could not resist gambling. Furthermore, the newspaper reminded the Chinese residents that gambling after the third offence in China would be punishable by death.[113]

On April 7, 1914, a party consisting of Cranbrook's mayor, the chief of police and two police commissioners, two city aldermen, the fire chief, and two reporters—all of them white—visited Chinatown to investigate conditions there as part of a city project to clean up the area, which they found to be "in deplorably wretched condition." The party was watched by numerous worried Chinese people, who congregated in the streets and alleys, as it visited several laundries, stores and restaurants.

While inspecting the laundries, the group found that the waste water from their businesses was transported to the yards in back of the buildings and collected in "small cess pools" there. These pools—which the group considered unsanitary—were covered with loose boards and the party worried that passersby might dislodge the boards and fall in.

Many of the buildings were "veritable fire traps" and it was clear that if a fire started, it would be impossible to stop it until the whole of Chinatown was destroyed. The way in which chimneys were built with stovepipes running through the walls increased the likelihood of a dangerous fire occurring.

The party continued its tour in a Chinese boarding house, and climbed on a "rickety shaky stairway" to the second floor where they found two bedrooms. One of the bedrooms contained thirteen beds, and the other, smaller room had five beds. The overcrowding caused by poverty was not considered by the inspection party with any sympathy; rather, it was eager to characterize the condition of the buildings as filthy and decrepit.

The members of the inspection tour concluded that the property owners in Chinatown should be forced to obey city bylaws and clean up and repair these buildings, regardless of their financial circumstances. In addition, they worried that Chinatown could pose a danger to the larger community should epidemic disease take hold.[114]

Various Court Cases and Incidents

In September 1908, the Chinese gambler Da Chu was tried in court. He was accused of having stolen six hundred dollars and an insurance policy and other papers from Mak See Lee in Chinatown. He was arrested and kept in jail. On August 19, he had a preliminary hearing before police magistrate Joseph Ryan, at which he elected to take a speedy trial. At the trial, Judge Wilson presided; George H. Thompson appeared for the crown, and J.A. Harvey, KC, and S.S. Taylor, KC, defended Da Chu.

Da Chu rejected the accusation, saying that he did not steal money, an insurance policy or any other papers from Mak See, and hide his "loot" in a woodpile, as the prosecution claimed. He said that he had spent the night with his cousin and did not go out, so he could not have stolen anything from Mak See.

Several witnesses were brought to court to testify, both for the prosecution and the defence. To ensure that key witnesses on both sides would testify truthfully, the so-called "King's oath"—also called the "chicken oath"—was required by the court. The *Nelson Daily News*, in its report on the trial, described this oath.

> At the mention of this ceremony a dead hush fell on the crowd of Chinese in court. One by one, they slipped out, except those

directly concerned,... There can be no doubt that the "King's oath" has some dread and awful significance for the Chinese, and it has been stated on good authority that not one Chinaman in a hundred will swear falsely if subjected to this test. It is called the "King's oath" since its terms are printed in [the] Chinese royal color.

The following is the mode of administering the oath. The witness writes his name... on a blank space in the paper, the name of the accused and curiously enough, the year of the reign of the Chinese emperor. He then reads it over, its terms amounting to the witness praying [for] the strict damnation of all his ancestors up to Adam and beyond, and of his descendants to the seventeenth generation if what he is about to say be not the truth.... Being ancestor worshippers the force of the oath can be understood to some extent.

Outside the court, four Chinese candles are lighted and four joss sticks... are arranged in a square and lighted also. The witness takes the yellow paper on which he wrote his name, lights it, drops it into a number of other secred [sic] papers, and when all are consumed, he lays a chicken on a block of wood and chops off is [sic] head with a cleaver. Returning to court he gives his evidence, which may be relied on.

The "chicken oath" was used for the first time in Cranbrook at Da Chu's trial. The ceremony, which used chickens from the local Morris ranch, attracted quite a lot of attention among the spectators who were present.[115] At the end of the trial, Da Chu was found guilty and sent to jail in Nelson for twenty-three months.

In October 1911, Gitata Nishiyama appeared in the Cranbrook police court, charged with misappropriating fifteen hundred dollars that he had borrowed from Mrs. R.J. Lum in July 1910. Nishiyama had borrowed the money supposedly to purchase shares in the H.K. Futa Lumber Company, a company in which Nishiyama had a financial interest. A mortgage on his interest was to be the collateral for the loan. However, Nishiyama purchased eighty shares at fifty dollars each in the Cranbrook Saw Mills company, which had taken over the Futa Lumber Company, instead. Nishiyama no longer had an interest in the company, making the mortgage held as collateral worthless. Although Nishiyama offered to repay the value of Mrs. Lum's loan in shares, she refused this offer, preferring a cash repayment, although she was willing to accept the shares as a security for her loan. Later on, Nishiyama pledged the value of his shares for another purpose, leaving Mrs. Lum with no security for her loan—hence the lawsuit. The case was adjourned until November 20, to allow more evidence to be assembled.[116]

The court case resumed on November 20, Judge Peter E. Wilson presiding. Mrs. Lum claimed the right of holding a security for $1,500, the money she loaned to Nishiyama, and the fraudulent transfer of $3,750, the stock in the Cranbrook Saw Mills Ltd. However, the evidence of the crown witnesses showed that both parties knew the money was a loan for investing in the H.K. Futa Lumber Company, the former Cranbrook Saw Mill Ltd. An agreement was prepared between them stating that Mrs. Lum should have a mortgage on Nishiyama's interest in the H.K. Futa Company.

In January 1911, Nishiyama had been allotted $3,750 in stock, according to the 'assessment of in the H. K. Futa Company, $1,500 of which was set aside for paying Lum. In cross-examination by Mr. Macdonald, Lum admitted that Nishiyama had offered to repay her with fifteen hundred dollars' worth of the stock, which she refused to take—demanding cash instead. She also admitted that she would not take the $3,750 in stock, if offered. At this time, the Cranbrook Saw Mill Ltd., negotiated and assigned all its stocks as collateral security to the mortgagee. Nishiyama joined in this assignment but did not assign $1,500 worth of his stock to Mrs. Lum, thus the charge of fraudulent assignment was not withstanding.

Testifying for the defence, witnesses stated that Lum had been offered the stock but refused to accept it, as such the $1,500 worth of stock had not been assigned to her. And the agreement between the parties did not oblige Nishiyama to hold more than $1,500 of the stock for Mrs. Lum. Further evidence showed that Mrs. Lum had already recovered judgment for the $1,500 loan. Therefore, Nishiyama was acquitted.

On July 29, 1911, the *Cranbrook Prospector* reported that "a Chink [sic], filled with Sam Suie [liquor] and 'hop' started a rough house in Chinatown.... He procured a large knife and... tried to butcher a number of celestials, but was finally locked in a room where he proceeded to amputate a finger of his left hand. Chief Dow was called and placed him in jail. Dr. J.M. Bell dressed his wounds and pronounced him insane. He will be taken to New Westminster."[117]

On August 1, 1912, the *Cranbrook Herald* reported on the death, supposedly by suicide, of Lim Chong.[118] Lim had been run over by a train. His head was crushed, and his slippers and cap were found a short distance from his body, which lay on the railway track in the CPR yards. His body was taken to the undertaker, F.M. McPherson, and a coroner's inquest was held, presided over by the coroner, Dr. Bell. Matt Barney, the CPR engineer who was backing up the train, testified that he did not see the body until one of the yard men alerted him to it. A Chinese witness identified the deceased man as Lim Chong. This witness had known Lim for over a year, but had not seen him during the past week. He reported that Lim had a wife in China, and had no money.

Witnesses R.J. Reburn and J.F. Belanger said they had found Lim's body lying between the rails, and "from the position of the body, they were of the opinion the deceased had not been knocked down, but had deliberately got on the track in front of the backing engine and had lain down with his head on the rail to await his fate." Cory Dow, the chief of police, thought that he had had Lim Chong in custody about a year earlier. Dow reported that Lim seemed to be suffering mentally at that time, but after being held for a while, he seemed to recover. After hearing the witnesses, the coroner's jury ruled that the death was accidental.

On September 13, 1912, Frank Eggleston, a drunk lumberjack, took out his knife and tried to stab Lee Dee, a well-known Chinese man who was walking on Van Horne Street. Lee managed to catch Eggleston's hand and was able to avoid a fatal blow, thereby saving his own life. His hand, however, had been cut and his body wounded. Constable Baxter arrested Eggleston and sent Lee to Dr. Bell, who dressed his wounds. Eggleston declared that he would kill all the "Chinks" in British Columbia, and he made no defence of his racist actions in the police court.[119]

Raids in Chinatown

According to a Cranbrook bylaw, every merchant, trader, or other employer of labour was required to pay a road tax. On August 24, 1905, the city police, assisted by the city treasurer, Nun H. Lockhart, made a raid in Chinatown and "secured the $2.00 road tax from 33 Celestials. The yellow men hung onto their coins, and threats had to be used before they would part with the coins. A number of the Chinamen hid under their beds and in other inaccessible places, and the police were fortunate in gathering so many coins in one night."[120] On July 15, 1906, the Department of Finance presented a cheque of $2,647.78, the money received from the road tax, to city council at its regular monthly meeting.

On December 12, 1912, Low Ling and twenty-two Chinese men were arrested for gambling in a house after a raid in Chinatown. Low Ling was charged with being the keeper of a gambling establishment. James O'Shea, counsel for the defence, argued that the Chinese individuals were engaged in a harmless amusement that did not constitute gambling as defined by the criminal code. Suey Hop was called on by the prosecution to demonstrate the fan-tan game. A.M. Johnson, the city prosecutor assumed the role of a player. On a table between Johnson and Hop, a large square was drawn on a piece of fabric. Each corner of the square was marked with a number, from one to four. Players would place their money on the number(s) of their choice. Once the players had placed their coins on the number at the corner that they chose, the dealer placed a handful of white beads in the middle of the square and counted the beads out in groups of four with a bamboo strip. The last group of beads, be it 1 or 2 or 3 or 4, won the game. And the round of games would start again for players. On the four numbers, Johnson placed bets of varying amounts. Police Magistrate Irvine was present to record the amounts of winning and losing by Johnson and the dealer. Twelve ways of betting were demonstrated. At the end of the twelfth round, Johnson did not lose or win any money! "It's a square game," said Suey Hop, who worked at the saloon. "The chances of dealer and player are even. And no commission is taken on amounts under 60 cents per betting."

By April 7, 1921, gambling in Chinatown was reported to be eliminated. In his report to a meeting of the Police Commission, Acting Chief Roberts stated that gambling in Chinatown had been entirely stopped.[121]

On Wednesday, April 1, 1914, police conducted a raid in Chinatown. There they arrested Jim Dick, Mah Lee, and two cousins, both named Mah Sing, in an opium den—opium had been made illegal in Canada in 1908. They confiscated five sets of opium-smoking apparatus, plus a small quantity of opium. The Chinese men appeared in the police court the morning of April 2, where they were fined ten dollars each and had to pay the court costs. The confiscated items consisted of "five long bamboo pipes with little lamps for cooking the 'hop' and the other accessories of the habit which provides the Celestials with sweet dreams of the Chinese heaven." These articles were displayed in the police chief's office and exhibited to curious visitors.[122]

In June 1914, Archie Herrigan, a police officer on night duty, learned that someone in Chinatown was smoking opium. He went there and found the suspected building, but all the doors of that building were locked. Herrigan found a telegraph pole next to the building. He climbed up the telegraph pole and entered the building through a window, "finding Mah Sing enjoying the seductive dreams from the poppy." Mah was taken into custody, and the next morning, he appeared before Magistrate Arnold who levied a fine of fifty dollars or six months in jail since it was Mah's second conviction on the same charges. Since the headline on the newspaper report is headlined "Secures Six Months Berth in City Jail," it appears that Mah served the jail sentence.[123]

In July, John Lee, a prominent merchant in Chinatown, was arrested for having opium in his possession and was fined a hundred dollars and the costs of the hearing. Another raid in Chinatown on Saturday night, July 4, 1914, resulted in the arrest of a dozen Chinese men who were suspected of possessing opium. The following Monday, they appeared in police court. One of them, Loui

Yea, was convicted and sentenced to serve six months in jail for possession and the others were discharged.[124] Kwong Sing, however, was found to have opium in his possession. He was detained in jail by Magistrate Leask. On November 7, 1914, he was deported to China.

Guomindang—The Chinese Nationalist League

The imperial Qing dynasty had ruled China for almost three centuries. In 1908, the Chinese community in Cranbrook received news that Emperor Guangxu (光绪皇帝) had passed away. His death was followed quickly by the death of the powerful Empress Dowager Cixi (慈禧西太后). Chinese businesses hung white flags to show that they mourned the loss of Emperor Guangxu and Empress Cixi. The last Qing emperor was Pu Yi, who became emperor at the age of two in 1908 when Emperor Guangxu, his uncle, died.

At the beginning of the twentieth century, a republican movement led by Sun Yat-sen had emerged in China, dedicated to overthrowing the Qing dynasty. Several of the Chinatowns in the Kootenay, including Cranbrook, formed local branches of the republican political party, the Guomindang, which was formed after the successful republican revolution.

In February 1911, Sun Yat-sen (孙中山) arrived in Victoria, BC, to raise funds for the Tongmenghui (同盟会), also known as the Chinese Revolutionary Alliance, among other names. The Tongmenghui was the predecessor of the Guomindang party; its goal was the overthrow of the imperial Qing dynasty and the establishment of a Chinese republic.

On January 1, 1912, the Xinhai Revolution (辛亥革命) led by Haung Xing (黄兴), a comrade of Sun Yat-sen and one of the founders of the Tongmenghui (同盟会), successfully overthrew the Qing dynasty and established the Republic of China. In March 1912, the Tongmenghui formed a new republican political party, the Guomindang, known in English as the Chinese Nationalist League. The members of the Tongmenghui formed the core of this new party. Sun became the first president (中华民国) of the new republic, but he soon handed this position over to Yuan Shikai (袁世凯), leader of the republican army (北洋军), who was able to force Emperor Pu Yi (溥仪) to abdicate.[125] To symbolize their new freedom, in 1912 Chinese men were asked to cut off their queues and foot-binding of women was henceforth banned.

On February 24, 1912, the *Cranbrook Prospector* predicted that "the whole of Chinatown will be in festive clothing on Monday evening, when local Chinamen will celebrate the inauguration of the new Chinese republic."[126] The Chinese community held a meeting on Van Horne Street at which several leading citizens delivered a series of speeches. Large quantities of fireworks were set off that night. The patriotic local Chinese merchants decorated their stores in Chinatown with bright colours and erected arches of evergreens across the streets.

On February 29, 1912, these festivities—which were concurrent with the Chinese New Year—ended "in a brilliant and exceptional programme. Over one thousand dollars was spent by local natives of the Celestial empire. The Cranbrook band was in attendance and a speakers' stand had been built in the street and in front hung a picture of Sun Yat Sen, the first president of the new Chinese republic, with his name below in colored electric lights. Several of the local Orientals addressed the audience, and P.E. Wilson, P. DeVere Hunt and R.E. Beattie spoke on behalf of the new republic.... Boxes of cigars, various liquid refreshments, candies and nuts were supplied to all."[127]

The last issue of *The Week*, another newspaper in the Kootenay, reported that

> the giant is awake, and awake with a vengeance. Not yet... to over-run the western world as a "yellow peril," but to set an example to the whole world how to transform a venerable autocracy into a republic, almost by a stroke of the pen, almost without the shedding of a drop of blood.... this remarkable episode illustrates, it must be taken as proof positive of the strength of character with which the most populous race in the world is gifted.... We have now four hundred million people,... enjoying for the first time in their history the freedom of constitutional democratic government, at liberty to elect their own representatives, and through them to voice the popular demand.... The new republic will have many problems to solve... [but] it must never be forgotten that the nation is the custodian of the most ancient forms of philosophy known in the world, and has an educated upper class, possibly more highly cultured than the leaders of thought in any other country. The interest centres on the policy which the new republic will adopt, whether one of expansion or of internal development. If the latter, then the world may breathe easily for a time. If the former, then a race so reflective, so patient, so impassive, and so determined, will have to be reckoned with in the not distance future. While it is impossible not to view with satisfaction the emancipation of so historic an empire, it cannot be doubted that this very emancipation may add to the responsibilities and anxieties of all the Great Powers.[128]

Indeed, the republican government faced many challenges. As president, Yuan Shikai invited Song Jiaoren (宋教仁) and three other former members of the Tongmenghui to join the new cabinet. Song, a political leader and a founder of the Guomindang, led the party to victory in China's first democratic election. His leadership and success in Chinese politics alarmed Yuan. On March 22, 1913, Song was assassinated in Shanghai, and Yuan was able to set himself up as a dictator. This triggered a second revolution in China led by Sun Yat-sen, who had already returned home to Guangdong.[129] However, Yuan remained in power until his death in 1916.

In January 1921, some of the Chinese merchants and well-known Chinese residents in Cranbrook initiated the establishment of a Guomindang branch in the city. An inaugural meeting took place at 102 Clark Avenue. Mak Kwong was elected president of the local branch and Wong Hong, the secretary. The *Cranbrook Herald* wrote that "the Chinese National League is a strong body all over the Dominion, and especially in the west, with many influential branches established in the Chinese colonies of the larger towns and cities." The paper commented that "while ostensibly a political body, being understood to stand in strong support of Sun Yet San [sic] and his republican ideas, the League still has very prominent moral, social and educational ideals to live up to, and is quite a strong factor in the life of the Chinese republic itself."[130]

After Yuan Shikai's death in 1916, China fell into turmoil as warlords, especially in the northern regions of China, competed for power, although Sun's party remained powerful in southern China, where it was known as the China Southern Constitutional Government. In October 1921, the *Cranbrook Herald* recorded that the local branch of the Guomindang had sent a message to the chairman of the United States Disarmament Committee (USDC), Elihu Root, who would be hosting an international disarmament conference in Washington, DC, seeking recognition for the China Southern Constitutional Government. The request emphasized that "the Peking Warlord government is unlawful and cannot represent our China."[131]

On October 13 of the same year, the *Cranbrook Herald* reported that members of the Cranbrook Guomindang had assembled to celebrate the tenth anniversary of the Republic of China. According to the newspaper, by living in Canada, many of the Chinese had learned of the great benefits to their homeland that a constitutional government could provide. However, the Chinese had also adopted this position after learning about its potential from Sun Yat-sen and other Chinese republicans. The officers of the Cranbrook branch were effective at communicating the republican message, and many Chinese in the city and its vicinity joined the organization.

A number of Cranbrook's citizens were invited to the tenth anniversary celebration. Eng Sing, then the president of the branch, presided over the event.

W.A. Nisbet, G.J. Spreull and Alan Graham were among the Cranbrook citizens who attended and who congratulated the local branch of the Guomindang on its achievements. As well, addresses from various members of the Guomindang were delivered in both Chinese and English. The evening wound up with a fabulous banquet featuring all kinds of Chinese delicacies.[132]

On October 20 of the same year, Eng Sing received a message from Guomindang headquarters in Vancouver stating that "President Sun Yet Sen [*sic*] of the southern republic had mobilized an army to move northwards against the imperialist forces."[133] The local branch was instructed to hang out the flag of the Chinese republic (中华民国国旗) to show support for the movement.

On November 10, 1921, the local Guomindang advertised that they would hold a three-fold celebration in their new building at No. 5 Durick Avenue. This celebration went on for a few days. A journalist from the *Cranbrook Herald* attended the grand opening in the new premises. Prior to the commencement of the event, Eng Sing, the president, and Joe Jack, the secretary, stood on a platform to greet their guests and members. Among the distinguished guests were Reverends R.W. Lee and Chew Ling of the Chinese Mission, Gee Yen Po from Trail, Mah That Ming from Nelson, and Hep Chong, Chue Gain, Gee Way Joe and several women from Cranbrook. After giving a speech welcoming everyone, Reverend R.W. Lee officiated at the opening ceremony. Reverends F.V. Harrison, E.W. MacKay, and W.T. Tapscott and Alan Graham and F.A. Williams congratulated the Guomindang. Messages of congratulations from Calgary, Alberta, and Trois Rivières, Quebec, and a message from Mayor Hicks regretting that he was unable to attend, were read out at the event. A group photograph of seventy people was taken outside the building, and then all the members and guests were ushered inside and invited to tea in the Mission Room. The journalist commented that "the Chinese Nationalist League has fixed up its new meeting place in an extremely comfortable fashion."[134]

On December 1 of the same year, this Guomindang branch sent another letter of protest to the United State Disarmament Committee, stating that they would not recognize the delegates sent by the Peking government. They protested the fact that the South China Republic, with a population of two million people, had no voice at the conference.

The year 1921 was thus a very busy time for the local Guomindang! And it had inscribed its name on the world map recognized by the United States.

The Chee Kung Tong

Many Chinese immigrants in Canada were members of the Chee Kung Tong (致公堂), also known as the Chinese Freemasons Society (中国洪门民治党). Originally this tong—tong is Cantonese for gathering place—was known as Hongmen but its name was changed to Chee Kung Tong in 1876. The first Chee Kung Tong branch was established in Yale during the Fraser gold rush (1858–1860). After gold was depleted in the Fraser Canyon, many Chinese miners, labourers and merchants migrated to Quesnel Forks in the north or to Similkameen and the Kootenay in the southeast of BC.[135] Members of the Chee Kung Tong might have arrived in Cranbrook as early as 1898, because Chinese labourers were already employed in various coal mines in the Kootenay region by that time. Its Canadian headquarters were established in Vancouver in 1892. In 1920, the English name Chinese Freemasons Society was adopted.

The Chee Kung Tong was an organization that helped the Chinese find employment and provided them with meals and lodging when they first arrived in the communities in which the organization had a building. If the organization did not have a lodge, key members like the president or secretary would help newcomers find a place to stay. The address or post office box of the Chee Kung Tong would be the contact address where it received notices from the headquarters in Vancouver, news from Guangdong and other places, and mail from the homes in China of its members. Many of the Chinese immigrants could not read or write Chinese, so the secretary of the organization or members who knew the Chinese language would read their letters to them. Quite often, members would ask the secretary to reply to family members as well as to help them send their earnings home. If the organization had a lodge or rooming house, it would provide recreation, usually in the form of card games and fan tan, for its members. Quite a few of the Chee Kung Tong organizations leased out their recreation rooms for gambling, since the organization needed funds to pay for housekeeping and to pay its utility bills. Usually, a lodge would have a hall for members to learn and practise kung fu or other martial arts and the lion dance—a traditional dance in which lion costumes representing joy and happiness were featured. Additionally, the organization would help the poor, take care of the sick and the aged, and hold funeral and burial services for deceased members.[136]

In February 1911, when Sun Yat-sen arrived in Victoria, BC, to raise funds for the republican revolution in China, the Chee Kung Tong pledged to support the Guomindang. Meanwhile, Sun also encouraged members of the Guomindang to join the Chee Kung Tong. As time went by, however, the older members of the Chee Kung Tong realized that their organization was on the verge of being displaced altogether by the Guomindang; as a result, the relationship between the Chee Kung Tong and the Guomindang grew strained, and they ultimately ended their co-operation.[137]

The date when the Chee Kung Tong was established in Cranbrook is unknown. However, on September 15, 1917, the management and objectives of the local Chee Kung Tong were published in the *Chinese Times* in Vancouver. In its message, the organization stated that its objectives were pure, undertaken with no thought of personal gain or recognition, and they honoured brotherhood and friendship among its members. It also reminded members to attend the event at which the first five founders (五祖) of the organization were honoured, and announced with pride that the Han people—the ethnic group to which most Chinese people belong—had been reinstated in the Hanzu (汉族)—the Chinese people recognized after the formation of the Chinese republic. The Chee Kung Tong organization had distinguished its ethnicity because the rulers of the Qing dynasty (1644–1911) were Manchu, a people from the northeastern provinces of China. Their notice stated that the organization would hold a dinner banquet for its members and guests. The proud message ended with the slogans, "Long Live the Chinese Republic" and "Long Live the Chee Kung Tong."

On October 27, 1917, the organization announced in the *Chinese Times* that it had held an event to honour Wan Yunlong (万云龙), one of key founders of the Chee Kung Tong, and hosted a dinner banquet at the Peng Fang Restaurant (鹏芳酒楼) to celebrate the event in Cranbrook. At this "double happiness" event, the organization also welcomed ten new members. Elders Lee Cao Zu and Lin Yin De were the masters of ceremony at the banquet. At the same time, funds were raised to help elder Ma Yan Yuan return home to China. Ma had served the Chee Kung Tong for more than ten years, but lacked the money needed to buy his ticket home. The funds were sent to the Dart Coon Club headquarters (达权社总部) in Victoria, so that a director there could purchase a ticket and arrange for Ma to sail home.

The Dart Coon Club is a division of the Chinese Freemasons Society that manages the finances of the society and provides resources for the society to carry out its functions and activities, including management of its lodge, and celebration of festivals such as Chinese New Year and Zhongqiu Jie (Mid-Autumn Moon Festival), and observation of Qing Ming (清明) in spring, Yu Lan Jie (盂栏) in summer and Chong Yang Jie (重阳) in autumn, the festivals at which homage is paid to deceased family members, including cleaning and sweeping their tombs in the cemetery. The elders of this division teach members the martial arts or kung fu for self-defence, as well as the art of lion or dragon dances.

Although progress and news about the Cranbrook Chee Kung Tong was published in the *Chinese Times*, the location of its lodge was not mentioned. Meetings and celebrations might have been held in restaurants, private homes or boarding houses. On July 22, 1921, however, an announcement was made of the grand opening of the lodge that stated its address as P.O. Box 757 in Chinese text—but no street address was listed. The grand opening of the lodge and the honouring of the five founders of the Chee Kung Tong would take place on August 6 or the fourth day of the seventh moon in the Chinese calendar. Members were encouraged to attend this event.

Resentment, Assault and a Tong War

At about the same time, Yang Gui Xing, a Chinese resident in Cranbrook, wrote to the *Chinese Times* to voice his resentment toward the Guomindang branch in town. He said the Guomindang branch had published his name in the *Xin Guo Min News* (新国民报), stating that he owed the party $120, funds he had promised to donate. That notice indicated he had been supportive of the party, otherwise he would not have committed to donate. But Yang had reasons for not living up to his commitment. The Guomindang branch in Cranbrook was corrupt and shameful, Yang continued. He said that he had donated funds to the party several times but received no receipt or "button," a kind of acknowledgement from the party. He believed that his donations were not reported to the party, otherwise he would have received an acknowledgement of some kind. He suspected the money he had donated thus far had been taken by certain director(s) of the party for personal use. Furthermore, the Guomindang had reminded him that his monthly membership fee of $14 was also due, and that he also refused to pay this, because he did not trust the Guomindang branch anymore. He recalled that in September of the previous year, he and his friend Chen Jing Ming had each donated $10 to support the military services in Guangdong, and they received no acknowledgement. The deficiency and corruption of the Guomindang branch had created his suspicion and mistrust of the party, and he therefore withdrew his membership in the Guomindang![138]

On January 30, 1922, a conflict within the Chinese community—characterized by the *Cranbrook Herald* as a "miniature tong war" or feud among the Chinese—took place between members of an unnamed Chinese organization and the Guomindang (Chinese Nationalist League). The name of one of the Chinese organizations involved was not mentioned in the *Cranbrook Herald* reports. The dispute was about fundraising practices in the Chinese community— one party wished to collect some of the profits from fan-tan games to donate to the Cranbrook hospital but the Guomindang preferred to rely on donations—and ended in a physical altercation among the parties. The consequence was injuries to Eng Sing, president of the local branch of the Guomindang, and Don Yin, another well-known leader of the Guomindang in Cranbrook. Sing was taken to the St. Eugene Hospital for treatment of a head injury. Charges and counter-charges were laid by the parties.

In the initial report by the *Cranbrook Herald*, it was reported that Wong See, a member of the Chinese community, had laid charges against Eng Sing, Ong Hon, Ciue Boo and Ung Oon for assault. Because he was in hospital, Eng Sing was unable to attend an initial hearing of the case. The charges and counter-charges were likely to be heard the following week, according to the *Cranbrook Herald*. G.J. Spreull would represent Eng Sing, and Herchmer, Nisbet and Graham would represent the others in court.[139]

A report the following week on the case reiterated that Wong See remained the plaintiff and Eng Sing and his associations the defendants in the case. Representatives from various branches of the Guomindang in BC and southern Alberta arrived in Cranbrook to attend the hearing, which was then postponed for eight days. An interpreter who had come from Calgary to assist with the trial was attacked as he got off the train in Cranbrook, and two people were convicted of this assault in late February.[140] The February 9 report speculated that an out-of-court settlement among the parties might be reached within a few days, and that "there is more to [the case] than appears on the surface."[141]

On May 16, the so-called Chinese assault case came up at the county criminal court, Judge Thompson presiding. However, the plaintiff reported in this case was Eng Sing and the defendants were now Wong See, who had been the accuser in the first reports, plus two others. Sir Charles Hibbert Tupper, counsel for the Guomindang headquarters in Vancouver, acted for Eng Sing, along with G.J. Spreull; W.A. Nisbet and A. Graham represented the defendants.

Eng Sing, the victim of the assault, gave evidence through an interpreter. After the assault, he testified, he was taken to St. Eugene Hospital where Dr. G.E.L. MacKinnon dressed his wounds. Dr. MacKinnon was a witness in the proceedings and described Sing's injuries and the treatment he had provided for Sing.[142]

The court case concluded by May 25, 1922. Wong See, one of the defendants, was fined a hundred dollars by Judge Thompson, and the other two defendants were discharged. This court case had created intense interest among the Chinese in the district.[143]

After the conclusion of this court case, the functions and activities of the Cranbrook Guomindang were no longer reported in the local newspapers. The *Chinese Times* would also no longer publish any news about the functions or activities of this organization, because it was the mouthpiece of the Chee Kung Tong. It is reasonable to assume that as time went by, the Guomindang may have dissolved like the other branches in smaller towns and cities across Canada.

Chee Kung Tong Stayed Alive

The Chee Kung Tong persisted in Cranbrook into the 1950s. On August 24, 1922, it announced in the *Chinese Times* that it would hold an anniversary celebration on September 24 at its lodge. All members and the public were cordially invited to this event.[144]

On December 10, 1923, the names of the board members were published in the *Chinese Times*. For this term, Lin Li Ben was elected president; Xu Pan Zhao, the vice-president; Liao Bi Shan, the Chinese secretary; Ma Li Tao, the English secretary; and Zhou Zhen Jia and Ma Xin Wei were two treasurers. In addition, the board consisted of five directors, two auditors, three advisors and fifty members.[145] On December 17, a general meeting was held and forty members donated funds to the organization; the individual amounts varied from fifty cents to five dollars and the total sum collected was ninety-six dollars.[146]

On the same date, the Cranbrook Dart Coon Club announced in the *Chinese Times* that members of the Chee Kung Tong had celebrated its twelfth anniversary.

On January 14, 1924, the Chee Kung Tong acknowledged the members and friends, listed below, for having donated money to the joss house and to its reading room—where the organization subscribed to the *Chinese Times* and magazines for its members and non-members to read.[147] It is interesting to note the name of one Chinese woman, Ms. Fok Rui Lian, who donated money to honour the five founders of the organization and the deity, Guan Yunxiang (关云翔), commonly known as Guan gong (关公), the Lord of Justice, a hero in the Three Kingdoms (189–280 AD) of Chinese history. Guan gong possessed four virtues—justice, loyalty, humanity and bravery—that members of the Chee Kung Tong admired and tried to follow.[148]

Donations to the Joss House

Names	Translation	Amount
顺利公司	Shun Li Company	$40.00
霍瑞连女士	Ms. Fok Rui Lian	$5.00
何月镶	He Yue La	$2.00
司徒轮	Szeto Lun	$2.00
陈宜谈	Chen Yi Tan	$2.00
保添	Bao Tian	$2.00
欧阳成	Ou Yang Chen	$2.00
周家亲	Zhou Jia Qing	$1.50
周享	Zhou Xiang	$1.50

何洪	He Hong	$1.50
林英罗	Lin Ying Luo	$1.50
余信统	Yu Xin Tong	$1.50
韩在明	Han Zai Ming	$1.00
郑永全	Zheng Yong Quan	$1.00
绉厚瑶	Zhou Hou Yao	$1.00
关松维	Guan Song Wei	$1.00
周华	Zhou Hua	$1.00
马桢三	Ma Zhen	$1.00
汤保	Tang Bao	$1.00
周乐全	Zhou Le Quan	$1.00
汤瓒	Tang Zhan	$1.00
周家简	Zhou Jia Jian	$1.00
张其表	Zhang Qi Biao	$1.00
廖长	Liao Zhang	$1.00
	Total	$74.50

Source: *Chinese Times*, January 14, 1924.

Donations to the Reading Room

Names	Translation	Amount
廖羽	Liao Yu	$5.00
骆记	Lou Ji	$1.00
周家简	Zhou Jia Jian	$1.50
马心直	Ma Xin Zhi	$2.50
	Total	$10.00

Source: *Chinese Times*, January 14, 1924.

A joss house was not a temple, but a Chinese hall or place where ceremonies and rituals took place. Members of the Chee Kung Tong burned incense and lit oil lamps in the joss house to honour Guan gong, and their founders. It was a community centre, a place for the lonesome single men to socialize with one another, and hold meetings and gatherings to celebrate festivals such as Chinese New Year and Zhongqui Jie (Mid-Autumn Moon Festival, an event of thanksgiving), and to observe Qing Ming (清明), Yu Lan Jie (盂栏节) and Zhong Yang (重阳), the festivals to commemorate deceased Chinese.

On March 21, 1924, the Chee Kung Tong received a request from its headquarters to hold a special memorial service to pay respect to Dr. Wong Fung Wah, a leading member, who had been killed in a car accident while attending a world conference in San Francisco. Dr. Wong was the principal of Pekin

University, a man of exceptional educational attainment. In the local Chinese lodge in Cranbrook, a picture of Wong was draped with crepe and the Chinese flag was lowered to half-mast.[149]

On August 8 of the same year, the *Cranbrook Herald* reported that the local Dart Coon Club had begun building new premises in Chinatown, next to the Chee Kung Tong lodge. The building was planned to be a two-storey building, 22 feet (6.7 metres) by 70 feet (21.3 metres), clad in metal to meet fire requirements. George R. Leask was contracted to erect this building, and at the time of this report, the foundation was underway.[150]

On February 27, 1926, the Dart Coon Club and the Chee Kung Tong, now called the Chinese Freemasons Society, celebrated Chinese New Year "with the most elaborate pyrotechnic display that the city has probably ever seen.... The fireworks were so thick that they rained on the ground in front of the Dart Coon [C]lub and the Chinese Masonic Temple like a heavy storm, and the noise resembled the air raids of London at their worst during the war [World War I]," reported the *Cranbrook Herald*. "Many hundreds of dollars' worth of fireworks must have gone up in smoke, as the litter on the streets the following day testified," continued the *Cranbrook Herald*, and "one elaborate piece consisted of a long chain, possibly a hundred feet long, made up of a continuous series of fireworks in all colors and degrees of explosiveness."[151]

On May 2, 1925, John Lee, an influential leader of the Chinese community, died of pneumonia. He was a notable member of the Chee Kung Tong and a well-known merchant in town and the district. His funeral service was carried out by the Chinese Freemasons Society and the Dart Coon Club.[152]

A canopy was erected in front of Lee's house, under which the body of the deceased was placed. Lum Lip conducted the service and called upon members of the different lodges and Lee's friends to come forward to give a reverent bow and to read out a personal eulogy. After all of them had paid their respects, Lum asked the people to form a circle around the coffin. Then the leader of the Chinese Methodist Mission read a scripture in Chinese, after which Chinese members of the mission sang two hymns in the Chinese language. After the hymns, Rev. E.W. MacKay conducted the ceremony in English. He said, "if our practices were more in accordance with the principles of the Christian religion it would be easier for these Chinese to appreciate Christianity." MacKay claimed that he was impressed with the simplicity and sufficiency of Christianity for the world's needs but was disappointed by the discord existing among Christians. After the ceremony, the Elks Band led the funeral cortege to the graveside. It was estimated that over sixty cars carried the Chinese and others in the funeral procession.

At the graveside, Rev. MacKay conducted the burial service. The Chinese non-Christian rite was not performed because Lee Look, the son of the late John Lee, was a Christian. The deceased was survived by his widow, five sons and a few daughters.

On June 3, 1926, the *Cranbrook Herald* reported that a fire had occurred the previous Saturday in a building behind the Dart Coon Club. The fire brigade arrived at the scene promptly to put out the fire. No occupants were affected, but damage to the building was estimated at four hundred dollars, which would be partly covered by insurance. The property, which was used as a rooming house and clubhouse, belonged to Chow Wing Kong and Associates. The building had three rooms on the upper floor, and the main floor was used as a clubhouse.[153]

On July 15 of the same year, another fire occurred in a closet under the stairway of the Chinese Freemasons Society hall. The fire brigade arrived and extinguished the fire using chemicals because coal oil was found on the floor and rolls of paper that were used to light incense were carefully placed nearby. In addition, several matches were scattered on the floor—so it was not advisable to extinguish the fire with water. The causes of the fire were under investigation at the time of this report.[154]

In 1942, an election ballot of the Dart Coon Club indicated that Wu Qi (吴其) had been elected as the president of the club, Huang Zhou Fan (黄卓凡) as its secretary, and Li Shu Yuan (李树元) as the public relations officer.

On February 5, 1949, the Chee Kung Tong published an acknowledgement in the *Chinese Times* of donations made by its members. The total sum that the organization received from thirty-eight members was ninety-three dollars.

In early 1952, the Chee Kung Tong and the Dart Coon Club acquired a new building on Seventh Avenue in Cranbrook. This building would be the home of many single Chinese men. An official opening was held, and elder Wong Yee Hon, the master of ceremonies, welcomed the guests and members to this event and then introduced the board members to the audience. Mayor Sang was invited to the grand opening, and he congratulated the two organizations.

Unfortunately, on February 21 of the same year, the *Cranbrook Courier* reported that a "Major Blaze Razes the Chinese Block." The paper reported that "a fire occurred at approximately 8:50 a.m. Lost in the blaze was the Felix Laundry, assessed value of improvements at $2450.00, the Chinese Dart Coon Club, a two-storey building owned by the organization, assessed value of $5000.00, and the Chinese Masonic Hall, another two-storey block under the names of Man Su, Lew Fhick Bow and Wong Lung, assessed value $2450.00." These values were based on the Cranbrook municipal assessments at the time.

The cause of the blaze was yet to be determined at the time this report was published, but it had affected a number of the Chinese who lived in these two buildings. The head and shoulder of one Chinese man were slightly burned. Other occupants of these buildings lost considerable money held in currency.

Flames from the tinder-dry wooden structures were fierce, with the heat so intense that firefighting was very difficult. The Sun Fick Café on the opposite side of the avenue and a small residence nearby smouldered and had to be doused with a fire hose. The blaze advanced quickly from the time the alarm was sounded. The entire fire department, led by Fire Chief James Gordon, arrived at the scene immediately, and a new fire-fighting apparatus—a triple combination of pumpers—controlled the blaze within forty-five minutes, but the buildings were impossible to save. A small dwelling at the rear occupied by Geo. Popoff, was also destroyed, although its charred walls and roof remained partially standing.[155]

On May 29, 1952, the *Cranbrook Courier* reported that members of the Chinese Freemasons Society had held a sod-turning ceremony to mark the rebuilding of its hall, as the original building had been totally destroyed by the recent fire. Supervised by Jim Sing, a Chinese businessman with an import-export business in Toronto, the first sod was turned by Wong Yee Hon, a past master of the order who was a member of the Chinese Freemasons Society for sixty-five years. Mayor Sang of Cranbrook, contractor Frank Jones of the A.E. Jones Company, and officers of the Chinese Freemasons Society were present at the ceremony.

Sing contacted members of the Chinese Freemasons Society across the country and gathered money and pledges, which enabled him as the chairman of the building committee to sign an initial contract of $25,000 with the A.E. Jones Company to erect a new, stuccoed building of 25 feet (7.62 metres) by 65 feet (19.8 metres) on the old site. This new building would provide accommodations with modern facilities for fifteen elderly members. Expansion of the building on the adjoining lot would take place in the near future, stated the lodge officers. The present new building was scheduled for an official opening ceremony on August 15.

Other members of the building committee were Harry Lim, who served as secretary; Lee Poo Wing as treasurer; Man Wah Sun, manager of the Sun Lee Yun Co. as the project's accountant; and Lee Hoy Hee to manage the building project. Included also were the Sam Yick Company, representing the Chinese Freemasons Society, and Mah Kong and Joe Lein from the Dart Coon Club. Mah was the supervisor of the project.

At the sod-turning ceremony, Mayor Sang, Alderman Burton, Mrs. Austin Millar of the Salvation Army, Mr. F.A. Jones and Mr. Hummel were present, guests of the Chinese Freemasons Society. Following, they sat down to a delicious spread in the banquet room of the Sun Lien Café. Proposing a toast to the new project, the mayor paid tribute to the Cranbrook Chinese citizens, whom he had found over his thirty years' association with them to be "honest, upright, community-minded and good citizens." The new project, he said, designed by them to assist the aged members of their community and carry on their charitable work, was of considerable importance in the community, and he wished them well in their new undertaking.

Sing expressed his thanks to the Chinese Freemasons Society and its patriarch, Wong Yee Hon. The latter, he said, had lost all his personal effects in the recent disastrous fire. And he predicted that many people would join the organization when they learned about the building project. He was also confident that an expansion to the building would follow in due course.[156]

The sod-turning event painted a bright future for the Chinese Freemasons. In reality, this beautiful picture soon faded away, as good news about and activities of the society can hardly be found after this year. Today, the Chinese Freemasons Society in Cranbrook no longer exists. But it has left a page of glorious history in the Kootenay.

A Rotary Governor

Jim Y.W. Chiu was born on August 5, 1950, in Guangdong. He immigrated to British Columbia in 1969 after completing high school in Hong Kong. He attended the University of British Columbia and graduated from the Faculty of Pharmacy in 1976. He then moved to Kelowna. In 1977, he married Helen, and the following year, they settled in Cranbrook, where they operated two Shoppers Drug Mart franchises.

Jim joined the Rotary Club of Cranbrook in 1990, and served as the club's president in 1994–95. He chaired the club's seventy-fifth anniversary celebration in 1997, and served as the governor's special representative in forming the Cranbrook Sunrise Rotary Club the same year.

Jim served as the assistant district governor from 1997 to 1999. He was also a Paul Harris Fellow and a Foundation Benefactor. His contributions to the Cranbrook community included serving in the Sam Steele Society, Big Brothers and Sisters, and the Canadian Diabetes Association. In 2000, he was elected district governor of the Rotary Club of Cranbrook. Jim and Helen had two children, Ryan and Andrea.

Unfortunately, Jim suffered from pancreatic cancer and passed away in 2018. After his death, Helen moved to Burnaby in BC's Lower Mainland.[157]

An Overseas Bride

In 1962, Eva Kwong from Taishan County (Toishan in Cantonese), Guangdong, immigrated to Canada to join her father in Cranbrook and to marry. Both her father and her husband worked in restaurants. When her father first began working in a restaurant, he had to peel about 150 pounds (68 kilograms) of potatoes every day. He received no money, only food and lodging, said Kwong.

James and Helen Chiu with Frank Devlyn, Rotary International President 2000–01 in San Diego, September 1999. Courtesy of Helen Chiu

When she arrived in Cranbrook, the city was a quiet place with a population of around four thousand people. Chinatown still existed on Seventh Avenue with about a hundred Chinese men and a few Chinese women living in the area. Many of these Chinese men were single and lived in the boarding house of the Chee Kung Tong (the Chinese Freemasons Society). This Chinese organization was the place where the elderly Chinese got together and socialized with one another. It was challenging for the board members to keep up the premises, since they had few resources. Eventually, the property was sold, and that marked the end of Chinatown.

Kwong recalled that many of the Chinese men in the city were labourers working in the coal mines. Some worked in the bush cutting logs for lumber companies. A few were market gardeners. Others performed odd jobs, such as carrying water, and chopping wood for restaurants and families. As time went by, these older Chinese men either passed away or left town. When Kwong arrived in town, she could find only one Chinese grocery store in the area where Chinatown had once existed.

During her first five years living in the city, Kwong stayed at home, preparing meals for the entire family and doing the household chores. She and her husband had two sons and one daughter. All her children attended school in Cranbrook. After they graduated from high school, her elder son and daughter left town and found work in other places. Her younger son, however, remained at home.

When Kwong started working as a helper in a restaurant, she received only seventy-five cents an hour. Later, husband and wife established the Golden Star Restaurant at 17 Twelfth Avenue South in Cranbrook (now called the Lucky Star Restaurant). In 1996, her husband had a heart attack and passed away. "His death was devastating to me," said Kwong with a hint of sadness. "I felt so lonely and helpless," she went on. She had no choice then but to operate the restaurant herself. She was thankful that her youngest son had remained at home and could assist her in managing the restaurant. As of 2001, she was the sole owner of the Golden Star Restaurant.[158]

Two Chinese Scientists

Cai Yi Hai (蔡义海 –译音) and Ma Zhong Lan (马中兰 –译音), husband and wife, were geologists in China. Cai came from Hunan, whereas Ma was a native of Taishan County (台山县) in Guangdong. In 1956, Ma graduated from college and went to work in Hunan where she met Cai. They fell in love and got married. After their wedding, they were sent to Guangdong by the Chinese government to investigate sources of water in Yegang Qu, Guangdong.

By then, Ma's father, Ma Yuen Tong (马 -棠 –译音), had already been in British Columbia for years. Apparently, he was sponsored by his older brother to immigrate to Canada. When Ma's father arrived in BC, he was only 15 years old, yet he went to work as a labourer. Later, he went home to get married, had a daughter, Ma Zhong Lan, and then returned to BC. In 1947, the Chinese Exclusion Act was repealed, and it once again became possible for Chinese people to immigrate to Canada. Reunification of families that had been separated as a result of the Exclusion Act was now possible. That provided the opportunity for Ma Yuen Tong to send for his wife to join him in BC. By then his daughter was a college student studying geology in Guangdong, so she did not join her mother in immigrating to Canada. Ma Yuen Tong lived a long life, dying at the age of 92.

In 1966, Mao Zedong (毛泽东), chairman of the Communist Party of China, launched the Cultural Revolution in China. Neither Cai Yi Hai nor Ma Zhong Lan felt that they could fit into the system. Since Ma's parents were getting old, they decided to immigrate with their children to British Columbia. When they left Guangdong, their daughter was 15 years old and their son was 9. When they arrived in BC, they spent a couple of weeks in Vancouver, visiting relatives and friends in the city. Meanwhile, they planned to move to Toronto. But Ma Yuen Tong advised them to move instead to Cranbrook where coal mining, the main industry in the Kootenay, would provide them opportunities to work in the coal mines as geologists. So instead they moved to Cranbrook; that also enabled them to stay closer to Ma's parents.

When Cai and Ma were in college studying geology, they had not been required to learn English. Instead, they studied Russian. When they arrived in Cranbrook, both husband and wife applied to work in coal mines. Ma was interviewed by one coal-mining company. Unfortunately, she did not get a position in that company due to her poor English. Cai was fortunate in being able to secure a job at the Chiseler Coal Mining Company as an analyst. Later, the company changed hands and became the BC Coal Company. He continued working for the BC Coal Company until it declared bankruptcy and he lost his job! Then he got a position at the Green Hill mine, another mining company, not as a scientist but as a driver, transporting coal to destinations where it was needed.

Meanwhile, Ma went to the College of the Rockies, a community college in Cranbrook, to study English. After half a year, she obtained a job as a dishwasher in a restaurant. Later, she went to work for the Town and Country restaurant, also as a dishwasher. These jobs helped Ma learn about the operation and management of restaurants, and in 1981, Cai and Ma established the Kowloon Restaurant in town. Ma was the full-time manager, while Cai continued to work at the coal mine. Unfortunately, the Kowloon Restaurant was destroyed by fire later on. The couple then opened the Champion House in the mall located at 300 Cranbrook Street North.

Ma was an optimist and did not feel sorry that she could not utilize her scientific knowledge in geology. She said that when a person ventured overseas, he or she had to adjust and adapt to his or her life in the new country. With her open mind and wisdom, she developed good friendships among her classmates at the College of the Rockies. While she was taking English there, she went home for lunch every day, even in winter. One of her classmates offered to give her a dollar so that she could buy coffee during lunch hour instead of walking home in the snow for lunch. She appreciated good friendships with her fellow classmates, and remarked that she did not encounter prejudice and discrimina tion living in Cranbrook.

During our interview, Ma said that she had two good reasons for immigrating to Canada: to be with her aged parents and to send her children to school in Canada. She was pleased that she had achieved her objectives. Her children were both university graduates. Her daughter was working in a large insurance company as a strategist, while her son was employed by the Toronto Dominion Bank as a stock market analyst. She was very proud of them, and happy with her life residing in Cranbrook.[159]

When the Exclusion Act was repealed in 1947, Chinese immigrants in Canada became able to sponsor their family members to immigrate to this country for family reunification. Both Eva Kwong and Ma Zhong Lan were Chinese immigrants who came to Canada to be reunited with their fathers. Both Ma and Kwong had to learn and speak English when they began working in restaurants and stores. In essence, it is fundamental for all new immigrants to acquire one of the official languages of Canada, either English or French, before they apply for Canadian citizenship.

Working in Cranbrook's Chinese Restaurants

The Bamboo Garden Restaurant was once owned and operated by Peter Mar and his wife. In 1974, Mar was sponsored by his uncle to immigrate to Canada from Guangdong. His uncle had his family with him and he owned the New Canton Café in town. Mar was only 18 years old when he arrived in Cranbrook. Soon after his arrival, he began working for his uncle in the café. His uncle paid him three hundred dollars a month and provided him with food and lodging.

"In those days, a restaurant needed many workers," said Mar. "In addition to hiring a chef, the restaurant owner(s) had to employ assistant cooks and kitchen helpers. For example, my uncle had to hire one person to peel potatoes, another one to cut beef from a half or quarter. Today, all the steaks are cut by wholesalers, and even hamburger patties are prepared by wholesalers before they deliver them. At that time, many restaurants burned wood for cooking, therefore, the owners hired people to chop wood for them." He paused and then continued, "In the 1970s, many restaurants were owned and operated by Chinese people. But in the 1990s many Caucasians began to operate restaurant businesses, in competition with Chinese restaurants. It is a relief for me that my wife and I own the business now, and we have no worries about paying mortgages because we own our business."[160]

Furthermore, he stated that the location of the Tamarack Centre shopping mall at 1500 Cranbrook Street North was in an area that had been occupied by Chinese vegetable gardens. Another vegetable garden was located between Second Avenue and Victoria Street. These vegetable gardens were owned by Chu Ban Quan, who hired Chinese men to work for him. In 1976, the area at Cranbrook Street North was converted to a shopping mall, because the younger generations were no longer interested in vegetable gardening.

Mar was happy and contented with his life. He said his happiest moments were when he met and married his wife. Together they raised three children, two boys and one girl. His mother-in-law used to live with them, but due to poor health, she was hospitalized. He and his wife as well as all his children made efforts to visit her in hospital regularly. His younger son was living with the family, and he visited his grandmother in hospital every day. The other two children, who were not in town, came home during the weekend to visit their grandmother in hospital.

Both Peter Mar and his wife found life agreeable and comfortable in Cranbrook although Mrs. Mar had encountered teasing from Caucasian teenagers when she started her job in town. They teased her because she had an accent in her spoken English. She said, in the early days, I was working as a cashier in a store. A group of kids who attended the junior high school nearby often came to the store to buy sweets and candy. Two of the mischievous kids loved to tease me. I tolerated them for some time until one day I could not take it anymore. I took them aside, told them my feeling and said that it was not right for them to tease me. After the incident, they stopped their teasing and became polite to me. I feel that was my accomplishment![161]

During our interview, Mrs. Mar compared the reasons why the old-timers and the newcomers left home and ventured overseas. She said,

Many of the old-timers [in China] were poor; they owned no farmland but cultivated crops such as rice, sweet potatoes and vegetables for landlords who paid them no wages. At harvest time, they took their produce to the landlords who gave them a meagre portion of their crops as a reward for their hard work. The peasants were poor and living in starvation, thus many of them left home and ventured overseas to find a better life for themselves, and to support their loved ones at home. And when they arrived in foreign lands, they still had to struggle to make ends meet, whereas the newer immigrants came here on their own accord and they were better equipped for dealing with a new environment. The new immigrants should not look back and think of their glorious days of the past in their home country, particularly in Hong Kong.

She paused and then continued.

When we come to a new country we have to adjust and adapt. Thinking of the good days in the past would hinder us from moving forward because those thoughts would not make us happy in the new environment, particularly when we might have to change jobs or have to find a job that paid or one that would give them prestige.

Deceased Chinese People Buried in Cranbrook Cemeteries

The table below shows that many Chinese and Chinese Canadians lived a long life in Cranbrook. Most deceased Chinese people were buried in the Cranbrook Old General Cemetery on Borden Road West. Those marked with an asterisk (*) were buried in the Westlawn Cemetery, located at Cobham Avenue West and Borden Road West.

Chinese Interred in Cranbrook Old General Cemetery and Westlawn Cemetery

	First name	Age	Sex	Occupation	Date of death	Years in BC
Ban Quan *	Lillian Martha	67	F	Unknown	1966-12-07	unknown
Ban Quan	William Andrew	31	M	Unknown	1915-07-14	31
Chew	Yim Kong	83	M	Logger	1957-12-02	44
Chin	Mabel	50	F	Pharmacist	1977-01-07	unknown
Chon	Tai Chu	65	M	Baker	1951-01-25	41
Chong	Fanny Hip	n/a	F	Unknown	1921-09-10	unknown
Chong	Lem Dad	69	M	Gardener	1960-08-19	unknown
Chong	Man	46	M	Unknown	1918-12-22	unknown
Chong	Wing	50	M	Labourer	1931-10-23	unknown
Chong	Yim Kong	83	M	Logger	1957-12-02	44
Chow	Sing	83	M	Barber	1959-05-25	47
Chow	Tome	57	M	Labourer	1935-03-08	unknown
Chow	Way	33	M	Unknown	1919-03-24	unknown
Chow	Win Wee	77	M	Gardener	1954-12-21	50
Chow	Yick Mah	78	M	Unknown	1949-12-13	unknown
Chow	Yue Ching	32	M	Labourer	1926-06-?	unknown
Chu*	Ban Quan	86	M	Prospector	1947-05-13	65
Chu	Jon Pon	82	M	Labourer	1952-04-15	64
Chu	Men Jun	79	M	Cook	1969-03-24	58
Con	Yue Chang	48	M	Unknown	1931-10-23	Unknown
Fang*	Tsick Kim	86	M	Unknown	1972-?-?	unknown
Fong	Yue	n/a	M	Unknown	1969-01-28	unknown
Lam	Hoy	n/a	M	Unknown	1967-11-11	unknown
Lee	Bo Chinese	46	M	Labourer	1938-02-12	unknown
Lee	Book Loy	57	M	Unknown	1926-04-19	unknown
Lee	Bow	78	M	Unknown	1936-09-12	unknown
Lee	Chong Fat	39	M	Labourer	1920-11-23	unknown
Lee	Chong	43	M	Labourer	1909-11-17	unknown
Lee	Chow Man	49	M	Unknown	1940-03-06	unknown
Lee	Edward	62	M	Unknown	1909-12-30	unknown
Lee	Ding	72	M	Store Owner	1956-01-14	30+
Lee	Do Wee	65	M	Storekeeper	1924-12-24	unknown

Lee	Gim	47	M	Unknown	1911-03-09	unknown
Lee	Guen Soy	51	M	Labourer	1921-06-03	unknown
Lee	Ham Fat	32	M	Labourer	1923-01-20	unknown
Lee	How	47	M	Labourer	1909-01-13	unknown
Lee	Hop	78	M	Cook	1961-02-21	57
Lee	Jack	80	M	Unknown	1929-04-29	unknown
Lee	John	58	M	Merchant	1925-05-02	unknown
Lee	Margaret	53	F	Housewife	1915-04-21	unknown
Lee	Shel Lun	26	M	Labourer	1909-10-27	unknown
Lee	Sick	78	M	Logger	1960-07-25	49
Lee	Soon	67	M	Cook	1961-07-20	48
Lee	Suey Chow	1	n/a	11-month-old	1929-06-01	11 months
Lee	Suey Shick	2	M	n/a	1938-09-21	2
Lee	Yew Ying	70	M	Cook/Labourer	1956-06-13	45
Lee	Yuen Ying	76	M	Unknown	1945-03-10	unknown
Lee	Ying	2	F	n/a	1913-09-10	2
Ng	Yee	n/a	M	Unknown	1958-05-11	unknown
Quan	Tom	n/a	M	Unknown	Unknown	unknown
Quen	Sing Yip	69	M	Unknown	1949-12-14	unknown
Wong	Chow	34	M	Unknown	1919-08-17	unknown
Wong	Dun Quai	74	M	Launderer	1934-01-05	unknown
Wong	Lim	61	M	Unknown	1917-12-21	unknown
Wong	Luck	70	M	Unknown	1918-04-15	unknown
Wong	Long	26	M	Unknown	1913-09-16	26
Wong	Mow	56	M	Labourer	1949-01-05	30
Wong	Sang	54		Cook	1951-07-28	unknown
Wong	Sue	58		Labourer	1939-03-07	unknown
Wong	Toll	78	M	Cook	1961-07-10	37
Wong	Tong	55	M	Labourer	1918-11-05	unknown
Yip	Quen Sing	69	M	Unknown	1949-12-14	unknown

Sources: West Lawn Cemetery Record and Vital Statistics, Cranbrook.

Conclusion

It is comforting to learn that the Chinese immigrants and Canadian citizens of Chinese origin in Cranbrook were successful in their careers and professions. Some of the old-timers, like the Chinese merchant John Lee, had acquired wealth, and Chu Ban Quan, the prospector and miner, succeeded in his endeavours. Both these Chinese men spent many years in Cranbrook and contributed to the growth and development of the city. Chinese Canadians have certainly left a memorable history in Cranbrook. The early Chinese immigrants had little choice but to tolerate racism in order to make life work in a foreign country as well as to support their family members in Guangdong. At the same time, they also contributed to the growth and development of the city, shown in the records of their trades and employment in the city and its vicinity.

Once the Farwell Town: Revelstoke

The City of Revelstoke is located on the banks of the Columbia River near the confluence of the Illecillewaet River, the meeting place of the Sinixt, Secwepemc, Ktunaxa and Sylix Nations.[162] Revelstoke is located within the traditional territory of each of these Indigenous peoples. The Sinixt are an Interior Salish people whose territory is located in the region now known as the Interior Plateau of BC and encompassed the headwaters of the Columbia River. Their language and culture are similar to those of the Okanagan and Secwepemc Nations.[163] The Secwepemc Nation is a nation of seventeen bands. Their traditional territory in south-central BC spans land from the Columbia River valley to the Fraser River valley and south to the Arrow Lakes. The Sylix people are part of the Okanagan Nation and their traditional territory crosses the international border with the United States. There are seven Sylix communities in BC today. The Ktunaxa traditional territory is adjacent to the Kootenay and Columbia Rivers and around the Arrow Lakes.

Revelstoke is approximately 641 kilometres east of Vancouver and 415 kilometres west of Calgary. Both the Trans-Canada Highway and the Canadian Pacific Railway pass through and link this city from British Columbia to Alberta via Roger's Pass in Glacier National Park. Mount Revelstoke National Park is located north of the city and Mount Begbie lies to the south. Highway 23 connects the city to the Mica Dam, which generates hydroelectricity for the Kootenay and is located on the Columbia River about 135 kilometres north of Revelstoke.

Revelstoke can be reached by air from both Vancouver and Calgary. In 1914, Parks Canada declared Mount Revelstoke as Canada's seventh national park in recognition of its unspoiled mountain scenery and subalpine wildflower meadows.

The Beginning of Revelstoke

In July 1882, Arthur Stanhope Farwell, a surveyor, received a letter from the chief commissioner of Lands and Works instructing him to survey the land between the international boundary and Kootenay Lake. He was to find out "the extent and character of the valley on each side of the [Columbia River], approximate area subject to overflow, average depth of flood water and the operations necessary to reclaim the lands."[164] The survey was also to include the Second Crossing, a townsite consisting of "a cluster of log houses and shacks… on the east bank of the Columbia [River], at which point there was a ferry across the swift-flowing, turbulent stream."[165] Farwell completed his survey, and on December 31, 1883, he handed in his report to the chief commissioner.[166]

In fall the same year, Farwell applied for a large tract of land twenty miles in length and four miles in depth on both sides of the Columbia River that included the townsite of Second Crossing. In May 1884, a fire destroyed many buildings in this townsite, but they were rebuilt shortly after. In 1885, "Farwell obtained by purchase a Crown grant under the great seal of British Columbia of 1,175 acres of land situated within what is known as the railway belt of British Columbia, a tract of land twenty miles [thirty-two kilometres] on either side of the CPR."[167] However, the railway belt—a corridor of land running along the railway line that the CPR could sell to raise money for its operations—had been conveyed by provincial statute to the Dominion of Canada in 1883 to allow it to recoup the expenses it had incurred building the railway from sales of land to settlers.[168] A complex law case regarding Farwell's possession of the land ensued, a case he ultimately lost.

Meanwhile, Farwell was advised by the provincial commissioner of Lands and Works to survey the land he had purchased. He did the survey himself and designed the townsite, which soon had "general stores, hotels, brothels and saloons" on Front Street.[169] In 1884, the *British Colonist* reported that "carpenters are busy altering and extending premises and erecting new buildings."[170] A journalist for the *Daily Colonist* reported in 1885 that "the town contains about 50 houses of a better class than those that stood there before the fire. Business is very brisk…. Mr. Farwell is selling lots briskly and new buildings are going up every day. The wagon road bridge, which is to run beneath the railway bridge, will be ready for use in ten days' time."[171] In 1886, "the Royal Hotel has had $4,000 expended on it in improvements, and will now accommodate about sixty guests."[172]

Farwell assumed the CPR tracks would run through his property, so he arranged to meet with Harry Abbott, superintendent of the CPR's Pacific Division, and offered to sell eighty acres of his land to the CPR so it could erect a train station. But W.C. Van Horne, vice-president of the CPR, wanted nothing to do with Farwell or his offer. Instead, the CPR built its station on a site about one and a half miles (2.4 kilometres) east of the Farwell townsite. A new townsite then began to develop in the vicinity of the railway station. Of the two townsites, a journalist at the *Kootenay Star* lamented that the CPR had not accepted Farwell's offer, causing the town to be "cut in two by a mile and a half of lonely, burnt-up timber." He thought the Farwell site would have made an ideal townsite, but due to the CPR's decision, "the two ends [must join] hands across the dividing stretch of forest [to become] a town of respectable dimensions."[173]

In the summer of 1885, the CPR had been on the verge of bankruptcy when the construction of the railway track reached Craigellachie. George Stephen, president of the CPR at the time, approached Edward Charles Baring, Baron Revelstoke—the head of an investment bank in the UK, Baring Brothers & Company—requesting financial assistance. Baring Brothers bought up the CPR's unsold bonds, enabling the railway to be completed.[174] On November 7, 1885, the last spike was nailed at Craigellachie by Donald Smith, one of the CPR's financiers—a historical moment at which the transcontinental railway was finally completed. The town at the CPR Station was renamed Revelstoke in 1886 in honour of Edward Charles Baring.

The court case the CPR mounted against Farwell disputing his right to the property took a number of years to resolve, which slowed down the development of the new town. Those who had bought lots in Farwell paid over their money and made improvements to their properties, but were unable to obtain the deeds to their properties. On March 14, 1893, Judge Burridge of the Exchequer Court found against Farwell in the lawsuit the CPR had initiated. He ordered "Farwell to execute to the Crown a surrender of the lands involved [the Revelstoke townsite]."[175] Farwell appealed this decision and the case went to the Supreme Court; the original ruling against Farwell was upheld. In 1897, the landowners at the Farwell townsite finally obtained clear title to their properties.

Eventually, the two townsites amalgamated into one and on March 1, 1899, the City of Revelstoke was incorporated. Florence "Frank" McCarty was elected the first mayor of the newly incorporated city.[176]

The First Chinese Labourers

During the construction of the Canadian Pacific Railway (1880–1885), Andrew Onderdonk, the contractor who oversaw the railway construction in BC, contacted agents to help him recruit Chinese labourers for the construction of the CPR in British Columbia. About two thousand Chinese labourers arrived from California, Oregon and Canada's eastern provinces, and another fifteen thousand Chinese labourers came from the four districts in the Zhujiang Delta in Guangdong, China.[177] The total number of Chinese labourers employed by the CPR was therefore about seventeen thousand men.

By the winter of 1883, the construction of the railway had reached Savona, BC, an area with less lofty granite hills, so construction of tunnels was not required. Onderdonk then dismissed a large number of the Chinese labourers, retaining some of them to continue with the construction between Kamloops and Craigellachie, and to do maintenance work on the railway line in winter.[178]

When the CPR rail from the east was connected to the line in the west at Craigellachie, on November 7, 1885, the many Chinese labourers were conspicuously absent from the photographs taken to commemorate the event. However, at least one Chinese man was present, even if he is not visible in the photographs. Wing Chung, one of the dismissed Chinese labourers, said he was there, standing behind the large crowd of people who attended this historic event.[179]

None of the dismissed Chinese labourers had been given tickets to return to their villages in Guangdong, nor had they earned enough money to pay for their passage home, so many of these unemployed Chinese men dispersed to various Chinese communities in Vancouver, Victoria, and New Westminster in the Lower Mainland to look for jobs and to find food and shelter. A good number of the unemployed Chinese labourers migrated to Revelstoke and other cities in the Kootenay region.

Wing Chung, one of the many Chinese labourers who were dismissed by the CPR upon completion of the railway, claimed to have been in attendance at the Last Spike event, though no Chinese men were photographed. Image 1796 courtesy of the Revelstoke Museum and Archives

The 1891 census listed ninety-six Chinese labourers who had previously worked on the CPR construction living in Revelstoke. These included Wing Chung, Wah Chung, Ah Hung, and Ah Ham, among others. Wing Chung, mentioned above, was also known as Sham Wah Ging (沈华劲–译音). He was recruited from Enping County (恩平县), Guangdong, in 1882 to work on the construction of the CPR. After he was dismissed by the CPR, he settled in Farwell, as the site of Revelstoke was known at the time. Later, he operated a store on Front Street.

Wah Chung (华 锺 – 译音) was another Chinese labourer who had immigrated to Canada in 1882 to work on the CPR construction. After being dismissed by the CPR, he found a job as a bellboy at the Glacier Hotel in Revelstoke. He was a well-liked person, known as Charley to his co-workers and many guests. In 1890, he purchased a store from another Chinese man, aquiring the building and the existing stock.[180]

How Ah Hung (亚行 – 译音) stayed afloat after being dismissed by the CPR is unknown for the first five years he lived in Revelstoke. But in 1890, he was working at a sawmill. On September 27 of the same year, his right arm was caught in a machine and the bones in one of his elbows, arm and shoulder were fractured. The doctors who attended him suggested that they

The stone cairn marking the location of "the last spike," which was ceremonially driven into the track to signify the moment at which the transcontinental railway was finally completed. Image 833 courtesy of the Revelstoke Museum and Archives.

amputate his injured arm. He refused. The doctors then warned him that when the fractured bones set, he might not be able to move or use his arm. As time went by, however, he healed, but he was no longer able to do heavy work.[181]

The Chinese labourers on the CPR mentioned above were just a few among the seventeen thousand Chinese men who constructed the CPR in BC. Many of them sacrificed their lives building the railroad. As the *Vancouver Sun* put it, "one Chinese worker died for every mile of track laid."[182] Yet their contributions and sacrifices were easily forgotten.

The Chinese Settlements: Chinatowns

Among the ninety-six Chinese labourers who had migrated to Revelstoke, the 1891 census listed eleven Chinese cooks. Four of them worked on steamboats, one at the Victoria Hotel, two at the Columbia House Hotel, one in Florence

McCarty's boarding house, and the other three were listed without addresses. Lee Yee, Wah Chung, Youei Zan and Wing Sam were merchants, and four other Chinese immigrants—Ah Chin, Hing Jim, Chung Lung and Lee Mun Fun—operated laundries. Yei Yan and Chong Yoo took up placer mining. Ah Hoong, Ah Tun and Ah Tim were listed as gardeners.

These Chinese immigrants settled in two locations in Revelstoke, effectively establishing two Chinatowns. Chinese businesses were mainly located on Front Street in the block between Benson and Hanson Streets on the west side of the city; others were located on First Street between Orton and McArthur Avenues on the east side of town.

Wing Chung, a dismissed CPR labourer, owned and operated a general store on Front Street. Wah Chung owned a general store and two houses on lots 7–9, block 10, and one more building on lot 1, block 11, on Front Street. Hong Chung had a general store in block 8 of Front Street. The Lon Chong Laundry was located on the riverside of block 3, Front Street, and the Shing Kee Laundry was situated between Benson and Hanson Streets. As well, Chun Tong, also known as China Pat, was the first owner of lots 16 and 17, block 18, on First Street. Eventually, lots 12 to 19 on First Street were all owned by Chinese people, operating as general stores, laundries and boarding houses. These areas along Front Street and First Street were commonly referred to as Chinatowns.

Events in Chinatown

In June 1890, an unpleasant incident occurred in one of the Chinatowns. Two white boys "proceeded to demolish things at a certain China house." Constable Redgrave arrested the boys; one was fined twenty-five dollars and the other was discharged. "The one who was made to suffer then complained of the [Chinese] woman for selling liquor." The woman was arrested but "was released without penalty." Several persons feared that they might be summoned as witnesses. "If these scrimmages and their consequences must occur, we do not care how soon they happen, if thereby law, justice and right-living sooner get to their places at the front," declared the *Kootenay Star*.[183]

In February 1891, Mr. Kellie, a member of the provincial parliament, visited Revelstoke to investigate public sentiment regarding "the granting of lands to railway companies, the employment of Chinese on public works, the payment of a $5 license fee by miners, and the enactment of a law allowing the appointment of municipal commissioners to assert the gold commissioner in expending public moneys."[184] A public meeting was called in a school hall; Mr. W.A. Jowett chaired the meeting and Mr. F.B. Wells acted as secretary, recording the minutes of the meeting. A crowd of white citizens attended the meeting and the topics were fully discussed and debated. At the end of the meeting, the attendees unanimously voted against all the issues, including the employment of Chinese people on private and public works—especially those funded by the government.[185]

This public meeting clearly indicated the existence of anti-Chinese sentiments within the white community. But, despite the alienation, many Chinese immigrants remained in Revelstoke, and some Chinese merchants did well in the city. For example, on November 21, 1891, Kioong On Lung bought out the business of Yee Lee, a general merchant with a business on Main Street (Front Street).[186]

The Chinese lived their own lives, observing and celebrating their festivals in the city. In February 1894, the Chinese community celebrated the Chinese New Year. A journalist at the *Kootenay Star* reported on the event as follows:

> The fun commenced at midnight on Sunday and continued without cessation till Tuesday night. During the two days the noise and smell of fire crackers and explosive dragons were the chief features of the celebration. On Tuesday a large Chinese flag was unfurled at Wah Chang's [store] and three large sleighs, decorated with flags and filled with Chinamen, were driven to the station and back and around town amid a continuous fusilade of fire crackers. In the evening colored rockets were sent up and bombs and dragons exploded, making quite a pyrotechnic display which brought out a large number of townspeople. The amount spent in the celebration this year was over $800, each rocket costing 15 [cents] and the big firework dragons $15 each. Suppers were given at Wah Chang's and Lun Ching's and presents to all white callers.[187]

At this Chinese New Year celebration, at least two Chinese merchants, Wah Chang and Lun Ching, attempted to reach out to the white residents of the town and invited them to join in celebrating the Chinese New Year for fifteen days.

In the fall of 1895, a Chinese cook named Sam, who worked in the CPR Hotel, mysteriously disappeared. On the evening of November 18, he called on some friends on his way home from work. After leaving his friends around ten o'clock, he was not seen again. At first, his friends suspected that he might have been killed by "one of the many devils which the celestials suppose to be lying in wait for them after dark." Other theories were that he might have been " 'removed' by members of the celestials' secret organization or else he took too large a dose of his favourite drug and in his delirium has wandered off."[188] The police subscribed to the latter theory.

However, three years later, in 1898, a skeleton was found near the Jordan Valley. A policeman and the coroner went there to examine the remains, accompanied by a number of curious citizens and led by the person who had found the skeleton, Ed White. The skeleton, which was missing its skull, was wearing a black coat. One of the party suggested that these were the remains of the missing Chinese cook. A doctor in the party stated that since the bones appeared to be those of a small man, this might be the case. The party continued searching the nearby area and found the skeleton of a dog, "part of a hat, boots, and a big open knife which lay hidden beneath the body."[189] Part of a canvas hunting coat was also discovered nearby but it did not appear to be the property of the skeleton. The discoveries led to conjectures about the cause of death but nothing definitive was established.

An inquest was held into this death. Although one of the witnesses testified that the clothing found with the skeleton "resembled exactly" a garment he had sold the dead Chinese cook, the jury returned a verdict that the remains were of an unknown person and that the manner of death was also unknown. Nevertheless, "some of the Chinese in town went up the mountain and found another big bone and some of the finger bones of the unknown dead man. The skull, however, cannot be found." Despite the verdict reached by the coroner's jury, the Chinese concluded that this was the missing Sam, and that he had been killed for the sake of his money. The Chinese community therefore undertook the burial of this person's remains.[190]

An Elaborate Chinese Funeral

Although there were certainly other deaths in the city, not all of them would have been mentioned in the local newspapers. However, on January 16, 1897, a correspondent from Revelstoke reported on the funeral and burial of Mark Sing (麦胜), a member of the Chee Kung Tong (Chinese Freemasons Society). The author commented that the event was "one of the strangest and most interesting ceremonies ever witnessed anywhere."[191]

The funeral was officiated over by the leader of the Chee Kung Tong in Victoria. The funeral was delayed, however, until "all the regalia and paraphernalia used in the ceremonies" arrived in Revelstoke from Victoria.

After having received all the essential items, the funeral procedure was carried out according to the rites of the Chee Kung Tong. It began with bringing out the deceased in a coffin from a tent where it had lain for about a week. Three tables containing a variety of foods were placed at the head of the coffin; the food represented the mourners' gifts to the spirit of the deceased as well as to the spirits of all those who had departed from this world. Different coloured banners bearing "some strange devices" surrounded the coffin. When the ceremony began, the leader, wearing a white costume, called out the name of the deceased asking him to arise. Hearing no answer, the leader announced that Mark Sing was dead. Then he read aloud from a scripture, and burned yellow papers, the symbol of ingots, at the foot of the coffin. Then the Chinese people who attended the ceremony took turns kowtowing to the deceased.

The funeral procession for Mark Sing, who was a notable member of the Chee Kung Tong, was so extravagant and attended by so many Chinese residents that it was reported on in the *Golden Era*, a newspaper published in nearby Golden, BC. Image 4100 courtesy of the Revelstoke Museum and Archives

Many local Chinese people attended the funeral and participated in the ritual. Some of them put on red and yellow vests with a Chinese character written in a disc on the front and the back of the vests. During the ceremony, a few Chinese musicians played their pipes aloud to frighten off any evil spirits.

At about 2:30 p.m., an orderly funeral procession was formed. The leader on horseback was followed by another horse without a rider, leading the procession. Three bands in the procession played on their way to the cemetery. A man carried a huge square flag that represented a general. Jim Hing, a Chinese man dressed in a yellow diamond-patterned robe and wearing a false beard, acted as the emperor of the underground world (阎皇), a supreme being governing the spirits of any deceased in the Flowery Kingdom! In addition, four men in black robes and hats were the guards of honour, and two men in purple carried lanterns to provide light for the spirit of the deceased to cross over dark [Yellow] river (黄泉). Many Chinese men in coloured vests carried flags of different shapes and sizes, and grotesque figures constructed of bamboo sticks and transparent coloured papers; these figures represented soldiers to protect the spirit of the deceased. The men wearing different coloured costumes in the funeral procession indicated their membership and rank within the Chinese Freemasons Society.

When the procession arrived at the cemetery, the burial ritual took place with the leader saying a prayer at the grave side. The coffin was then lowered into the prepared grave and the cemetery undertakers filled in the soil. Food, clothes and other articles were burned for the spirit of the deceased.[192]

It was an extravagant and brilliant affair and must have cost a good deal of money, commented the newspaper reporter: "If such are the obsequies over Mark Sing, what must be those of some big tyhee like? Apparently, nearly 80 Chinamen attended the funeral."[193]

Hard Times, Struggles and Casualties

The year 1897 was an unfortunate period for both the Chinese and the white communities. The cost of living was inflated. The prices of some essential food items published in the *Revelstoke Herald* on January 18 of that year were high: milk cost 10¢ a quart; butter was 20¢–30¢ a pound; eggs were 30¢ a dozen; and potatoes, oats, and flour were all very costly.[194]

In May 1898, Low Chung and Yo Sing quarrelled. Chung used an axe to hit Sing, inflicting two severe wounds on Sing's head. Immediately, Chung took a train to Vancouver. Dr. Cross, the Medical Health Officer, and Police Chief Bain were called to the scene. Dr. Cross sent Sing to the hospital to get his wounds dressed. Chief Bain arrested Chung and sent him to jail.[195] Up until the date of his imprisonment, he had been a porter and laundryman at Glacier House.

An avalanche in Rogers Pass on January 31, 1899, swept away a train sta-tion and a roundhouse. The avalanche killed seven people, and injured two oth-ers. The dead included William Cator, the station agent; Mrs. Cator; the Cators' two children; Frank Corson, the night operator; James Ridley, a CPR wiper; and a Chinese cook, Ah Ham, reported the *Revelstoke Herald*.[196] Three Chinese labourers in a bunkhouse nearby escaped without injury.

On September 2, 1905, the *Kootenay Mail* reported that "a Chinaman was found dead in C. Snyders boarding car." Dr. Cross held an inquest the same day the body was found and ruled that the man had died from natural causes.[197] The same newspaper—the *Kootenay Mail*—reported on an accident on July 16, 1913, in which a west-bound passenger train ran over a Chinese man a short distance from the roundhouse. It seemed that the man was deaf and could not hear the train approaching.[198] These casualties were just a few that occurred in Revelstoke and its vicinity. Many Chinese immigrants in Revelstoke's China-town also passed away due to illness, suffering from diseases such as tuberculosis and asthma, overdoses of opium, and starvation.

The Destruction of Chinese Residences

Until fall 1899, a group of Chinese people lived in about a dozen cabins just north of the city. In September 1899, Dr. Cross, the medical health officer, made a tour of inspection of these buildings and ordered that they be destroyed be-cause of a perceived risk that they might be the source of an epidemic. One Chinese man protested the destruction, saying he would relocate to California instead. The editor of the *Kootenay Mail* heard this complaint and stated in the newspaper, "If more of his countrymen in Revelstoke could be made to arrive at the same decision it would be a blessing to the town."[199] The following week, these cabins were burned to the ground, and the inhabitants were left homeless.

> Officers Bain and Plumber commenced applying the torch, and even then, many of the occupants would not leave until almost forced out by the flames. It is said that one Chinaman's feet was smoking before he left his bunk.
>
> After the fires were well started there were chinks [*sic*] running in all directions, carrying blankets, pots, pans,…asking, 'Wha' fo?' 'Walla matter?', and cursing in Pigeon English the white man and his laws…though the celestials had been notified to leave several days before the cabins were fired.[200]

Dr. Cross was congratulated on his decision to destroy these buildings and he was informed in a complaint published by the *Kootenay Mail* that "north of the railway are several shacks which are just as bad as those burned; one of these, a horribly filthy place, is a laundry." Yet, the paper went on,

> it is extensively patronized by the white residents of Revelstoke: it makes a specialty of washing for families. Dr. Cross should turn his attention to the vile dens on Front street, which are…more of a menace to the health of the town as there is a large white population in the immediate vicinity.… Gambling and opium smoking are here constantly indulged in by the celestial sons and sons of heaven.
>
> It seems that the only way these people can be got rid of is through the sanitary laws, and by keeping a very close watch on them it is believed that many of them can be driven from the town. Still it is the white residents of Revelstoke who keep them here. They do this by purchasing fruits, berries, vegetables, etc., from them and employing them in every way possible.[201]

These complaints about conditions in Chinatown continued throughout 1899 and into 1900 and 1901. The mainstream community was unsympathetic to the crowded conditions that prevailed in Chinatown due to poverty and which was exacerbated by the destruction of Chinese homes in September 1899 and they were intolerant of pastimes such as gambling and opium use that were foreign to the mainstream culture. There was no appreciation among the white population of the cultural differences between them and the Chinese; rather they were looked upon at best as exotic curiosities and at worst as slum-dwellers. The Chinese community was plagued with repeated invasions by white officials looking for reasons to drive them out of Revelstoke and extremely ugly descriptions of the buildings and businesses in Chinatown were repeatedly published by the local newspapers. Indeed, in concluding a story about the conditions in Chinatown, the *Kootenay Mail* stated that "this is not a nice story to print but the *Mail* has no apology to offer for doing so, believing… that the facts should be laid before the public so that measures may be adopted to do away with the evil."[202]

Such news reports about Revelstoke's Chinatowns prompted the city council to delegate the city clerk to write the following letter to J.D. Sibbald, MP, Land Agent at the CPR Revelstoke Station:

April 27, 1901

Dear Sir,
I am directed by the City Council to address the Land Department of the Canadian Pacific Railway through you, with a view to enlisting the sympathies of the Land Department on the side of a certain persons on Second Street in this City who had petitioned the City Council to use its influence with the CPR to prevent the selling of property on that street to Chinamen.

According to the statement of these petitioners it would appear that Chinamen are negotiating for the purchase of a lot between Lots 4 and 10 in Block 37 (or 27) with the intention of erecting thereon a Chinese boarding house and a store. As you are aware a very good class of buildings are being erected in this vicinity, and a Chinese house [will] undoubtedly depreciate the value of property on this street. The petitioners, Messrs. McLeod and Pettipiece have built very good residences on the Block referred to, and it seems inappropriate that their property should be ruined by the proximity of such undesirable neighbour as Chinamen would be.

Yours truly
City Clerk

This plea was aimed at preventing the expansion of Chinatown through the sale of CPR land.

The Chinese Joss House

The Chinese joss house on Front Street was built next to the fire brigade. It was the building of the local chapter of the Chee Kung Tong (Chinese Freemasons Society).

On October 30, 1901, the *Revelstoke Herald* reported that the fire system at the No. 1 station was "nothing but a source of annoyance and trouble ever since it was installed... [the] wires are naked and sagging about between poles, some of them as much as 275 feet apart.... The hose reel and chemical engine are stored in the old No.1 fire hall, which is rapidly falling over against the new Chinese joss house."[203] The newspaper went on, pointing out the deficiencies of the fire hall and its systems, and urging the city council to address the issues—implying that the Chinese joss house had taken up the space the fire hall needed to dry and store its hoses.

Located on Front Street, the Chinese joss house served as a hub of the community and the location of the local chapter of the Chee Kung Tong; its grand opening was marked with the lighting of firecrackers and hanging lanterns. Image 3103 courtesy of the Revelstoke Museum and Archives

Regardless of the negative coverage in the newspaper, the Chinese joss house held a grand opening on November 20, 1901, reported the *Revelstoke Herald*. The opening ceremony began at 3:00 a.m. with an explosion of fire-crackers, and "during the day there was an incessant sound of fire crackers and explosives. Several citizens witnessed the opening ceremonies, and the local Chinamen appeared in gay attire on the occasion."[204]

The report stated that "the Chinese celebrated the opening of the new joss house with a vast expenditure of fire crackers outside and prayer sticks [incense] inside the building. The temple was visited by considerable numbers of people on Sunday.... All of the furniture had not arrived, but what there was on view was well worth a visit. Tables in front of the picture of Gee Hing, the tutelary divinity of the shrine, were spread with a lavish display of Chinese confectionery and preserved fruits, in the midst of which the joss [incense] sticks smouldered with their faint incense-like fragrance. A large hanging lamp with paper figures revolved continually by the familiar device of a current of air, attracted a good deal of attention. On the balcony outside are stacks of ceremonial banners, halberds etc., of curious design and considerable value. Altogether there was much worthy of observation by the white visitors to the joss house."[205]

The large hanging lantern (走马灯) with its paper figures revolving continually as a result of an air current is a rare artefact. This lantern is usually lit during Chinese New Year, and at Zhongqui Jie, the Mid-autumn Moon Festival. The traditional Chinese, especially farmers, believe that the speed of the revolving paper figures indicates the kind of harvest, good or poor, to expect that year.

In many traditional Chinese communal buildings, the Chinese set up an elaborate altar with an urn of ashes for inserting incense sticks to honour the divinities such as Guan Yin (观音), the Goddess of Mercy, and Guan Yun Xiang (关云祥), the Lord of Justice, whom they believed would bless and guard them. The latter was a legendary hero in the period of the Three Kingdoms (220–265 BCE).

Whether any of the divinities mentioned above were being honoured in this Chinese joss house was not mentioned in the news reports. This building no longer exists in Revelstoke, and many of the Chinese old-timers either passed away or left town and relocated to Victoria, or Vancouver, New Westminster and other cities in the Lower Mainland. The brief history of this joss house can only be traced from references in the Chee Kung Tong magazine. Fortunately, the Revelstoke Museum and Archives has kept an image of the joss house, recording an important illustration of Chinese-Canadian history in the city.

A joss house is different from a Chinese temple; it is a communal building in a Chinese community. Both a joss house and a Chinese temple would usually have an altar and at least one caretaker to offer incense to the Almighty and other divinities every morning and evening. In a joss house, there are no monks, priests, or nuns, or disciples of Buddhism or Taoism to recite scriptures or say prayers daily. In a temple, however, monks, nuns, or priests pray and read scriptures at least three times a day—in the morning, at noon and in the evening.

In 1911, Dr. Sun Yat-sen visited and held a meeting with the Chinese residents of Revelstoke. In his acknowledgement printed in the Chee Kung Tong (Chinese Freemasons Society) bicentennial magazine, Sun expressed his appreciation to the members of the Chee Kung Tong in New Westminster for hosting a welcoming reception and their support for the Chinese revolution. He said that after he left New Westminster he had travelled to a good number of towns and cities in BC, including Revelstoke.

When Sun visited the various towns and cities in BC, many Chinese immigrants organized receptions and dinners to welcome him. They supported his mission, a strong indication that they were mindful of China, their homeland. The defeat of the Qing dynasty and the success of the Chinese revolution

Cover and interior pages of the Chee Kung Tong (Chinese Freemasons Society) bicentennial magazine. Featured in this issue is an article, written in Chinese, about Dr. Sun Yat-sen's 1911 visit to Revelstoke. Images courtesy of Mr. Shui Lee, chair of the Chinese Freemasons Society chapter in Kelowna were imminent, stated Sun. He told his countrymen that funds were very much needed to support the revolution. He reminded the Chinese in Revelstoke that they were needed to collect donations and raise funds for the revolutionary cause. The funds should be speedily gathered and sent to Mr. Liu Ru Fang and Mr. Sham Fa Shen in Vancouver. Sun further stated that he would next take a night train from Revelstoke to Calgary. The message from Sun was printed in Vancouver's Chinese newspaper on March 29, 1911.[206]

The Chinese joss house in Revelstoke offered accommodation and took care of the members of the Chee Kung Tong, especially single Chinese men who had no wives or other family members with them. Sun Nui, a member of the organization, passed away at the age of 63. His funeral took place from Howson's Undertaking Parlors but the Chinese ritual for the deceased was performed in the joss house.[207]

In June 1920, a group of Chinese residents led by the Chee Kung Tong donated money to the Revelstoke Hospital. Reprinted below is the letter sent from the Chinese community to H.H. McVity, the secretary of the Hospital Drive Committee.[208]

Dear Sir:

On behalf of several of the Chinese residents of Revelstoke who wish to show their appreciation of the fine treatment which their countrymen have received from the Revelstoke Hospital, we beg to hand you herewith a cheque in your favor for $184.50, which has been subscribed by those whose names are on the attached list.

Wishing you and your committee every success in your efforts to clear off the debt of the hospital.

Yours respectfully,
Wong Chung Lock, Wong Juen Yuen

The Names of the Donors

Names of donors	Amount
Chinese Free Masons	$50.00
Wing Wo Co.	$10.00
Kwong Chang Lee	$10.00
Mike Pat	$10.00
Kwong Hong On Co.	$10.00
Wah Chung	$10.00
Kei Dick House	$10.00
Sun Shung Wing Co.	$10.00
Wing Chung	$10.00
Kwong Seng Yuen Co.	$10.00
Man Sang Co.	$10.00
Windsor Café	$5.00
BC Café	$5.00
Mar Eulie Lee	$5.00
Mar Sam	$5.00
Wo Ken	$5.00
Houi Sam Toy	$2.00
Wong Chung Hei	$2.00
Wong Que	$2.00
Wang Chee Chung	$1.00
Wong Fon	$1.00
Chen Do	$1.00
Ying Gen	$0.50
Total	$184.50

Source: *Revelstoke Review*, January 22, 1920, 3.

In March the following year, members of the Chee Kung Tong made another donation to the Revelstoke Hospital toward its purchase of x-ray equipment.[209]

Donations of the Chee Kung Tong

Names of donors	Amounts
Chee Kung Tong	$20.00
Wing Chung	$10.00
Wah Chung	$10.00
Sam Won (CKT Secretary)	$10.00
Chop House Restaurant	$5.00
Windsor Restaurant	$5.00
BC Café	$5.00
Kwong Chong Lee Co.	$3.00
Wong Kue	$2.00
Wing Hang Wo Co.	$2.00
Kwong San Yuen Co.	$2.00
Huoe Yee	$1.00
Houe Lee	$1.00
Houe Chee	$1.00
Houe Jui	$1.00
Charlie Sing	$1.00
Man Sang	$1.00
Chow Chew Gun	$1.00
Chin On	$0.50
Chong Hing	$0.50
Fong Ling Sing	$0.50
Total	$82.50

Source: *Revelstoke Review*, June 3, 1920, 1.

The Chinese Laundries

In the 1891 census, four Chinese laundries were recorded in Revelstoke, including the Lon Ching laundry. As time passed, more laundries opened, including the Shing Kee laundry, located on block 8 at the town site; Wong Sing on Douglas Street in block 8; the Nam Sing laundry on Second Street in block 22; the Mar Eulie laundry on Fourth Street; and three other Chinese laundries, including the Kwong Lee laundry.[210]

In December 1895, a small fire occurred in the Lon Ching laundry. The fire brigade arrived at the location in time to put out the fire; the roof had caught fire from a defective chimney, but the damage was slight.

In 1898, Nam Sing applied for a permit from the city council to erect a building to house his laundry on First Street East. The white community protested against his application. Sing was then advised to erect his house on Second Street. He accepted the proposal, but the residents on Second Street also objected to having a Chinese laundry located on the street, saying that if the laundry was not good enough for First Street, it would not be good enough for Second Street either. However, the Nam Sing laundry did open on Second Street, according to the records held in the Revelstoke Museum & Archives.[211]

On November 2, 1901, Buker & Saxton, proprietors of the Steam Laundry Company, posted "A Challenge" in the *Revelstoke Herald*.[212] The challenge stated: "We challenge anyone in Revelstoke to give substantial reasons for supporting Chinese laundries. In exchange, we offer to give 10 good reasons why Chinese laundries should not be patronized." The same newspaper also reprinted a suggestion from the *Nelson News* as to how to deal with Chinese laundries. It said that local health officials should enforce the rules forbidding Chinese laundrymen from using saliva to moisten clean and dry garments before ironing; instead, they should use a mechanical device to dampen the clothing before ironing it.[213]

In spite of such negative messages, by 1911, thirty-four Chinese laundries had been established in Revelstoke.

In February 1913, the West Kootenay Steam Laundry placed yet another advertisement in the *Mail Herald* advising people not to patronize Chinese laundries. The notice, headed "White People," admonished Revelstoke's white citizens to: "Be reasonable! Don't send your hard-earned money to China! Remember, we are here to do your work and we employ local white labor only. Be progressive, and have your washing done by the West Kootenay Steam Laundry. Regular collector and delivery service."[214]

By this time, Nam Sing had moved his laundry from block 22 to lot 6, block 27, on Second Street. In 1914, however, Nam Sing was unable to pay the property tax due. The City of Revelstoke scheduled his property for a tax sale auction at $88.04, the amount due on December 31, 1913. This amount had to be paid prior to the auction day on September 14, 1914, if Nam Sing were to retain his property.[215]

Meanwhile, with much anxiety, Nam Sing successfully negotiated with A.H. Sing to give him the sum of $510 to purchase his property so that he could pay for the delinquent taxes, including costs and expenses. Nam Sing was thus able to pay his property tax, although the transfer of the property between these two Chinese laundrymen took place on September 16, 1914.[216]

In November of the same year, Nam Sing was also charged with non-payment of his trade licence. He appeared before J.H. Hamilton, the police magistrate. He was "fined ten dollars and costs, a distress order made or in default thirty days."[217]

These episodes at the Nam Sing Laundry illustrate the resentment the white laundries held toward Nam Sing, if not the entire Chinese laundry industry, at that time.

The Mar Eulie Laundry on Fourth Street West was successful. In 1893, Mar had arrived in Revelstoke as a young boy with his father. After working as a laundry man for some years, the senior Mar handed the laundry business over to his son and returned home to Guangdong to spend his sunset years, where he passed away several years later. In 1919, Mar Eulie purchased a house and operated a restaurant on Mackenzie Avenue in the neighbourhood of the Chinese quarters. He continued to operate the laundry business for forty years. Meanwhile, he sponsored his brother to come to Revelstoke to help out with the laundry business, and his two sons, who lived and worked in Kelowna. However, he visited his wife and a daughter and a few grandchildren in Guangdong only once in the forty years. In 1933, he handed over the laundry business to his brother and returned home to China to be with his family.[218]

Wong Kwong, a Famous Chinese Man

In 1899, Wong Kwong arrived in Revelstoke, where he worked for the CPR. Although the transcontinental line had been completed by then, a good number of subsidiary lines needed to be built. Since he was fluent in both English and Cantonese, Kwong was hired by the CPR to recruit Chinese labourers for the construction of bridges and tunnels throughout the Rockies. Being a Chinese scholar, Kwong read Chinese letters for the single Chinese men who could not read the written Chinese language, and helped these single men to write and/ or send replies to their home villages in the counties of the Zhujiang Delta, Guangdong. Kwong also fed and provided accommodation for the labourers in the winter season when construction work could not be carried out.

In 1907, Kwong went home to Guangdong where he married. He brought his wife, Yee Von, a young Chinese woman with bound feet, to Revelstoke. This couple established and operated the Kwong Lee Laundry, and he built a house near the laundry shop for his wife and family. Together, they raised five girls and four boys in that house. Kwong also established a store that imported Asian foods for the workers, and built a rooming house near his home for the Chinese labourers. He was a blessing to the Chinese-Canadian community in his time.

Kwong was a member of the Guomindang (中国国民党), the Chinese Nationalist League. In 1911, when Dr. Sun Yat-sen arrived in Revelstoke to raise funds for the Chinese revolution, he stayed with the Kwong family.

Between 1915 and 1932, Kwong established a business in Edmonton, and in the meantime, he also had an interest in the Big Eddy Shingle Mill located in Revelstoke. Yet he also remained employed by the CPR. When the construction of the Connaught Tunnel commenced on April 2, 1914, he joined his fellow countrymen in constructing the tunnel, carrying rocks on his back, according to the late George Kwong, a grandson of Wong Kwong, in an interview published in the *Vancouver Courier*. "The construction crews did not have machinery to carry stuff at that time, so they hauled huge rocks on their backs," continued George. "The labourers were paid $0.50 cents an hour and they worked for 10 hours per day, whereas the white labourers were paid $1.00 an hour."[219]

In 1932, while driving a team of horses, Kwong stopped to look at one of the horses. That mare kicked him in the head, killing him. His funeral was sponsored by the Guomindang. His obituary in the *Revelstoke Review* stated that Wong Kwong "is survived by his wife, four sons and five daughters: Sam, Jean, Kim, Lun (Doris), Clara, John, Mary, George and James (Jim).… Pallbearers were H. Wong, J. Wong, Wong Yuen, Wong Kim, Wong Lok and Wong Kid."[220]

Kwong's remarkable wife Yee Von continued to manage and operate the laundry business, and raised her children in the city. After her children had completed high school, she sent them to trade schools, colleges and universities. All her children had good careers and a few of them became professionals. She is discussed in more detail below.

The Market Gardeners

Besides working as labourers, cooks and kitchen helpers, and operating laundry shops, general and grocery stores and restaurants, many early Chinese immigrants became market gardeners, cultivating root crops and vegetables in Revelstoke and its surrounding area. These Chinese had been small-scale farmers in southern China and once the gold mines were exhausted and the railway constructed, they returned to what they knew: growing crops. These Chinese gardeners peddled and sold their produce directly to the general public.

There were conflicting opinions about the Chinese market gardeners at the time. In 1885, for example, Judge Begbie, testifying before the Royal Commission on Chinese Immigration, applauded the Chinese market gardeners for supplying fresh produce within BC. He testified that "they are the model market gardeners of the province, and produce the greater part of the vegetables

Wong Kwong (right, seated) and his family. Kwong was a member of the Chinese Nationalist League and ran a successful laundry and Asian imported goods store.
Image 1795 courtesy of the Revelstoke Museum and Archives

grown here." He concluded that he "did not see how people would get on here at all without Chinamen."[221]

In April 1901, on the other hand, Dr. Fagan, the provincial health officer, after a visit to Chinese market gardens in Victoria, issued a "Warning to House-holders Who Buy Produce From Oriental Market Gardeners."[222] Believing that the practices of the Chinese market gardeners could spread diseases such as typhus, he reported that he

> found that in nearly all the families in which typhoid infection occurred it was the custom to get vegetables from Chinamen. Now, it is not generally known, but a fact, that vegetables can, and often do, carry infection. Of course, most vegetables are purified by boiling, but many—such as salad and celery—are served raw. This, no doubt, is the cause of more trouble than is generally supposed, and therefore, I thought it my duty to visit some of the gardens…. In many of them pigs are kept. There is no pretence of

keeping the place clean. The pens are simply an abomination: the yards just as bad. In two instances, I saw offal lying around, and from its condition must have been there for some days.... This is bad, but nothing compared to the dirty habit all these Chinamen have of preserving the urine for the fertilization and whitening of vegetables. Each garden has a barrel always full of urine; which is allowed to decompose so that plenty of ammonia develops. The vegetables are then freely sprinkled with this. Outside this disgusting practice, the health aspect is grave, because these vegetables, unless cooked, will carry typhoid or other diseases, just as sure as milk or water. I would recommend that this matter be actively dealt with.

Dr. Fagan concluded that

the large number of private residents in the city who are accustomed to purchase their vegetables from the Chinese peddling vendors... should carefully consider the above report.[223]

Contrary to Dr. Fagan's belief, it is now appreciated that urine is an acceptable form of plant fertilizer.[224]

Charlie Sing moved to Revelstoke in 1913 and established a market garden. During the summer and fall, he drove his horse and cart through the streets of Revelstoke, selling his produce. He was popular with the local children and often had children tagging along for a ride when school was out.[225]

In March 1916, delegates of the commercial market gardeners from the BC Interior declared at a meeting that public markets in Revelstoke and other places where farmers sold their produce had flourished until Chinese market gardeners began peddling their produce from house to house in BC's towns and cities. They believed that the Chinese peddlers had killed the public markets. This was essentially a conflict between larger-scale farming operations and the small, local farming operations of the Chinese.

Some delegates advocated asking the government to pass a law controlling peddling on the streets, but it was pointed out that such a law was unconstitutional, since no one could be prevented from taking out wares and selling to any customers. It was finally decided to turn the matter over to a committee that would thoroughly investigate the whole question of public markets, and their relations with producers and consumers.

No follow-up about this investigation and any actions taken by the committee to deal with the Chinese market gardeners who peddled and sold their produce on the street could be found in any contemporary newspapers. Perhaps the many customers of the Chinese market gardeners appreciated the freshness of the produce and the convenience of having them come to their homes with their fruits and vegetables.

Raids in Chinatown in the 1920s

One Saturday night in February 1920, the city police force visited a gambling den in the house of Wong Ly at 19 First Street East and arrested twenty Chinese men for gambling. The gamblers were incarcerated until the following Monday because Dr. Hamilton, who was also the police magistrate, was busy attending his patients. In the police court, Messrs. W.I. Briggs appeared for the crown, and Geo. S. McCater for the accused. Bail was set at $100 for Wong Ly, and the other participants paid $50 each. Later, when the case was brought forward to Police Magistrate Hamilton at the police court, no charges were laid due to lack of evidence as well as the death of the late police chief, James Cleland.[226]

In April 1920, the city police, armed with a warrant, visited 19 First Street East at noon to search for opium. One Chinese man, Won Gar, was caught in the act of smoking, and another man, Lee Hoy, was found with a smoking outfit in his bunk and some opium on a tray nearby. These men were arrested and their pipes and gear confiscated. When their case came up before Police Magistrate Hamilton on the following Monday, W.I. Briggs appeared for the crown and Geo. S. McCarter for the accused. Mak Jok acted as an interpreter for the accused men.

The defence maintained that Won Gar used opium to numb pain caused when he was severely beaten by an Italian in Golden recently. Won King, Won Gar's brother, who lived in Vancouver, had advised him to smoke opium for seven weeks before he would see a beneficial effect. Won was unwilling to pro vide his brother's address in Vancouver; his story therefore did not convince the magistrate, who happened to be a medical professional. Consequently, he was fined fifty dollars plus costs or two months in jail. Neither was the magistrate persuaded that the smoking outfit found in Lee Hoy's bunk could by chance have belonged to any of the other forty individuals present in the building at the time the arrests were made. The judgment of this police court case was recorded into the police logbook accordingly.[227]

On February 17, 1921, the *Revelstoke Review* reported on another raid by Chief Spratt and P.C. Edwards at a Chinese building located at 23 First Street East that resulted in gathering in four Celestials with smoking outfits and opium, in addition to considerable other paraphernalia in their possession. The accused were released on bail, and appeared to answer to the charges before

Police Magistrate Hamilton. They were found guilty and fined $20 each and costs, a total of $81.20 or in default, six months hard labour in each case. These cases were tried under the new amendment of the Opium, Narcotics and Drug Act, which the government had brought forth to curb the defence. W.I. Briggs appeared for the prosecution and Geo. S. McCarter for the defence.[228]

On February 24 of the same year, another seven Chinese men were fined twenty dollars each for smoking opium. These seven Chinese men, employed at the Pole Camp, two miles north of Malakwa, were caught by the Provincial Police with opium in their possession. They were tried by a Malakwa justice of the peace who found them guilty. Each man was fined twenty dollars, which they paid.[229]

On March 11, 1925, Lee Gow and Wong Kar were charged under the Drugs and Narcotics Act. They appeared before Stipendiary Magistrate Maxwell. W.J. Briggs appeared for the prosecution and R.B. Russel, KC, of Vancouver for the defence. At the trial, Corporal Ball of the RCMP described his search of the premises of Kwong Sang Yuen where Lee Gow was the manager. Ball found part of an opium-smoking outfit and a small amount of opium. Dr. Hamilton testified that Lee was suffering from an acute rheumatic affliction and that he (Hamilton) had prescribed him the opium to alleviate his suffering. Lee was then discharged.

Two charges were laid against Wong Kar for possessing opium and a complete outfit of opium-smoking equipment that he had concealed between his bed sheets in the premises of the Wing Hang Wo Company. He pleaded guilty and was fined twenty-five dollars.

Chinese Merchants and Businesses

Many early Chinese immigrants ventured overseas—especially to Gam Shan, the gold mountains—to seek for good fortune and wealth. They always dreamt that one day they would return home to build a house, buy a plot of land where they could cultivate crops, and to enjoy their sunset years with their loved ones and family members.

Wong Tong was one of these men. Wong lived in Revelstoke for nearly forty years, was highly respected, and eventually became a wealthy merchant. But at the age of 73, he retired and wanted to go home to Guangdong to enjoy his retirement. So in January 1921, he went to Vancouver with the intention of catching a boat to sail home. Shortly after he arrived in Vancouver, however, he died. A funeral service for him was held at the T. Edwards Co. Chapel with Reverend B.H. Best officiating at the ceremony. Wong's son took his father's remains and sailed home to China on the *Empress of Russia* for the burial.[230]

On December 13, 1922, a notice was published in the *Revelstoke Review* stating that "the partnership between the undersigned members carrying on as general merchants at No. 19 First Street, Revelstoke, under the firm name of Kwong Hong, On Wo Kee, Yick Yuen & Co., that on the 24th of November, had been dissolved in so far, as Woo Sou Lum had retired from the partnership. The business would be continued under the aforesaid firm name by the remaining partners, who would assume all debts and liabilities of the firm and to whom all accounts owing to the firm were to be paid. Woo Sou Lum, Wong Toy, Eng Chong, Wong Chew Lai, Wong Yick. Witness: W.I. Briggs."[231]

Other Chinese merchants who were successful in the city included Wah Chung, Wing Chung and the amazing Mrs. Wong Kwong, also known as Yee Von Kwong, Wong Kwong's widow.

Wah Chung (华钟 -译音) was born in 1859 and immigrated to Canada from Guangdong in 1882 to work on the construction of the CPR. As mentioned above, he was dismissed by the CPR in November 1885, the year the transcontinental railway was completed. In September 1890, he bought the store building and stock of Kwong Fook On (广福安) in Revelstoke and operated a general store on Front Street.[232]

By 1895, Wah Chung owned two more houses on lots 7–9 in block 10, and one more building on lot 1, block 11 on Front Street.[233] Before he immigrated to Canada, he and his wife had a son, Bing Wah Chung, born in 1883 in Wah Chung's home village in Guangdong. Junior Chung was also known as Charlie Chung. At the age of 16, he came to Canada to join his father.

In BC, Wah Chung married Oie Gam (爱金 -译音), a young woman in Victoria. Gam was born in 1861 but at the age of 2 she immigrated to BC with her parents from China. She and her family resided on the coast for more than twelve years. Then her parents returned to China, leaving her in Victoria. After she married Wah Chong, she moved to Revelstoke to live with him.

Since Gam could not find fashionable clothing to meet her taste in Revelstoke, she went to Nelson in early October of 1898 to look for trendy outfits. In Nelson she stayed with a friend of her husband's and met Lang Jo, who was once a laundryman in Trail. Lang mentioned the name of a country woman of hers whom he said was living in Kuskonook, and encouraged her to visit that town. She loved to meet someone from China, so she went there with Lang. When they arrived in Kuskonook, she could not find this woman, so she wanted to return to Nelson. Instead of taking her back to Nelson, however, Lang took her to a group of three Chinese men, one of whom was Wong Sang, a notorious smuggler. Together they boarded the steamer *Ainsworth* going south toward the international boundary with the United States. By 1:00 a.m. the next day, they had arrived at Rykerts on the boundary and disembarked. There Gam realized that she had been entrapped and tried to escape. Her captors loaded their revolvers, pointed them at her and forced her to follow them. Apparently, these men had a contract with Wong to lure and bring Chinese women for him to sell in San Francisco.

Meanwhile, customs collector Hill received a telegram about the abduction. He gathered a few deputies and began to track down the smugglers. After several days of pursuit, he located the smuggling party on a Great Northern Railway train, bound for Helena. After passing Port Hill, the smugglers, together with Gam, walked a long distance until they arrived at a point about ten miles (sixteen kilometres) from Bonner's Ferry, where they secured a wagon and passed through the town in the night. The party of officers was after them in hot pursuit but could not find them because the smuggler abandoned and hid the wagon in the bush near Bonner's Ferry. They boarded a train at Leonia, Idaho, where a car was waiting for them. They travelled a few miles farther and left the car at the sidetrack west of Kalispell, Montana. At Kalispell, they boarded a train bound for Helena. On October 10, Hill and the officers arrested the smuggling party, including Gam, at Great Falls. They were kept in jail until October 14 when they were brought up for trial for illegally entering the United States. Gam pleaded guilty and proved her residence in British Columbia, stating that she had been taken to the US against her will. Gam was released and Hill took her back to BC.

Wong Sang, when brought up for trial, produced a registration in the US but he had left the state without complying with regulations, so his registration became void. He was deported to China. Lang Jo claimed that he was a merchant in San Francisco but he had no documentation to prove it. He was also deported to China. The other two men in the kidnapping party were sent to jail, one to Missoula and the other to Butte.

Officer Hill then took Gam back to her husband, Wah Chung, who was overcome with great joy. Chung had thought he would never see his wife again.[234]

As time went by Chung acquired quite a few properties in the Lower Town (where Farwell had been) and later on First Street, including the house of a Japanese woman, Jennie Kiobara. When Jennie passed away, there was no one to take care of her dead body. Chung stepped in and asked an undertaker to bury her, and he paid for her burial plot as well as a grave marker.

By November 4, 1905, Chung had purchased a restaurant on Front Street and sold groceries—"a splendid supply of fresh vegetables from S.D. Crowie's ranch"—which Chung leased for several years.[235] He also owned the Chop

The Oyster and Chop House, located on Mackenzie Avenue, was owned by successful Chinese merchant Wah Chung. Chung also owned a general store on Front Street. Image 174 courtesy of the Revelstoke Museum and Archives.

House Restaurant on Mackenzie Avenue until 1919. Clearly, he was a very successful Chinese entrepreneur in Revelstoke.

Chung was also a generous and benevolent merchant, assisting and serving as a patron to many Chinese in town. His wife passed away on August 15, 1929, at the age of 68 after a long period of illness. Her obituary stated that she had been married to Chung for fifty years. Her funeral was held at her residence on First Street East. Her casket was placed on a decorated table under a specially constructed canopy. A profusion of flowers and wreaths surrounded the casket. A large crowd of Chinese people, some wearing white, attended the funeral. Reverend W. Vance officiated at her funeral.

In July 1932, Wah Chung himself passed away at his residence on First Street East at the age of 74. He had lived in Revelstoke for over half a century and was connected with restaurant, grocery and hardware businesses. His funeral, attended by a large number of people, was held from his late residence. He was survived by two sons, one in Revelstoke and the other in Chicago. The funeral was conducted according to Chinese tradition, with his body lying under a canopy in front of the family residence. The funeral service was officiated at by Reverend W.S. Beams.

Wing Chung, the Chinese labourer dismissed by the CPR in 1855, owned and operated a general store on Douglas Street in Revelstoke. On April 19, 1899, he publicly announced the purchase of a business from Hip Chung on Front Street and relocated his store there.[236] The goods he sold in his store included produce, different kinds of supplies and foods, and imported articles such as silk handkerchiefs, umbrellas, and shoes from China.[237] Later he added more rooms to the building to provide accommodation for his family at the back of the store.

On November 4, 1905, Wing advertised the goods he carried in his store in the *Kootenay Mail*.[238] These included "the best assortment [of Chinese and Japanese goods] ever landed in Revelstoke. Items for sale included tea services, plates, baskets, cane chairs, handkerchiefs, flower pots, umbrella stands, lunch baskets, smoking jackets, silk goods, gold fish, and "the finest stock of candies and fruit in town." Clearly, he aimed to meet the needs of many people in the Revelstoke community, not just the Chinese.

Directly across the street from Wing's store was the Chee Kung Tong (Chinese Freemasons Society) lodge. Wing had joined the society and was elected as a secretary of the Revelstoke chapter.

Wing married three times in his life. His first wife did not live long with him as she was in poor health. She died on December 13, 1910, at the age of 38. The day of her funeral, the weather was bitterly cold, yet many Chinese in town wearing heavy jackets or coats, snow boots and hats attended the funeral. Her body, dressed in silk garments, was placed on a stuffed bed covered with a satin canopy, which was transported to the cemetery on a large sleigh. The Chinese people walked behind the sleigh scattering small pieces of rectangular bamboo papers with tiny holes in the middle. In the cemetery, the bed that held the deceased was lowered into a grave and then it was filled up with dirt. More bamboo papers were scattered on the dirt and cups of white wine and tea sprinkled on the grave. Large amounts of food, including steamed chicken, roast pork, rice and dried fruits, were left at the gravesite.[239]

Jung Ling was Wing's second wife, a cheerful, friendly and highly respected woman. The couple had four sons—Henry Quan Sam, Jack Hung Sam, Sham Lai Mee, and Kay Sam.

Eventually Jung Ling developed asthma. In 1920, husband and wife took a trip home to Enping, Guangdong. On their return trip, when the boat arrived in Shanghai, Jung Ling had an asthma attack and she died there on December 22, 1920. Wing took his deceased wife in another boat to Hong Kong for burial, after which he took the *Empress of Russia* to return to Vancouver. He spent a week on the coast before returning to Revelstoke.[240]

Jung Ling, wife of Wing Chung, was highly regarded in the community. She died of asthma complications during a trip to Shanghai and was buried in Hong Kong. Image 1797 courtesy of the Revelstoke Museum and Archives

Later, Wing married again. It is unclear if he went back to China and returned with his young wife, a small woman with bound feet, or if he sent for her from Canada. This marriage was blessed with another two sons, Owen Sam and Ming Sam. All Wing's sons were educated in Canada and in China, except Sham Lai Mee, and they all went on to have good careers.

Henry Quan Sam moved to Sicamous after high school and worked in a local hotel. He had a wife picked for him by his parents in China but he did not marry or even meet her. In his old age, he moved to Vancouver and spent his sunset years there.

Jack Hung Sam was a court interpreter and worked in the Kamloops court for several years. He became the English secretary of the Kamloops Chinese Freemasons Society. On August 17, 1932 he died at the age of thirty-four and the Kamloops freemasons held a spectacular funeral for him. The coffin was laid open, and huge masses of floral tributes were placed on tables at the foot of the casket. Beyond the flowers was another table laden with many kinds of Chinese foods. Hundreds of Chinese and many white citizens gathered in front of the lodge of the Chinese Freemasons Society on Victoria Street West, Kamloops, to say farewell to Jack. The funeral ceremonies were directed by Wey Suey, the chief of the society, with Charlie Lim delivering the funeral oration. Many Chinese present at these funeral rites were moved with emotion. Jack's father, Wing Chung, and other relatives from Revelstoke, the Okanagan and the coast were present at his funeral.

The funeral procession began from the Freemasons' lodge on Main Street and travelled along Third Avenue and St. Paul Street to the cemetery in the Miller Addition where Jack Hung Sam was buried. The procession was led by a Chinese band on a truck. Leaving Chinatown, the name of the deceased was called out by the mourners, and rectangular pieces of yellow paper were scattered on the street at intervals. At the graveside, rice, roast chicken, cigarettes and the belongings of the deceased were placed in the grave. More gold and silver papers were burned, so that money would be available for the deceased in the afterlife.[241]

Five of Wing Chung's sons in Vancouver, BC. Left to right: Kay Sam, Sham Lai Mee, Henry Quan Sam (from his first marriage), and Owen Sam and Ming Sam (from his second marriage). Chung's sixth son, Jack Hung Sam died young, at the age of 34. Courtesy the Revelstoke Museum

Sham Lai Mee worked in a local restaurant after graduating from Revelstoke High School. He met and married Helen E. Hartel, and they had a son, Donald. When World War II broke out, Mee enlisted in the army and became the first Chinese Canadian to join the BC Dragoons. Shortly after, he was promoted to the rank of Regimental Sergeant Major, and became a chief cooking instructor. When he was discharged from the service in 1946, he moved to Vancouver where he worked at Hastings Mills. No information about his earlier marriage was noted except that he married again and added three more children, Lyle, Shirley and Catherine, to his family. In 1972, he was named the chef of the year by the BC Chef's Association.

Kaye Sam was married but had no children. He lived and worked in the Vancouver area; his last employment was as a bartender at the Bayshore Inn.

Owen Sam settled in Vancouver's Chinatown after he completed high school in Revelstoke. He suffered from tuberculosis and was hospitalized for a long period of time and spent lots of time with his half-brother Henry.

Ming Sam was married and had one daughter. He lived, and taught Chinese school, in Vancouver's Chinatown for a number of years; he then found employment with BC Ferries. He moved to Victoria where he lived until he passed away.

Their father, Wing Chung, moved out of the house on Front Street after his children had left the nest, and relocated uptown to the 200 block of First Street East. He had farmland and timberland in the Revelstoke area but he did not understand the tax system. Consequently, he lost most of his properties, as the government sold his lands to cover outstanding property taxes that he had not paid. After World War II, Lai Mee took his father, Wing Chung, to Vancouver to live with his family, so that the old man was closer to his sons. On December 26, 1955, Wing Chung passed away and was buried in Mount Pleasant Cemetery with Reverend Andrew Lang officiating at the burial service.[242]

Yee Von, a Remarkable Woman

When Wong Kwong died, he left a considerable amount of debts to his wife, Yee Von. At that time, their children ranged in age from 5 to 22. Yee Von, a hard-working woman, continued with the laundry business, the livelihood of her large family. Early in the year her husband passed away, their eldest son, Sam, was hospitalized at the King Edward Memorial Sanitorium at Tranquille, BC.[243] Jean, the second child, took up nursing. Soon after the death of Wong Kwong, Yee Von's third child, Kim, married Peter Wing in Kamloops. All the children remaining at home helped Yee Von operate the laundry business. Yet all of them attended school in Revelstoke. As time went by, Yee Von managed to pay off the debts incurred by her deceased husband and to send her other children to colleges and universities to obtain a higher education. All her children had good careers, and quite a few of them were professionals.

Sam, being the first child and the oldest son, assisted his mother in operating the Kwong Lee Laundry after he was discharged from the sanitorium. Later he ventured out and engaged in restaurant businesses. He married Fern Lew, and they had three sons and one daughter. He owned and operated several restaurants in the BC Interior. He died in 1973 at the age of 63.

Jean became a registered nurse at the Queen Victoria Hospital in Revelstoke. She graduated from the Royal Columbian Hospital in New Westminster, the first Chinese nurse in Canada.

Kim, the third child, who married Peter Wing and moved to Kamloops, had no children but the couple lived a happy life. Ron Kwong, their nephew (the son of John Kwong, Yee Von's fifth child and second son), often stayed with them and helped out in the orchard that Peter had acquired from George Oishi, a Japanese immigrant. The orchard became the gathering place for the Wing family; Peter's parents and siblings visited them often. Their visits kept Kim busy preparing tea, snacks and meals—especially for her parents-in-law. Kim and Peter were involved in the Kamloops Methodist Church. When Peter joined the International Rotary Club, his involvement in the Rotary gave him and Kim an opportunity to meet people from many nations as well as to travel to overseas conferences. In 1965, Peter was elected as the mayor of Kamloops, the first Chinese-Canadian mayor in BC's history. After Peter retired, the couple moved to Vancouver. In 2007, Peter had a stroke and passed away. Kim remained in Vancouver; her nephew Ron helped and looked after her until her last day.

Doris, Yee Von's fourth child, worked for a silk importing company in Vancouver. She married Dr. Stanley Chinn, a research scientist. They moved to Saskatoon, where Stanley worked for a research council.

Clara, the fifth child, was another registered nurse. She married Kenneth Lim, a Vancouver businessman. She continued with her nursing career at the Vancouver General Hospital and eventually became the director of the Nursing Support Service. Unfortunately, Kenneth drowned while fishing. Clara dedicated herself to her nursing career for forty years, and was awarded both the Queen's Medal and the Order of Canada in recognition of her distinguished service.

John, the sixth child, owned and operated two restaurants in Revelstoke. At the age of 5, his parents sent him back to China to attend school, and he stayed in the village school for two years. He was infected with liver flukes, became ill and returned to Revelstoke where he was cured. Like his siblings, he helped his mother operate and manage the Kwong Lee Laundry. He married Mary Mochinzuki, a Japanese woman from Lillooet, and returned to Revelstoke to operate the Manning Chocolate Factory and the Chalet Restaurant. As well, the couple owned and managed two restaurants in Revelstoke, according to his son, Ron Kwong.[244] John passed away in 1974, survived by his wife and three children—one son and two daughters.

Mary, the seventh child, took up nursing and became a registered nurse in Vancouver General Hospital. She married Dr. Wilson Lee and moved to Chatham, Ontario, where Lee set up a pediatric practice. Mary continued her nursing career at the Chatham General Hospital and became involved in local politics. In 1986, she was elected as an alderman (councillor) in Chatham.

George, the eighth child, spent his childhood and received his education in Revelstoke. After school, he helped his mother in the laundry business. He often rode on a bicycle for five miles (eight kilometres) on a route to collect twenty-five cents' worth of laundries for his mother! When World War II broke out, he left high school in 1943 and joined the armed forces. None of his brothers joined the army because Canada then did not give the Chinese in this country the right to vote. He did not care about that since he believed that one day after the war ended the Chinese in this country would be enfranchised—and in 1945, Chinese members of the armed forces were indeed allowed to vote, followed in 1947 by an amendment that re-enfranchised all the Chinese in Canada.

George fought with the First Canadian Army in France, Belgium and Holland, and did not see another Asian face in Europe until his unit captured a German-held monastery in Belgium. One of the three hundred monks liberated by his unit came from China, and he lamented that the Germans had destroyed the painting of Christ's last supper. While George was fighting in the Belgian city of Bruges, he was shot in the legs and a shrapnel fragment flew off a bomb or other explosive device and hit his back. After having the shrapnel removed from his back, he kept it as a souvenir! The Canadian army did not give him a rank, so he remained as a "buck private." He met Janet Grant, who became his wife, while he was in hospital in England. Grant, a Chinese descendant, was a qualified nurse and served in the British Nursing Corps.[245]

Jim, Yee Von's ninth and last child and her fourth son, was born on February 17, 1927, in Revelstoke. He lived through the Great Depression and World War II. He married Beverly, an English woman, and together they had two sons and a daughter. Jim was a loving husband, a caring and kind father, and he loved cooking for his family. He was one of the first Asian chartered accountants, had an uncompromising work ethic, and successfully built a career in western Canada as a senior executive at one of the largest steel and pipe manufacturers in North America—IPSCO in Regina, SK. When he retired, he and his wife moved to Sorrento, BC. Soon after the death of his wife, he relocated and settled in Kelowna to be closer to his children. On June 8, 2020, he passed away at the age of 93 in Kelowna. He was survived by his children, four grandchildren, a great-granddaughter, and many nephews and nieces, and fondly remembered by his family and friends as a caring and kind person.

Yee Von and Wong Kong, however, lost one daughter, Yew Kwong, in March 1925, when the young girl was only 6 years old; she died from abdominal pains/trouble. She was an endearing girl, loved by her parents, her siblings and many of the Chinese in Revelstoke Chinatown. Her funeral was held in the Howson funeral parlor with Reverend W.W. Abbott officiating.[246]

Other Chinese Deaths

Besides Yew Kwong, there were other Chinese deaths in Revelstoke in the 1920s and beyond. In March 20, 1923, John Lee, a Chinese tailor, aged 40, could not meet his financial obligations and took his own life by hanging himself on the branch of a tree at the Cashato Ranch, a location south of the city. His dead body, suspended on the tree branch, was found by a couple of boys cutting wood for the ranch. The boys immediately reported the incident to Fred Markland, the provincial constable. The body of Lee was brought down from the tree and taken to the city, where the coroner examined Lee's remains. A coroner's jury consisting of W.E. Johnson, foreman, John Daly, G. Graham, Dan Chisholm, E. Norberg and Louis Thompson was presided over by Coroner W.I. Briggs. The jury ruled that the deceased had committed suicide. His funeral was held the following day with Reverend J. Wesley Miller officiating in English and Reverend T.F. Cheong from the Methodist Church, Kamloops, in Chinese. After leaving Howson's Parlor, the funeral procession went to the Chinese National League building on First Street East where further ceremonies were conducted; Wong Jung read an account of the deceased's life there. At the graveside, Reverends Miller and Cheong officiated at the burial ceremony.[247]

On November 2, 1925, Lan Lou Sing, aged 31, the wife of Charlie Sing, died from consumption (as tuberculosis was known then), and was interred in the same cemetery. Sing was a Chinese restaurant keeper in Revelstoke.

On December 7, 1942, Chug Lee passed away at the age of 65 in Revelstoke. He had lived in the city for thirty-two years, and worked in the roundhouse cleaning engines, one of the crew who serviced passenger trains. His wife and family were in China.

On November 14, 1945, Yip Kong Hong, aged 79, fell on the pavement trying to avoid an automobile and fractured his skull. The automobile was driven by Michael Defoe. No blame was assigned to anyone for the accident. Yip was taken to the Victoria Hospital in the city. Dr. Sutherland, who had known and attended him, said that he had poor vision and impaired hearing. George P. Echlin, manager of the Revelstoke Drug Company that employed Yip doing occasional odd jobs, said that the man was blind in his left eye and had no hearing in his left ear. Yip died the following day.[248]

On February 8, 1951, the *Revelstoke Review* reported that Wong Lock, aged 69, a resident in the city for over forty years, had passed away. Funeral services were held at Brandon's Parlors, and Reverend H.S. McDonald of the United Church conducted the funeral rites. The deceased's son, Wong Kee Chung, came from Grand Prairie to attend his father's funeral.

Below is the list of deceased Chinese Canadians who were buried in Mountain View Cemetery.[249]

Chinese Interred in Mountain View Cemetery

Last Name	First Name	Date of Death	Age	Locations		
				Block	Row	Plot
Chang	Wong	Unknown	Unknown	D	3	34
Chong	Wong	1940-09-01	65	C	1	46
Chong	Tsoa	unknown	Unknown	D	2	26
Chow	Sey	As above	As above	F	7	13
Chung	Lung	As above	As above	F	4	43
Chung	Sam Choy	As above	As above	D	4	36
Chung	Tiu	As above	As above	C	6	63
Chung	Wing	As above	As above	F	3	29
Foo	Choo	As above	As above	F	2	23
Get	June	1926-0?-0?	As above	D	2	33
Git	Mary Hung	1945-01-05	87	G	11	14
Hing	Tsoa Chang	1931-03-16	71	D	2	26
Hong	Yip Kwong	1945-11-14	81	D	2	44
Hong Wong	Bill	1923-02-01	46	F	6	26
Hoy	Kee Sing	1956-12-19	91	F	3	62
Jae	S.J.	unknown	unknown	F	7	11
Jug	Lee	1942-12-07	65	D	4	43
Kee	L.	unknown	unknown	F	3	46
Kee	Nun Kong	unknown	unknown	F	7	12
Kwong	John Hon	1932-02-0?	unknown	F	1	15
Kwong	Maizie	1925-03-05	6	F	6	29

Kwong	Wong	1932-02-10	56	F	1	13
Lee	On	unknown	unknown	D	1	25
Lee	Tim	unknown	unknown	D	2	25
Lee	Ton	unknown	unknown	F	5	14
Let	Wong	1935-07-20	47	F	4	11
Mine	K.	unknown	Unknown	F	7	14
Ming	Ham	1923-06-12	70	C	2	60
Moe	Sam	unknown	unknown	G	12	17
Nui	Ng Sun	1920-01-15	63	F	6	24
Po	Woo My	1941-01-02	60	D	3	35
Sing	Charles	unknown	unknown	G	4	14
Sing	John	1929-03-04	58	D	2	29
Sing	Lee	1924-09-12	41	F	5	28
Sing	Mrs. Charles	1925-11-02	31	F	5	30
Sing	Wong Lay	1952-07-28	74	G	11	15
Sue	Chen	unknown	unknown	F	3	23
Tan	Chao Chi	unknown	unknown	CO	5	56
Wai	Choy	1941-01-04	81	D	4	35
Wong	Baby	unknown	unknown	C	2	60
Wong	C.T.	1941-04-19	50	D	4	34
Wong	Chee King	unknown	unknown	B	12	34
Wong	Goon	1967-04-08	81	G	2	14
Wong	Kar	1944-05-18	64	D	1	27
Wong	Lock	1951-02-02	69	G	5	11
Wong	Mow	1927-12-31	63	D	2	32
Wong	You Fung Too	1954-01-27	70	G	11	13
Yee	Fook	1947-03-23	77	D	4	37
Yick	Woo	1950-07-14	77	G	6	10
Yuen	Wong	unknown	Unknown	F	6	22
TOTAL	**50 burials**					

After the repeal of Head Tax and the Chinese Exclusion Act in 1947, the Chinese immigrants became able to send for family members in Guangdong and have them join them in Canada. When family members arrived, many of them preferred to live in the Lower Mainland of BC or larger metropolitan areas in other provinces. Consequently, many Chinese residents in Revelstoke left town to join family members in other large cities. As Ron Kwong put it, at the time when the family of Wong Kwong left town, only four Chinese families remained in Revelstoke.

Conclusion

The beginning of Farwell Town and the establishment of Revelstoke were formidable. Arthur Stanhope Farwell, a surveyor, went to court to challenge the CPR company, a big corporation in Canada. Although Farwell did not win the legal battle, his courage and bravery was admirable. The construction of the CPR in Revelstoke brought many Chinese labourers to the fledgling city. After they were dismissed from the railway's labour force, they settled in Revelstoke where they established two Chinatowns. Quite a few of these Chinese operated laundry shops and offered services to the white people in the mainstream community. Some of them cultivated land and grew root crops, vegetables and fruits, and sold their produce door to door to the white families, saving them from taking trips to the market. The health officer, however, declared that the Chinese gardens were filthy, because the farmers fertilized their gardens with urine. He denounced the Chinese gardeners, destroyed their farms, and offered no alternatives.

Indeed, the living conditions in the Chinatowns in the early days were poor—polluted and overcrowded. The burning of their huts and shacks without offering better and affordable housing did not help the Chinese settlers to live healthily; rather, it manifested the prejudice and discrimination the Chinese residents in Chinatowns faced. Many of these settlers were labourers who had constructed the CPR, an essential piece of infrastructure that brought trades to Canada and merchandise to Canadians, Europeans and people in other ethnic groups in this country. Indirectly, the Chinese immigrants had assisted the development of the Canadian economy, but they needed education to improve their living conditions and earn acceptance as Chinese Canadians in the mainstream society.

Some of the Chinese settlers established and operated grocery stores and restaurants in town. These businesses helped the Chinese to make a good living and maintain their relationships with one another. The presence of the joss house showed that members of the Chee Kung Tong (Chinese Freemasons Society) had arrived in Revelstoke. This organization helped the Chinese immigrants in town and its vicinity, both practically and to retain Chinese heritage and culture. This organization also attempted to reach out to the mainstream community by donating funds for the local hospital so it could purchase an x-ray machine.

Wong Kwong, a labour contractor and owner of the Kwong Lee Laundry, died young in an accident and left his wife, Yee Von, to fend for a family of nine children. Yee Von was a capable and resourceful woman who raised and nurtured her children, and continued to operate the family's laundry business with the help of her children whenever necessary. All of her children had careers, and some became entrepreneurs or professionals. Her resilience and strength are truly admirable.

In the early days, the Chinese immigrants experienced prejudice and discrimination in Revelstoke. However, many of them lived well and made a good life for themselves and their families. They indeed left a page of remarkable and unforgettable Chinese-Canadian history in Revelstoke.

The Queen City: Nelson

The City of Nelson is situated on the extreme western arm of Kootenay Lake in the Selkirk Mountains region of British Columbia's southern interior. This is in the traditional territory of the Ktunaxa and Sinixt First Nations. Nelson lies at the junction of Provincial Highway 3A and Highway 6, about 663 kilometres from Vancouver in the west, 340 kilometres from Calgary in the east, 340 kilometres from Kelowna in the north and 237 kilometres from Spokane, Washington, in the south. Travelling by air from Vancouver or Calgary to Nelson takes only an hour.

Nelson has a vibrant shopping area and more than 350 well preserved heritage buildings, many of which reveal Nelson's colourful history. It has been fondly referred to as the Queen City by its citizens "because there are millions of lights glowing around the city that makes it look like a crown fit for a queen."[250] The downtown core is the centre of the arts, tourism, and commerce, including small manufacturing and home-based businesses; it is also the administrative centre of the Regional District of Central Kootenay. Its back country offers recreational sports throughout the year. The network of trails on Toad Mountain, which is approximately ten kilometres southwest of the city, are excellent for hiking and biking in the summer. When snow covers the mountain in winter, its slopes are perfect for backcountry skiing. A downhill skiing resort, Whitewater, is also located near Nelson.

The Discovery of Silver

In the fall of 1886, Osner and Winslow Hall, together with a party of placer miners from Colville, Washington, arrived at the headwaters of the Salmon River to search for gold. They accidentally discovered silver with traces of copper instead. The Hall brothers took samples of the mineral ore to Colville for assay. The report they received astounded them, indicating that the mineral ore contained high-grade silver. This discovery encouraged the Hall brothers to return to the area in the spring of 1887 and stake claims on the northeast side of Toad Mountain to mine for silver.[251] The news of the discovery quickly leaked out and attracted about four hundred people to the area to prospect and mine the precious metal. These miners set up tents along Ward Creek at the present townsite of Nelson.

At the same time, the Hall brothers established the Silver King Mine on the northeast side of Toad Mountain approximately seven kilometres southwest of Nelson. Mining operations began in 1889, producing both copper and silver ore. The ore was originally brought down from the mountain by pack trains and shipped to Butte, Montana, for smelting. A wagon road was constructed mainly for the purpose of delivering silver ore to the smelter in the south. Later, the Silver King Mine established its own smelter in Nelson and erected a tramway just over seven kilometres long to bring ore from the mine to the smelter. Although at this time, businesses and industries were discouraged from employing Chinese people by both provincial and federal legislation, it is likely mines in the Nelson area employed Chinese labourers to work in the mine, as was the case in other parts of British Columbia, regardless of the legislation.

The Silver King placer mine, as well as other mining operations, was known to ignore legislation and hire Chinese labourers. Image C-07791 courtesy of the Royal BC Museum and Archives

In the spring of 1890, the company constructing the Columbia and Kootenay Railway was pushing its workers to finish the Nelson line. The construction crews reportedly consisted of 160 British or Canadian people, 65 Italians (there was prejudice against the Italians as well as the Chinese, so they too were singled out in the newspaper accounts), and 175 Chinese labourers.[252] The contractor for this CPR line believed that if the Chinese labourers were treated kindly, they would do more work than the same number of white workers. To encourage them, he gave each of his Chinese labourers a pound of fresh beef each day, and he even attempted to learn the Chinese language so that he could communicate with them effectively.[253] Because of this, the Chinese labourers were often referred to as the "pets" of the CPR.

As the infrastructure was put into place and the population of the settlement increased, G.M. Sproat, the gold commissioner and a magistrate, laid out a plan for the townsite.[254] In 1897, the city was incorporated, named after the then-lieutenant governor of British Columbia, Hugh Nelson.

The Earliest Chinese Immigrants

On September 6, 1890, the *Nelson Miner* reported that

> Chinese [placer miners] have taken up a number of claims on Bird [Eagle Creek], the first creek west of 49 [Creek] and distant about 10 miles from Nelson.... They have already made as high as $5 a day to the man, [and sold the gold dust to their 'Tyee' in Nelson]... Chinese are better placer miners than whites, for the reason that they work the ground closer.[255]

This story shows that Chinese immigrants had already arrived and settled in Nelson by 1890. In the same year, a notice for the election of fire wardens issued by the government agent for the West Kootenay District also provides evidence that Chinese immigrants had settled in the city. The notice stated that three fire wardens would be elected in Nelson, and that every male inhabitant aged 18 or older could be elected to serve as fire warden for a one-year term—except for Chinese and First Nations individuals.[256] The 1891 census listed 103 Chinese railway labourers in Lower (West) Kootenay and 43 Chinese labourers working mainly as cooks, miners and laundry operators. In August of the same year, the *Nelson Miner* reported, "The authorities have suppressed gambling in Nelson. They should now devote a little attention to suppress the Chinese dens and opium joints... in various parts of the town reserve. Of course, these pets of the CPR must not be treated too harshly in the enforcement of the law."[257] This comment alongside the election notice shows that anti-Chinese sentiment had already surfaced in the city. Similarly, on February 10, 1892, the *Ainsworth Hot Spring News* stated that "not a single hotel or restaurant at Nelson now employs Chinese help," and advertisements in the *Nelson Economist* and the *Nelson Daily News* clearly revealed discrimination against the Chinese in Nelson.[258]

The *Ainsworth Hot Spring News* article continued, saying, "If private families would do likewise, the Chinese question as far as Nelson is concerned, would solve itself. Efforts are also being made to establish a well-equipped white laundry in the town." This remark was directed at a few prominent Nelson families such as the Davys, the Humes and the Applewhaites who employed Chinese "houseboys."

The Chinese Laundry Men

Two early Chinese immigrants who operated laundries were Mar Sam, whose laundry was located on Vernon Street, and Wah Sing, whose laundry was on Ward Street.[259] On July 7, 1884, the *Nelson Miner* reported that Mar Sam had participated in a race on Dominion Day open only to Chinese runners—the two-hundred yard dash—and won the first prize of $5.00. Three other Chinese men—recorded in the news report as Ah Sing, One Lung and "Whiskers," whose Chinese name was not "pronounceable"—also took part in the race.[260] By 1892, two other Chinese businesses were listed in the *British Columbia Directory*: Hip Chong, a baker, and Sin Lee, a tailor, both on Ward Street.[261] On December 15, 1894, Mar Sam sold his laundry to Mar Ming, but he continued to participate in the laundry business by "picking up and delivering laundry around town with a child's wagon."[262] By 1898, business licences for laundries included Yee Chong, Kwong Wo, C. Young & Co, and Wing Kee.[263]

On August 14, 1899, a petition from residents of the neighbourhood around Kootenay Street and Hall Mines Road that demanded the closing of a Chinese laundry was read at a city council meeting. In reporting on the petition, the *Nelson Economist* claimed that "these people are dangerously unsanitary in their habits. They herd together in hovels that a white man would not use for his cattle."[264] Countering this petition, a letter was also read at the meeting from the landlord of the property that pleaded on behalf of the Chinese. "He based his request on the extraordinary ground that he was an 'old timer,' whereas those who desired the removal of the Chinamen were recent arrivals," commented the *Nelson Daily Miner*.

In June 1905, Lip [Hip] Chong Laundry was charged with an infraction of a city bylaw regulating laundries. This laundry was using water from a well sunk in

Mrs. Applewhaite with her son and a Chinese servant. Image 94-31-23 courtesy of the Nelson and District Museum, Archives, Art Gallery and Historical Society

Mar Sam's Laundry operated on Nelson's Front Street, and on Vernon Street before that, for almost sixty years. Image courtesy Greg Nesteroff

the owner's washroom in his house, which was built on swampy ground. Such water was considered by officials to be undoubtedly "full of contaminating filth." Although the defence argued that it was beyond the purview of the city council to regulate such matters, the court determined that there was a bylaw in place requiring laundries to use the city's water supply. Hip Chong was therefore ordered to pay a fine of $25 plus legal fees, or in default of the payment, serve one month's imprisonment in the local jail.[265] It is unknown which option he chose.

Around 1912, laundry man Mar Sam returned to China to visit his wife and while there fathered three children. Yorkie Mah was his eldest child. When Mar Sam returned to Nelson, he did not bring his wife and children with him. Upon his return he established the Mar Sam Laundry at 510 Front Street.[266]

Mar Sam's son Yorkie, however, immigrated to Nelson when he was a teenager. Yorkie worked briefly in Nelson's LD Cafe. Later he worked at a restaurant in Trail and then became a pastry chef and butcher. In 1945, he established the Kootenay Foodland on 1402 Bay Avenue in Trail. Mar Sam then moved to Trail to live with Yorkie, who made sure his father did not gamble away all his savings. After his wife moved to Hong Kong later on, Sam joined her in that city to retire. He died in Hong Kong in his nineties.[267]

Other Events in the Chinese Community

By 1894, the Methodist Mission had arrived in Nelson, and had begun holding services in its building at the corner of Silica and Ward Street. By the early 1920s a Methodist church had been established at 342 Josephine Street.[268]

Reverend Silas Ng of the Methodist Church in Vancouver visited Nelson a couple of times to conduct services in Chinese.[269] The *Tribune* reported with an approving tone that "one Chinaman has been induced to embrace Christianity… [and] had quit gambling and smoking opium…."[270] Also, a good number of the Chinese desired to learn English, and to help achieve this purpose, many of them attended church and Sunday school regularly, whether they were Christians or not. The Epworth League of the Methodist Church conducted English classes for some Chinese who attended church services, especially in winter.[271]

Sadly, on December 7, 1898, the *Nelson Daily Miner* reported that Len Lung, a destitute Chinese man, had been found dead from opium poisoning in his shack on the waterfront. Lung had been ill for a long time, and was living in poverty with no prospect of getting well. He became very despondent, so he took opium to end his life. A post-mortem examination confirmed that his death had been caused by an overdose of opium.[272]

On the night of Hallowe'en 1898, Chief W.J. Thompson and the members of the Nelson fire brigade visited the Chinese settlement for the purpose of collecting the road tax imposed under bylaw no. 86 of the city. Around 8:00 p.m., members of the brigade proceeded to the houses where most of the Chinese men congregated nightly to play fan-tan, smoke opium and indulge in other Chinese pastimes. The first place they visited was Wo Kee's store on Vernon Street where about thirty men were playing or watching a game of dominoes. These men scrambled to escape, but firefighters were posted at every exit, so they returned to the room and protested against their capture in the Chinese language. Chief Thompson pulled out a receipt book and called on the men to pay their taxes. Most protested they had no money, but the chief told them to "dig up or go to jail." Some then produced the money and some borrowed it from friends. Several, however, were unable to, so they were ordered to an inner room to wait for a decision from the tax collector.

The firefighters visited more houses facing Vernon Street and several laundries in the area, collecting a total of about $150 from the Chinese. When the raid was completed, about a dozen men were unable to pay the taxes, but they were released on a promise to appear at city hall the next day. One man complained, "This is the worst country I ever saw. I pay tax on property, I pay taxes and taxes and taxes and I have no vote for the mayor."[273] His complaint highlighted the fact that the Chinese had been disenfranchised yet still had to contribute financially to support laws they had no say in formulating. In total, the city collected taxes from about 140 Chinese residents, but another 50 or 60 remained outstanding. (Those figures meant the Chinese accounted for one-seventh of Nelson's adult population at the time.)

On April 29, 1899, Yong Jo, another Chinese man, passed away. His funeral and burial were described in the *Nelson Daily Miner*:

> The body was taken up to the cemetery on a wagon, surrounded by burning joss sticks, with a number of Chinamen following on foot behind. On reaching the grave the body was lowered down, the earth filled in.... More joss sticks were lit, and then an impossible Mongolian [*sic*] produced a large and mysterious looking bundle. This was unrolled, and found to contain the clothes, bedding and other belongings of the defunct.... These were, one by one, solemnly burnt....
>
> The dear departed being thus provided with raiment and bedding on his long journey to the "never, never," his thoughtful friends proceeded to supply him with the necessary sustenance. Accordingly a small but sufficient store of chicken, rice, and fruit was placed handy at the foot of the grave.[274]

A Chinese "high priest" officiated at the funeral ceremony. The reporter concluded by noting that Yong Jo could not yet rest altogether in peace until his bones were reburied in his native soil. The assumption was that one day in the future, the bones of Yong Jo would be exhumed and sent back to his village in China for final burial, so that his spirit would rest in peace.[275]

In late November of 1910, Der Ming, a Chinese man living on Front Street near Cedar was fined $100 by Police Magistrate William Irving in the city police court for selling liquor without a licence; $50 for having opium in his possession for sale; and $50 for keeping a disorderly house. The alternative to the fines, which added up to $200, was one year's imprisonment. In the charges brought against Der Ming, Constables Reid and McLeod stated that the building where the accused had lived for some time had been closely watched for a considerable period. Women had been seen to go there and the place was frequented by Chinese people. On a Friday night, the two officers went to the building and saw Der Ming rush away. Inside they found a woman named Carrie King. Later they found a complete opium-smoking apparatus, which was produced in court, and which included one tin vial filled with opium, and another that was practically empty. Also seized were three opium jars, a pipe, seven bowls for the pipe, an opium knife, two opium needles upon which the drug was heated before being placed in the pipe bowls, a lamp filled with oil, small rags for wiping the needles, and a pair of scissors.

A large stock of liquor was also found in the building, together with a number of glasses, a corkscrew and a beer opener. The liquor consisted of one partly filled bottle of Scotch whiskey, one bottle of *sam sui* (Chinese whiskey), two bottles of beer, and a number of empty beer, whiskey, *sam sui* and gin bottles.

The evidence provided by Carrie King, who was called by Mr. Johnson, was to the effect that she had spent two days in Der Ming's shack. During that time, she had purchased some whiskey and smoked four pipes of opium. Nine or ten Chinese individuals visited the place while she was there. At the request of Mr. Johnson, the charges against King were withdrawn. However, she was given twenty-four hours to leave the city. Both Der Min and Carrie King spent the night in jail, none of the fines having been paid.

The afternoon of the next day, Dr. Gilbert Hartin, the city's medical officer, and Sergeant Ellis, together with Donald Guthrie, chief of the fire department, visited the "shack" in which Der Ming conducted his "nefarious" business. Without hesitation, Dr. Hartin condemned it as being a menace to public health. The fire department would burn Der Ming's building down in the near future.[276]

The Chinese Settlement: Chinatown

In the early days, many of the Chinese immigrants settled on the west side of Vernon Street, and Wo Kee, an employment agent and grocer, was also located on Vernon Street. The newcomers leased lots in this area from the CPR. In May 1898, the CPR wanted to build new freight sheds where the Chinese settlement was located, and the city felt that the area was too good for a Chinatown. This led to a meeting between Acting Mayor Teerzed and L.A. Hamilton, the CPR commissioner. The meeting concluded with an agreement that the CPR could lease the land on Lake Street in blocks 61 and 71 to the Chinese. These blocks were in the CPR allotment and the presence of a Chinese community would not interfere with anyone, meaning among the mainstream community.[277] In addition, the city council passed a resolution stating that renting buildings to Chinese merchants on the main streets of the city should be discouraged "as they are detrimental to the city's best interests."[278] As a result of the decision regarding the CPR, an eviction notice was issued to the Chinese residents and businesses, ordering them to leave Vernon Street and relocate themselves onto Lake Street.

At the same time, "a petition was adopted by the City Council… extending the fire limits so as to include block 69 and also block 4. Why these two blocks should be singled out:… A rumor had been going the rounds for some days past that that ever-growing Chinese element in the city had their almond eyes [sic] on this particular section, and that arrangements were about complete by which they were to get possession of it…. If all this be true… the people of the east end are fully justified in making a very vigorous protest and in taking every possible precaution to keep the pigtails from settling in their midst."[279]

Respected community member and merchant Kwong Wing Chong's shop is prominently shown in this 1890s image of Nelson's Chinatown. Image E-09183 courtesy of the Royal BC Museum and Archives

Although an eviction notice had been sent out, not all the Chinese residents and merchants left Vernon Street. Kee War and Long Yick, the two Chinese stores, and Wo Kwong and Yee Chong, the two Chinese laundries, were still listed on Vernon Street in the 1899 *British Columbia Directory*. Similarly, Kwong Wing Chong, Wo Kee and Yick Sang Lung, the three Chinese general and grocery stores, were found on Vernon Street.[280]

On February 10, 1899, the *Nelson Daily Miner* reported on the Chinese New Year celebration.

> Nelson's Chinese colony is by no means a small one.... The Chinamen were at home yesterday to [welcome] their friends—whether white or yellow—as it was the first day of their New Year celebration....They keep an open house and not only exchange the compliments of the season with one another but take pleasure in receiving and entertaining their white friends.
>
> Yesterday afternoon and evening a large number of citizens found their way to "China Town" and visited the different establishments. In these the Mongolians were assembled resplendent in the gorgeous hues of their native dress. Some gambled while

others dispensed refreshments in a lavish manner. Native drinks and sweetmeats were abundant and the more favored of the guests not only received all they could comfortably drink or eat at the time but were presented with parcels of nuts and candies to take home with them. The houses were decorated in the most tasty Oriental manner.

In the evening the festivities confined themselves pretty well to gambling… but firecrackers kept up a fusilade until a late hour. The more prosperous Celestials will keep up the celebration for at least a week, the laundry men will knock off work for a couple of days and those who are servants in private houses will celebrate just as long as their masters or mistresses will allow them.[281]

This event not only showcased Chinese customs and culture but also demonstrated that the Chinese settlers were making attempts to show hospitality and to reach out to the mainstream society.

Still, young white boys were often seen teasing and making life miserable for the Chinese. The *Nelson Tribune* wrote,

Nelson has a smart lot of boys, but many of them have been permitted by their parents to run wild, and as a consequence they have become a general nuisance. One of their chief delights has been playing tricks upon the Chinese, particularly in throwing stones. A few days ago, a Chinaman was coming down a side street and was made a target by a gang of young hoodlums. He was struck on the jaw by a rock, which almost smashed his face in. The police are getting information against these young rascals…. Parents should keep their boys under more home influence, and a good, healthy castigation would improve many of them and keep them out of court.[282]

On May 19, 1900, the *Nelson Tribune* reported on an impending marriage between a leading Chinese merchant, Kwong Kay, and a recently arrived Chinese woman, Ah Gee. The marriage was a unique occurrence in the Kootenay at this time—Ah Gee was only one of three women in Nelson. The reporter visited Chinatown and came upon Wo Kee, another Chinese merchant, who took the reporter to the house of the affianced couple. Wo took him to the house but left him outside. Shortly after, Wo came out, mumbled a few words to the reporter, and left. At that instant, a brunette woman peeped out from inside and quickly shut the door. Following this, Kwong, the groom, appeared from his store and told the reporter that his bride-to-be had been born in China and had arrived from Victoria the previous December. Kwong said since he was a Christian, the couple would marry in church. In fact, he was trying to arrange the wedding ceremony with Reverend H.S. Lakehurst for that very morning! Kwong added that he didn't want news of the marriage to spread in the Chinese community since they would make too much of a noisy fuss![283]

On September 12, 1900, the entire city was charged with excitement and festive with banners, flags, and coloured streamers welcoming Lord and Lady Minto—Canada's Governor General and his wife. Elaborate ceremonies and parades were organized, and Nelson's Chinatown was not to be outdone. The *Nelson Tribune* reported, "Front Street was lit by long strings of paper lanterns, and in front of the Chinese stores several hundred celestials… exploded strings of firecrackers and giant bombs, burned joss sticks in bundles, and banged their brass cymbals…. As their excellencies' carriage passed, the din was ear-splitting, but the Governor-General seemed to be intensely amused."[284]

Chinatown at this time was bounded by Ward, Josephine, and Hall Streets running north-south, and Front, Lake, and Vernon Streets running east-west, and included a few Chinese living on Silica Street.[285]

In 1901 the commissioner of the federal Royal Commission on Chinese and Japanese Immigration visited Nelson, and he interviewed Kwong Wing Chong, a prominent Chinese merchant in Chinatown, and Mar Sam, the laundry owner. Kwong estimated that 325 Chinese people lived in Nelson. This included 50 cooks and domestic servants, 20 workers in four laundries, 40 woodcutters, 50 workers in twelve market gardens, 10 merchants, and another 150 unemployed individuals. However, Mar Sam reported that there were actually ten laundries, employing 50 men.[286] The same year, the *Nelson Economist* reported that Nelson had a Chinese population of 277 citizens, making it the largest Chinatown in BC's Interior.[287]

In the interviews, neither Kwong nor Mar had mentioned any Chinese women in the Chinese community. But Kwong's wife lived with him in a suite on the upper floor of his general and grocery store on Vernon Street. Mrs. Kwong apparently did not speak English, and her feet were bound. "Her tiny feet were so small that she could barely totter around the room," observed Helen Dickson Reynolds when she and her mother visited the Kwongs.[288] Reynolds noted that "Mrs. Kwong bowed and smiled politely but let her husband to do all the talking. She was dressed in rich silks in the old Chinese fashion of a loose blouse falling over the loose trousers, and ornamental shoes on the tiny distorted feet. She tottered around carrying a tray of cups of delicate scented tea, and Chinese candies." As time went by, the Kwongs had three sons.

Despite the interviews conducted for the royal commission, the 1911 census recorded the population of Chinatown as only about eighty, including thirty people each at 200 Josephine Street and 312 Hall Street. There was only one woman among them.

In the same year, Chinatown suffered a series of fires in late August. On August 21, fire occurred in two houses at the corner of Lake and Hall Streets. On August 22, the buildings of a Chinese ranch located near Willow Point just outside of Nelson were destroyed; the damage was estimated at $5,000.[289] It was believed that the fires were the work of an arsonist; the *Nelson Daily News* speculated "that there is a firebug at work in the city who has particular animus against the Lake Street, Chinatown and waterfront districts."[290] The chief suspect identified by the police left town before he could be charged — and the fires ceased.

In 1922, the following businesses were found in Chinatown. The list is a sample only, and not a comprehensive list of the Chinese businesses at that time.

Hip Chong Laundry, 118 Silica Street
Kwong Sang Wing Co., Chinese store, 612 Front Street
Kwong Ton, choy suey and noodles, 305 Josephine Street
L.D. Café, Gee Kay and Hym Sing, 419 Baker Street
Lee Kee, shoemaker, 612 Front Street
Man Hing & Y Co., dry goods and groceries, 610 Front Street
Mar Sam Laundry, 510 Front Street
On Tai, Chinese store, rear 612 Front Street
Royal Café, Le Quong, proprietor, 504 Baker Street
Sing Chong Laundry, 312 Hall Street
Standard Café, Wong Soon, proprietor, 320 Baker Street
Wing Lee, Chinese store, 602 Front Street
Wo Kee, Chinese store, 394 Hall Street[291]

The Chinese Market Gardeners

The Chinese market gardeners who remained on the CPR flats had cultivated the land into greenery, producing vegetables for the citizens of Nelson. Some Chinese gardeners had moved to the mouth of Grohman Creek, where they cleared land for growing vegetables. Others lived on the land at Cottonwood Creek and at the foot of Cottonwood Falls. They had "achieved wonders in the way of clearing and getting their new locations under cultivation. Every foot of the ground that could be possibly used has been put in shape," claimed the *Nelson Miner*. In April 1902, City Council received a letter about imposing a tax on the sellers of fruits and vegetables that triggered a lively debate during the council meeting. Mayor Fletcher believed that the public was strongly against enforcing a prohibitory law on the Chinese gardeners who produced and supplied vegetables for the community. But the aldermen argued that the Chinese should be taxed or a licence fee imposed on the Chinese peddlers who sold fresh produce door to door. Alderman Irving was of the opinion that the Chinese should be allowed to peddle their vegetables but that they should also be charged $25 for a licence. Alderman Hamilton felt that $10 per year for a licence or tax was plenty. Alderman Selous argued that if a licence fee or tax was enforced, the Chinese market gardeners might stop delivering or selling produce from door to door. Then it would "necessitate the housewives 'putting on their best, bib and tucker and walking down town every day to a market for fresh vegetables for breakfast or lunch....'" Finally, it was decided that a letter should be sent to the Attorney General requesting advice as to whether the council could impose a licence on the Chinese peddlers.[292] The response from the Attorney General was not located but it seems from Chinese complaints about taxes that licensing fees were indeed imposed on the Chinese peddlers.

Charlie Bing [Soo Bing Quan] (苏炳坤) was a renowned Chinese market gardener and rancher as well as a Chinese cowboy in the Kootenay. Bing was born in Hong Kong on October 22, 1882, but nothing was known about his family and his childhood since he did not want to talk about them. According to immigration records, he arrived in Victoria on March 13, 1900.[293] Shortly after that, he moved to the Midway area where he farmed and worked in mines and logging camps. He cut wood and hauled it for the lake steamers. By 1904, he had a small herd of cattle and an eighty-five-acre ranch that straddled the Canada-US border. He also had a garden that won prizes at the Greenwood Fall Fair in 1911, 1912 and 1913 for yellow onions, pumpkins, celery, corn, squash and tomatoes.[294]

Bing was an excellent horseman, "a Chinese cowboy who'd ride anything with four feet, if he could get [his] leg over it," commented W.S. Wilson, a journalist for the *Vancouver Province*.[295] Very often he was called upon to track down strayed horses that had been lured away by wild mares at night. By the next morning, those strayed horses would be kilometres away in the mountains, and the owners of these strayed horses would call upon Bing to find and bring the strayed horses back for them. When Bing received such a request, he would take off alone into the mountains to round up the horses, and return them, along with a few wild ones, to the owners.

On July 4, 1912, Bing entered and won the cowboy race at Rock Creek.[296] The following year, he participated in the race again but did not win. He was riding alongside a cowboy with a very vicious horse, which wheeled suddenly and planted both its heels on Bing's horse; one foot hit and broke Bing's leg. Shorty Perasso, the operator of a garage in Nelson, took him to hospital where he had a cast put on the fractured leg. A few weeks later, when the cast was taken off, the leg had been set at an angle and was about an inch shorter than his other limb.

Bing returned to China in 1922 to get married, and had the leg re-broken there and pulled back into shape by a series of rope tourniquets that enabled him to walk normally.[297] Then he brought his bride, Yee Shee Coan (谢氏好安), to Nelson. They were one of the first few Chinese families who settled in Nelson. Bing's wife could not speak English and lived on their farm, somewhat isolated from the community. Fortunately, she had a cousin, Frances, living in Cranbrook who often visited and conversed with her. The visits of Frances were delightful moments for her.[298]

Bing and his wife had eight children: Winnie, James, Eva, Johnnie, George, Mary Helen, Nellie and Bill. These children enjoyed their years on the farm and

An old truck from the 1940s sits on the Bing property at Willow Point, just outside of Nelson. Charlie Bing was a renowned Chinese market gardener and rancher, and his riding abilities made him a local legend. Image courtesy Greg Nesteroff

developed a respect for the wildlife and wilderness around them. The Bing family had one of the finest vegetable market gardens on the North Shore at Willow Point, about eight kilometres from Nelson. They supplied produce and pork to Nelson restaurants and private homes, as well as to mines in Ymir, Salmo and Sheep Creek. Bing handled all the deliveries, and as the children got older, they did the bookkeeping.

On March 13, 1944, fire consumed the home of Charlie Bing. Neighbours came running to help out and managed to save most of the household belongings. Bing lost everything, including his home and farm, because he had not insured his house and property.[299]

In 1969, Bing passed away at the age of 86 in Kootenay Lake General Hospital. Besides his wife, he was survived by his three sons, Johnnie, George and William, and his five daughters, Winnie (Mrs. S. Smith), Eva (Mrs. J. Wrangler), Mary (Mrs. F. Parker), Alice (Mrs. McKay), and Nellie, and sixteen grandchildren.

The Mar Family

The 1921 census records that Mar Juck [Jack] (马泽 -译音), aged 55, immigrated to British Columbia in 1888, and went to Nelson to work as a storekeeper on Front Street. Around 1905, he went back to his village in Guangdong to marry Lee Shee (李氏 -译音). The couple had a son, Shu Tong. Later, Lee and their son joined Mar in Nelson, and the couple then had another son, Shu Ling, in 1910, and a daughter, Hon Wan, the following year.

All the Mar children went to school in Nelson. In 1922, Mar Shu Tong graduated from the local high school. He wanted to continue studying at the University of Washington, but his parents had made an arrangement for him to marry a girl whom he had not met in their home village in China. They wanted him to go back to the village with them and his siblings to marry the girl. Shu Tong resisted the marriage arrangement. With the help of a former classmate, a Chinese girl in Vancouver, he managed to avoid travelling with his family to the village. On the day when the boat was to set sail from Vancouver, Shu Tong hid in the home of his former classmate in Vancouver. The wedding obviously could not take place without the groom. Later, Shu Tong found a job with a Chinese morning newspaper in Vancouver.[300]

On November 30, 1922, Shu Tong wrote to the *Nelson Daily News* informing the community that he had not sailed home with his family to China, and had instead remained in Vancouver working in the office of the Chinese newspaper. He said that he disliked the Chinese tradition of arranged marriages, but he understood the disappointment of the Chinese people in Nelson in him because he had disobeyed and upset his parents and challenged the Chinese culture. It was his own doing, he said, and he had not been influenced by the Chinese Nationalist League. Besides, he enjoyed the company of the young people in Vancouver.

As a resourceful and determined young man, Shu Tong managed to enroll at the University of Washington eventually. In 1937, he graduated with a bachelor of arts, with a major in international law and diplomacy. In June the same year, he travelled to China for a visit. Shortly after the invasion of China by the Japanese, he returned to Nelson, and raised funds to support the Chinese republican government against the Japanese invasion by showing newsreel footage of the Japanese invasion to many Chinese communities in BC. In 1938, Shu Tong's father, Mar Juck, passed away in his home village in Guangdong, and in 1941, Shu Tong became ill with pneumonia and passed away at the age of only 36.

By then, Shu Tong's brother, Mar Shu Ling, had already married Kung Yook Poy in the family's home village in Guangdong. In 1934, their first child, Mar Woo Hym (馬和謙)—also known as Lawrence Mar—was born. The following year, Shu Ling returned to Nelson where he worked as a cook in the Club Café. Two years later, World War II erupted. Shu Ling was drafted but was not sent overseas to serve Canada due to thyroid enlargement. He was assigned to the home guard, patrolling West Kootenay hydro dams. Because he was able to speak both Chinese and English, he was often called on to interpret in court. He was a well-liked person, but he missed his deceased brother, Shu Tong, and his own family, which was stranded in Guangdong. It took fifteen years before he would see his wife and son in Nelson.

In 1947, the Chinese Exclusion Act was repealed, so the Chinese in Canada could send for their family members and reunite with them in Canada. Shu Ling immediately sent for his wife, Kung, and his son, Lawrence, who were still living in the village in Guangdong. In September 1950, mother and son escaped to Hong Kong before the People's Republic of China tightened passport restrictions. In July 1951, they finally arrived in Nelson from Hong Kong. It was the first time that Lawrence had seen his father since infancy! When they first arrived, the family lived in Chinatown. The following year, a baby son, Allen Mar, was born. After the birth of his younger child, Shu Ling bought a house in the residential area and moved the family away from Chinatown. Meanwhile, he entered into a partnership with Fred Wah Sr., Jimmy Wong and Seto Howe to operate the Diamond Grill, a Chinese restaurant.[301]

The death of his beloved brother and the long absence of his family had affected the personality of Shu Ling; he became a quiet and reserved person, seldom socializing with people in the Chinese community other than his partners in the restaurant business. It is unknown when he retired from the restaurant business. In 1993, he died at the age of 83.

When Lawrence arrived in Nelson, he was already 17 years old, yet he was admitted to grade 6 in school. "It is pretty difficult for a young Chinese person at that age to learn another language," he said. "I was lucky to stay in school until I reached grade 10. Then I quit school and worked with my father in the Diamond Grill."[302]

At the time of his arrival in Nelson, there were a little more than three hundred people in the Chinese community. It consisted of five families, and the rest were single men, said Lawrence. Most of the Chinese were merchants operating restaurants and grocery stores. However, he remembered that his father had told him that there were a few Chinese organizations, including the Chinese Freemasons Society, the Chinese Empire Reform Association and the Chinese Nationalist League in Nelson's Chinatown.

The Chinese Freemasons Society

During the Fraser Gold Rush (1858), members of the Hongmen Hui (洪门会), known later as the Chee Kung Tong and even later as the Chinese Freemasons Society, arrived in the Fraser Valley from San Francisco, Oregon and Victoria, and established chapters of the organization in various gold rush towns including Yale and Lytton.[303] Therefore, it is no surprise to find Hongmen members in Nelson. Their lodge was located first at 521 Lake Street (from 1921 to 1946), and was then relocated to 605 on the same street.[304]

As shown in the photograph opposite, the Chinese name on the society's building was Minzhidang (民治党), the name given by Dr. Sun Yat-sen (孙中山). In 1911, Sun had arrived in Vancouver to raise funds for the Chinese revolution. He joined the Chinese Freemasons Society, helped the organization write its constitution, and changed the name to Minzhidang, the People's Governing Party. The Chinese Freemasons Society mortgaged its buildings in Victoria and Toronto to support Sun and the Chinese revolution. In turn, Sun promised the Minzhidang two seats for the Chinese Freemasons Society in the Chinese parliament should his own party, the Chinese Alliance Party (中国同盟会), succeed in overthrowing the Qing dynasty and forming a republican government in China. Meanwhile he invited members of the Minzhidang to join the Chinese Alliance Party, and encouraged its members to take up Minzhidang membership. On October 10, 1911, the Chinese Alliance Party succeeded in overthrowing the Qing regime and in 1912 formed a republican government in China. But no seat in the parliament was allotted to the Minzhidang.

The Minzhidang, or Chee Kung Tong, building. The building was christened Minzhidang, meaning the People's Governing Party, by Dr. Sun Yat-sen during his visit in 1911. Image 2007.052.020 courtesy of the Nelson and District Museum, Archives, Art Gallery and Historical Society

Meanwhile, some old-timers or senior members of the Minzhidang realized that the intrusion of the Chinese Alliance Party members and their attempts to absorb the Minzhidang would gradually eliminate the society altogether. So these society members, using the name Chee Kung Tong (致公堂), placed a large plaque with the name, Chee Kung Clubhouse (致公会所) written in Chinese characters, on the wall inside the building.

The Chee Kung Tong in Nelson acted as an employment agent to find jobs for its members in the early days. "When a new Chinese immigrant arrived in town he went to the Freemasons, identified himself and the Freemasons would offer free accommodation to him for a few days until they found a job for him or he found an employment himself. Then he had to pay rent," said the late Cameron Mah.[305] "When I first arrived in town, I noticed many jobless old folks sitting around in the building," Mah continued, "Apparently, many of them shared beds taking turns to sleep on them."

Nelson's Chee Kung Tong building had two floors. Mah recalled that a small hall, a reading room, a coffee room and a kitchen were on the main floor, and accommodation provided for the members on the upper floor. Chinese newspapers such as the *Chinese Times*, published in Vancouver, and Chinese books and magazines were available for members to read in the reading room. The society also helped connect its members to their families in their villages in Guangdong, to provide interpretation services and supports for members who needed them, and to reach out and interact with the mainstream community.

On September 17, 1910, the Nelson and Kaslo chapters together announced in the *Chinese Times* (大汉公报) that they would hold a grand opening of the reading room. All members were welcome to attend. On December 12, 1929, the Nelson chapter was registered as a society. The following year on May 12, this chapter donated $283 to the Vancouver Chinese Freemasons Society headquarters so that the *Chinese Times* could purchase a printing press. The names of the donors were acknowledged in the *Chinese Times*.

On July 22, 1921, the Nelson, Kaslo, and the Trail and Rossland chapters together made a joint announcement in the *Chinese Times* that they would host the third national convention of the Chinese Freemasons Society on August 12 in Nelson.[306] Delegates from the headquarters and members from various chapters in BC, Alberta and Ontario arrived and attended the three-day convention held in Nelson. The convention began on August 12 and adjourned on August 15. The conference was a success, a great celebration and memorable occasion, reported the *Chinese Times*.

On November 18, 1928, the four Chee Kung Tong chapters received news from the headquarters in Vancouver that Cao Mao Shen (曹懋森), president of the Vancouver Chinese Freemasons Society, would visit the Kootenay. On the day of Cao's arrival, members of the four Chee Kung Clubhouses went to the ferry terminal in Nelson to welcome Cao and ushered him into a hotel operated and owned by Li Guang Yu (李广育) in Nelson.

That evening, the four chapters held a banquet to welcome Cao and invited all the members in the region to attend because a general meeting was to be held after the banquet. At the beginning of the dinner, the chair of the Nelson chapter, Li, welcomed Cao. Following the introduction, Cao addressed the assembly and reminded members to honour the five founders (五祖) of Hongmen Hui (the Chinese Freemasons Society), to be loyal to the organization and to respect and assist one another. The banquet and meeting ended at 11:00 p.m.

On July 7, 1937, the Japanese bombed the Marco Polo Bridge in Beijing. This incident triggered the second Sino-Japanese War in China. In 1938, the four chapters of the Chee Kung Tong formed a unit known as the Nelson Chinese Freemasons Anti-Japanese Salvation Association to raise funds to support the war efforts. The board of the Salvation Association consisted of three chairmen: Ma Lin Da (马 林大), Zhou Zai Xian (周在铣) and Zhang Pei Lu (张培禄); three vice-chairs: Zhu Guang Li (朱广礼), Hu Zhang (胡长) and Wu Ang (吴昂);

five Chinese secretaries, six English secretaries, four treasurers and nineteen committee members.

Members of the Chee Kung Tong, Chinese residents in the community and the general public were asked to donate funds generously to support the war efforts. As well, anyone could purchase Chinese bonds for five dollars each. Those who could not afford to pay the five dollars in one payment could purchase the bonds by installment. Their names would only be announced in the *Chinese Times* when they had paid the full amount. Monies from the sale of bonds together with donations would be sent to the Chinese government in Chongqing (重庆), Sichuan Province, China.

After World War II ended, the Anti-Japanese Salvation Association was dissolved but the Chee Kung Tong continued to serve its members and reach out to the mainstream community. Many of its tenants had aged and some had passed on. Quite a few of them went home to China, so fewer people lived in the society's building.

When the Chinese Exclusion Act was repealed on May 14, 1947, many single men, especially those who lived in the Chee Kung Tong building, sent for their families in their home villages in Guangdong to come to Canada and be reunited with them. When their families arrived, they moved away from the society's lodge and lived with their families in the city; some moved with their families to the Lower Mainland, where the Chinese community was larger and a better variety of Chinese food and cultural activities were available to them. Gradually, fewer and fewer people lived in the association building so the revenues of the Chee Kung Tong dwindled. The building was getting old but utility bills and property tax had to be paid, said the president of the Chee Kung Tong in the 1960s. "Since we could not manage the building, we sold the property to a Caucasian and used the money to pay off some debts. We kept the rest of the money to carry out functions without the building," continued the president. "We, the members of the Chee Kung Tong, usually gathered together to celebrate Chinese New Year with a dinner in a restaurant, and observed Qing Ming festival. We went to the cemetery during Qing Ming to pay respect to the deceased Chinese who were buried there."[307]

The Chinese Empire Reform Association

In March 1904, posters containing Chinese characters were found posted on some walls in Chinatown. Caucasians were curious about the posters, but none of the Chinese residents would translate the messages since the posters referred to the reform movement (维新运动) in China and the formation of the Chinese Empire Reform Association (CERA), also known as the Protect the Chinese

Emperor Society (保皇会). At that time, China was still ruled by Empress Dowager Cixi (慈禧太后), who persecuted the Chinese reformers; six of the key reformers were arrested and beheaded. But Kang You Wei (康有为) and Liang Qi Chao (梁启超), the leader and scholar of the reform movement, had escaped. Generally, people in the mainstream community did not know about the political situation in China, so they assumed the reluctance to translate the posters was due to the supposed secretive nature of the Chinese people, who did not want to share the messages with other races. However, a journalist with the *Nelson Daily News* was persistent in his efforts to learn what the posters said, and he asked several Chinese individuals in town about them. One Chinese man suggested that the journalist ask Wo Kee, the employment agent, who was fluent in English. So the journalist approached Wo Kee for a translation of the Chinese posters. Wo told the reporter that the message was about Kang You Wei (康有为), the founder of the CERA, his advocacy for the Reform Movement in China, and how Kang came to Canada, as well as about the existing buildings of the CERA in Vancouver and Victoria. He went on, telling the reporter that Kang had established newspapers in Hong Kong, Shanghai, New York and San Francisco, and had raised funds to carry out the work of CERA. The posters in Nelson called on the Chinese in Nelson's Chinatown to contribute funds to the CERA. Wo further stated that Emperor Guangxu (光绪皇帝) was strongly in favour of the reform movement, without mentioning that Emperor Guangxu had been placed under house arrest on Yintai, a small island in the Summer Palace in Beijing, by Empress Dowager Cixi. Wo praised Kang, and told the journalist that Kang was currently in Hong Kong.[308]

In October 1905, Lee Jak Tin (李泽田 – 译音), the Canadian president of the CERA, arrived in Nelson from Rossland on a coast-to-coast tour of the country. On Sunday, October 8, Lee spoke to nearly three hundred local members about the latest developments within the association. Poon Yin (潘殷 – 译音) translated Lee's message for the local press. Lee gave an inspiring talk, saying that although the association was in its infancy, its members could be found on every shore of the Pacific Ocean, as well as in every city in China. Wealthy members were pooling funds for developments in China. Lee further stated that the membership dues were only four dollars a year, and the fee provided lifetime protection, free burial upon death, and an honorarium paid to the family of a deceased member. In addition to this minimal fee, each member might purchase any number of shares in the association's joint stock company. The money so subscribed would be used to build hotels in Chinese cities, found steamship and railway lines, and establish a banking system.

Lee was in Nelson for several days. On the second day after his arrival, members of the CERA branch in Nelson held a banquet for him. Lee said the purpose of his tour was to strengthen the bonds among the branches of the CERA, with an emphasis on brotherhood shared by all members. He reminded his fellow members of the sacrifices and risks taken by Kang You Wei, the founder of the association, and urged them to keep in mind the aim of bringing China abreast of other nations in commerce, industry and education. He informed his audience that China would build a railway network in the densely populated districts in the country. A paper or note system would replace the silver coins—a cumbersome and wasteful currency system that required the frequent transportation of large quantities of the metal from point to point. A modern postal service would be slowly established. Science and western cultures would be taught in schools and colleges. Discussing the boycott of American goods, Lee advised his audience not to ask for American goods nor to keep them. After his speech, he gave each member in the audience a metal badge/ button engraved with the image of Emperor Guangxu, flanked by two flags— the flag of the Qing Empire and that of the CERA.[309]

In November 1908, both Empress Dowager Cixi and Emperor Guangxu died, and the Qing government came under the control of Yuan Shikai (袁世凯), a powerful warlord and successful military commander, although Emperor Henry Puyi (溥仪皇帝), just a little boy, was still sitting on the throne.[310] On February 12, 1912, Puyi, the last emperor, was forced to abdicate from his throne by Yuan, ending the 267-year rule of the Qing dynasty in China. The reform of the empire was no longer needed, once the empire itself ceased to exist.

The Chinese Nationalist League

Prior to the formation of the Chinese republic (中华民国), the Chinese in Nelson were watching the turbulent situation in China closely, and raised funds for the revolutionary efforts against the Qing regime. Their fundraising methods included selling revolutionary scrip at twenty dollars per certificate. If the revolution were successful, the revolutionary scrip would be redeemable for forty dollars per certificate. "The gamble is appealing strongly to the Chinese residents of this country," said the *Nelson Daily News*.[311] A journalist from this paper was curious and approached Quong [Kwong] Wing Chong, a prominent merchant in Nelson, to find out more.

"Well, the Manchus have become frightened or they would not have made the emperor promise a constitutional government," said Kwong. But he did not want to comment on whether the purchase of the revolutionary scrip was a good or poor investment. The general opinion of the local Chinese, however,

The Chinese Nationalist League Building. During the Chinese Revolution, the Chinese community in Nelson raised funds in support of the revolutionary efforts. Image 003.027.002 courtesy of the Nelson and District Museum, Archives, Art Gallery and Historical Society

was that even if the revolutionaries did not succeed in establishing a republic with Dr. Sun Yat-sen as president, the movement might lead to the formation of a constitutional form of government with a parliament whose members were elected by the people.[312]

On October 10, 1911, the uprising in Wuchang (武昌革命) led by Huang Xing (黄兴), one of the leaders of the Chinese Alliance Party, succeeded in defeating the Qing army, ending the feudal monarchy presided over by the Qing dynasty and leading to the formation of the Republic of China. Dr. Sun Yat-sen became the provisional president of the republican government with Chinese Alliance Party as the governing party. The Chinese Alliance Party then changed its name to Guomindang (国民党), also spelled Kuomintang) or the Chinese National League. In December of the same year, Chinese residents in BC began to cut off their queues, following Sun's advice that this was a sign that they were no longer controlled or governed by the Manchus. In truth, however, the political struggles and the chaotic situations in China still existed.

After the success of the Wuchang uprising, Sun had to negotiate with Yuan Shikai (袁世凯), a powerful military and government official in the late Qing dynasty, to remove Emperor Henry Puyi from the throne. Yuan was the most suitable official to carry out this task, since he was an influential mandarin in the Qing court. In order to achieve this mission, Sun stepped down and handed over the presidency of the republic to Yuan. Yuan, however, as the president of the Chinese republic, abused his powers, overriding the constitution. He declared himself the emperor, although his reign as the Hongxian emperor (洪憲皇帝) lasted only eighty-three days, primarily due to growing revolts in Yunnan, Guangxi, and Guizhou provinces against him, as well as his declining health. He died on June 6, 1916, at the age of 56.[313] After Yuan's death, the provisional constitution was reinstated and the parliament reconvened.

Around 1912, a group of Chinese individuals had established a chapter of the Guomindang (Chinese Nationalist League) in Nelson. The board members of this chapter consisted of Charlie Chow, Dar Wing, Chan Kai and Mee Chalk, among others. In 1917, they collectively purchased the lot and building at the corner of Josephine and Lake Streets.[314] On August 26, 1917, the grand opening of the chapter took place. There were 125 Chinese people from Nelson and the surrounding areas who attended the opening ceremony. In his opening remarks, Mee Chalk, the president of this branch, emphasized the importance of the Three People Principles (三民主义) of the political party, namely People's Nationalism, People's Democracy and People's Livelihood, the doctrines of Dr. Sun Yat-sen (孙中山).[315] A certificate was presented to the chapter by the Guomindang headquarters in Canada on the opening of the chapter.

The portrait of Dr. Sun Yat-sen was flanked by the two flags of the Republic of China; the right flag with five coloured stripes was the first national flag of the republic from 1912 to 1928, whereas the one on the left is the flag of the republic of China from 1917 to the present day in Taiwan. The certificate stated the mandates, and the constitution of the chapter was the same as that of the headquarters; members of the branch were enjoined to stay united in fostering the Three People Principles.

Mee also announced that the board of the Nelson Guomindang would make attempts to educate its members in the ways of doing businesses and carrying on trades in Canada. They would assist both members and non-members to find employment in the city and the surrounding regions. A reading room was set aside for members and non-members to read Chinese newspapers and magazines so that they could learn about the political situation in China and the modernization of the country.

The building would also provide hostel facilities for single Chinese men.[316] In January 1920, the chapter held a secondary anniversary celebration in the building and celebrated Chinese New Year at the same time. As time went by, members gradually departed from the Guomindang party. On March 12, 1920, Zhou Tian Cai (周添才), a Chinese resident in Nelson, announced in the *Chinese Times* that he had joined the Nelson Chee Kung Tong and left the Guomindang in Nelson.[317]

In the late fall of 1920, Lao Xiang (劳祥), an elderly Chinese labourer, injured his legs badly at work, and had to be admitted to hospital for treatment. Since he had been a member of the Nelson Guomindang since 1916, he asked the political party for assistance. But the party gave him the cold shoulder, treating him like an old rug or a scrap, stated Lao in the *Chinese Times*. When the Nelson Chee Kung Tong learned about Lao's injury, they not only paid his medical bills but also bought him a ticket to sail home to China, so that he "would not die in a foreign country." He was grateful to the Nelson Chee Kung Tong, and wrote his farewell message in the *Chinese Times* to express his gratitude to the Nelson Chee Kung Tong for its kind assistance and generosity, and his disappointment and frustration with the Nelson Guomindang. He urged his fellow Chinese not to join the Guomindang.[318]

Huang Chao Lin (黄潮林) also expressed his regret at having joined the Guomindang in the *Chinese Times*. On October 21, 1921, he left the political party on the advice of his fellows, and declared that he would not be responsible for any undertakings of the Nelson Guomindang effective on that date.

Despite these complaints, the Nelson Guomindang marched on with dignity, especially under the leadership of Mah Fong, the son of Mah Loong (Lung). Shortly after the imposition of the five-hundred dollar Head Tax on Chinese immigrants, Loong arrived in Nelson and established the Sam Sing Laundry with Mah Sing, and Sing Lee. "Sam Sing" means three wins/successes in Cantonese. Loong used his Head Tax certificate as a visa several times to visit his family in Tin Sum village (田心村), Taishan (台山县) county, Guangdong. After one of his trips, he returned with his son, Fong, to Nelson. When Fong arrived, his first job was working as a porter at the Hume Hotel, and meeting guests at the CPR train station to unload their luggage and take them to the hotel.[319] Later, he returned to his village in China and built a beautiful house. Upon his return to British Columbia, he joined the Guomindang, and became the president of the BC organization. While he was in office, the Nelson Guomindang chapter announced in the *New Republic*, the Guomindang's newspaper, that the party would hold its twenty-fifth anniversary celebration at 514 Lake Street on August 26, 1942. All members were welcome to attend.

In 1943, Fong died at the age of 35 in Vancouver General Hospital following an operation for liver cancer.

During World War II (1939–1945), the Guomindang and the Chinese Communist Party (中国共产党) in China were allies defending the country. After the war, civil war between the Communist Party and the Guomindang resumed. The Communists won the war and on October 1, 1949, its leader, Mao Zedong (毛泽东), declared the establishment of the People's Republic of China. Chiang Kai-Shek, the leader of the Guomindang, fled with his defeated army to Taiwan. Many loyal Guomindang members believed that one day in the future Chiang would lead his troops back to mainland China and the Guomindang would eventually govern the country.

In 1947, the Canadian Chinese Exclusion Act was repealed and the Canadian Chinese regained the right to vote.[320] As a result of the repeal of the Chinese Exclusion Act many Chinese men in this country sent for their wives and children to reunify their families. Many family members arrived, boosting the Chinese population in Nelson to 250 individuals. In January 1952, the Nelson Guomindang hosted the Chinese New Year celebrations in its building at 524 Lake Street for three days. More than a hundred members from the Chinese community attended the celebrations. Statements in writing about the homeland and pictures of the noted Soong family[321] and of Chiang Kai-shek were framed on the walls of the Guomindang building. Chinese music floated in the air, while firecrackers exploded outside the building to welcome the arrival of the Chinese New Year.

One of the gatherings in these three days included a dinner for the Chinese families in the city. Many of them were the wives and children of the Chinese residents who had arrived in the city less than a year or so ago. On that night, a special room was set aside for the youngsters. The adults gathered in two other rooms. All of them were served fabulous Chinese cuisine. The delicacies consisted of braised bamboo shoots, a variety of mixed seafoods, stuffed Chinese mushrooms, burnt almond chicken, sweet and sour spareribs, bird's nest soup, and sliced chicken on bean shoots.[322]

It was also the installation night for the newly elected officers of the Guomindang. President Fred Wah took over from the past president, Woo Sing. Joe Hing Wing was elected vice-president and Wong Doong became the secretary. "The New Year brought the opportunity for greater efforts to fight the worldwide enemy—Communism," emphasized President Fred Wah.[323]

Jimmy Der spoke briefly about the expectation that the future would see a release of the Chinese homeland from the hold of the Reds, the Communist Party. The final event of the evening was the honouring of the chefs: Woo Sing, Jimmy Wong and their helper, an unnamed youth who had immigrated to Nelson from China only two months earlier.

As time went by, it became obvious that the Guomindang would not return to power and become the governing party in mainland China. The activities and functions of the Nelson Guomindang gradually faded away. On August 2, 1974, fire destroyed the building at 524 Lake Street and sadly claimed the life of Wah Der, at the age of 69, a well-known Chinese Canadian in Nelson.

The Chinese Youth Association

In early 1952, some of the Chinese youths in Nelson formed a basketball team, the China Clippers. This basketball team worked out zealously, until they were ready to participate in the district competition. "This squad of New Canadians ranging in age from 16 to 21 had caught on quickly to our Number Two Winter sport... and most [of them] got by with little or no understanding of English," remarked the *Nelson Daily News*.[324] The team had been practising diligently every week under the management of Sam Brown and the teaching and guidance of Don Bates and Bud Godderis, reported the newspaper, and had recently bought their own uniforms.

They had already played three games; all were played against the Nelson high school Bomberettes. They achieved their first win against this girls' team. The China Clippers hoped to arrange a competition with the boys' teams in Castlegar and Kaslo teams. Although handicapped by a lack of height, they made up for it with quick hands and fast footwork. On the team there were

The China Clippers, a youth basketball team formed in 1952, with their coaches. Image 2003_66_4 courtesy of the Nelson and District Museum, Archives, Art Gallery and Historical Society

three Mahs: Teddy, Ken and Sammy, and eight Wongs: Albert, Allen, George, Yin, Johnny, York, Joe and Lorne.

In 1954, about twenty of the Chinese Canadians got together to form the Nelson Chinese Youth Association. Lawrence Mar, one of the founding members, said, "Not all the Canadian Chinese in town were included in the China Clippers. There were quite a good number of young people with nothing to do after school, so we formed the club to have some fun and to socialize with one another."[325] "We found it awfully lonely at times," echoed Donald Quon, another founding member. "We formed the Chinese Youth Association so that we would have a place to meet friends and make new ones."

On the evening of May 19, 1954, about fifty young people plus a few adults turned up at 648 Lake Street in Chinatown where the young people elected officers for their club. The following Chinese Canadian youths were elected to serve in various position in the association, 一九五四－中青职员表－第一届.

Executives and Directors of the Chinese Youth Association, 1954

荣誉会长 黄世重	Hon. President: Yick Wong
主席 正李锦宁 副黄国忠	President: Allen Wong Vice-president: John D. Joy
文书 正黄国威 副黄国忠	Secretary: Wen Won, John D. Joy
康乐 正谢缤赞 副马述舜	Entertainment Committee: Sammy Mah, Donald Quon
财政 正黄军郁 副雷浩念	Treasurer: Yorkie Goo, Louis Wong
中文组 正 黄仲平 副 盘国强	Chinese Class Committee: Hank Wong, Bing Pon
英文组 正黄炎洪 副谢珍卿	English Class Committee: Jimmy Wong, Jean D. Hingwing
宣传组 正朱德灼 副谢峰	Propaganda/PR Committee: Shick Gee, Yonie Der
核数组： 马和笈，李文活 谢灼俞， 黄汉文	Auditors: Lawrence Mar, Dick Dar, Moon Mah, Albert Wong
杂务组： 朱炎焜，黄定邦	General Duty Officers: Larry Yee, Henry Wong
外交顾问： 关富烈， 谢英铨	Advisory & Public Relations: William Wone, Fred Wah

A couple of weeks later, the club held a ribbon-cutting ceremony to celebrate the grand opening of the Nelson Chinese Youth Association with elders giving speeches. A tea party was held for all who attended the event.

The club's board had two language committees, the English and the Chinese committees. The English language committee was to organize and teach newly arrived Chinese immigrants English, whereas the Chinese language committee was responsible for teaching Chinese reading and writing to those who were interested in learning the language. The association also formed a band. "In the band we played Chinese music, mostly Chinese opera in Cantonese music," said Lawrence Mar. "The instruments we played included saxophone, violin, erhu, guitar, clarinet and banjo."

The association also published yearbooks. Fred Wah Sr., Jean Hingwing, Donald Quon, Lawrence Mar and others contributed articles and poems in both English and Chinese. Hingwing wrote the following narrative that was published in the 1954 yearbook:

Members of the Nelson Chinese Youth Association playing musical instruments. Image 2003.066.002a courtesy of the Nelson and District Museum, Archives, Art Gallery and Historical Society

My friend Mrs. Der was a shy, lovely little woman, with few interests in life. She spent most of her waking hours in a windowless kitchen in her flat. One day she said to me, "I think of you often, dear. It doesn't seem right you should have to live on that back street."

I was then living in an apartment facing a fine view of the Kootenay Lake.

"Isn't a back street," I protested.

"There are no streetcars on it," declared Mrs. Der.

"Well," I retorted, "you can't see the streetcars on your street."

"No," she admitted, "but I can hear them going by..."

This piece of creative writing reflects the loneliness of a Chinese woman without English language skills living in a foreign land. The sound of the passing streetcars was the only means for her to imagine the environment in which she lived.

The public relation officers of the Chinese Youth Association did an excellent job of reaching out and introducing the association to the community. They asked the Chinese merchants in town to subscribe and advertise their businesses in the yearbook, a way to earn revenue for the club so it could carry out various kinds of activities. Indeed, thirteen Chinese merchants advertised their businesses in the 1954 yearbook. Below are the names of these merchants.

English Names	Chinese Names	Address	Manager
C. Bing's Garden	苏炳园	R.R. 1 Nelson	Soo Bing 苏炳
Cameo Café	宝石餐厅	616 Baker St.	Mah Cheng Lun 马程伦
Chung King Chop Suey	重庆酒家	624 Front St.	Zhu Bing You 朱炳有
Diamond Grill Café	钻石餐厅	543 Baker St.	William Wone 关富烈
Hing Wah Store	兴华宝号	624 Front St.	Wong Sai Chung 黄世重
Liberty Food Store	自由大货仓	636 Baker St.	Der Ying Hey 谢应喜
Ramsay Camera	照相店	497 Baker St.	Lin Shi 林世士
New Star Café	新星餐厅	429 Baker St.	Der Ying Chun 谢英铨
Salmovogue Café	流行餐厅	Salmo, BC	Chu Fook Shiu 朱福修
Standard Café	标准餐厅	377 Baker St.	Wong Shu Wing 黄树荣
Sung Chung Laundry	成昌洗衣馆	312 Hall St.	Der Lai Yan 谢礼彦
Sun Sang Garden	新生园瓜菜	CPR Flat	Wong Bing Kou 黄炳球
Wing Lee Store	永利宝号	602 Front St.	Wong Guang Xi 黄广习

The public relations committee also invited some of Nelson's important citizens to visit the club and to participate in some of the activities with the Chinese youths. Many visitors were impressed by the operation of the club and the activities the young people carried out. They wrote congratulatory and encouraging messages, including one letter from the Nelson City Council, to the organization. The following is a transcript of a letter the club received from the Nelson City Council.

Mr. Allen Wong,
President, Chinese Youth Organization,
319, Josephine Street, Nelson, BC.
June 10, 1954

Dear sir:
At the last regular meeting of the City Council, the Council had the pleasure of welcoming a new club into the city, "The Chinese Youth Organization", and I have been directed to express the council's appreciation of this venture and to extend its best wishes for success in all your endeavours.

Yours Sincerely,
Signed: Acting City Clerk

Many members were very keen to play basketball. On October 25, 1954, these young people formed the Nelson Chinese Youth Basketball Team.

Bill Wong, the coach, wearing a black jacket, is standing in the back row on the left. The two captains, and Lawrence Mar and Zhou Yu Lin (周俞冧), hold the basketball with the name of the team in the front row. The girl in the back row standing on the right is Jean D. Hingwing, the score keeper.

The team rented the gymnasium in a public school for practice every Wednesday evening, and spent about four hundred dollars to purchase a couple of basketballs and a uniform for each player. On December 1 of the same year, the team was invited by the local high school basketball team for a friendly game. The score was 51 to 38 for the Chinese—not bad for the Chinese team since they did not have a professional or gym teacher to coach them. Besides basketball, these young people also loved to play ping pong inside the building, especially during winter.

When Christmas arrived, they decorated their premises, held a Christmas party for all, including their parents and siblings. A Santa Claus was present to distribute gifts to all the young people. Then they had the winter break.

After the new year, life returned to normal and basketball practices were carried out as usual. The team had a couple of competitions with the local high school as well as with the Kaslo basketball team.

In 1955, Lawrence Mar was elected as the president of the association, and Jean D. Hingwing became the vice-president.[326]

Executives, directors and board members of the Chinese Youth Association in 1955. Image courtesy Lawrence Mar

"Unfortunately, the Nelson Chinese Youth Association only lasted for 3 or 4 years because members were moving away from Nelson; some went to other towns and cities to find jobs," said Mar, "and those who graduated from high school left for post-secondary institutions in the Lower Mainland. After they graduated from colleges or university, they seldom returned to Nelson, as this city is a tourist haven with very few jobs for young graduates."

"All our children were raised here but they are now living in the Lower Mainland where they work," added Mrs. Mar.[327]

A Venerable Chinese Canadian

The late Cameron Mah Kin Shum (马健燊 – 译音) was saluted as a pillar of the Chinese Canadian community in Nelson.[328] In 1959, he arrived in Canada under the sponsorship of his grand-uncle, Mah Ye Sun (马乂珅). His immigration journey began when his father received a letter from his grand-uncle in 1955, saying that he could secure a birth certificate and an application form to sponsor a young boy to come over to Canada. Mah recounted his story, saying that[329]

> after receiving the letter, my father kept the news to himself for more than two weeks. He did not want to break the news immediately as he knew I would be the chosen one, the oldest among his five children—four sons and a daughter. He was happy because I would have the opportunity to go to the gold mountains, but at the same time, he felt sad, as I was only 9 years old, too young to venture overseas. When my mother heard the news, she burst into tears and said to my father that I didn't know how to cook rice and wash clothing.
>
> My mother said that if I were to go to Canada, I would suffer in the foreign land. I comforted her and then asked her to teach me to do the household chores so that I could stand on my own feet in the gold mountains. Reluctantly she nodded, looked at me painfully and held me in her arms.

He paused and then continued.

> Unfortunately, it took more than two years for the immigration application to get through. And in 1957 my granduncle had a heart attack and died. But my parents still wanted me to immigrate to Canada because they believed life would be good in the gold mountain. Also, they heard that the overseas Chinese in Canada were very kind and helpful to one another, especially to new immigrants.

When the immigration application was approved, my parents went around the village to borrow money so that they could buy me an air ticket to fly to Vancouver. But it was not easy to borrow money from the village folks because most of them were poor. Anyway, my parents borrowed $10 or $20 from some families in the village and managed to gather a sum of $200 US for me to immigrate to Canada. Before I left home, my mother bought me a whole bunch of clothing and a couple of pairs of shoes but all of them were oversized. She believed I would grow into them eventually. She was right. Within two years I outgrew all the clothing and shoes.

Finally, I left home and arrived in Vancouver in 1959, and found my way to the St. James Hotel on Hastings Street. When I was staying in the hotel, I missed home, and a lump in my throat surfaced whenever I was alone. As a "man," I could not cry; I could only feel the pain in my heart! Fortunately, Mrs. Woo, the owner of the hotel, was very kind to me. I was supposed to pay $2 a day for room and board but she did not take any money from me, knowing very well that I could not afford to pay.

Before I left home, my parents told me that my grandfather, Mah Fong, had died from liver cancer in Vancouver when he was in his thirties. And he was the president of the Chinese Nationalist League in British Columbia. Although I had had my great-grandfather, Mah Loong, in Nelson, he had died of old age before I arrived in Canada! In short, I had no relatives to take care of me or to help me out after I landed in Vancouver.

Mah sighed and looked away. A hint of sadness surfaced on his face. Then he continued to narrate his experiences.

While I was staying in the St. James Hotel, I met Mr. Wong, the proprietor of the Hop Lee Laundry in Kelowna. He told me that his friend, Yorkie Mah, who had two restaurants in Castlegar and a hotel in Trail, would probably help me out. He asked me to follow him to Kelowna so that he could arrange for me to see Yorkie. So, I went to Kelowna with him to meet Yorkie who then hired me as a dishwasher in one of his restaurants in Castlegar. As the restaurant only opened in the late afternoon, I went to school there and got admitted to a grade 3 class. But before I went to school in the morning, I had to mow the lawn and clean

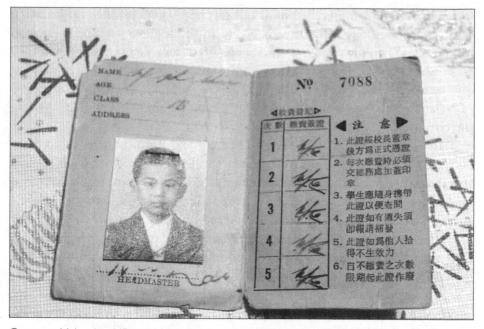

Cameron Mah school ID card. Mah immigrated to Canada in 1959 and was considered a pillar of the Chinese community in Nelson. Image courtesy Greg Nesteroff

the windows of the restaurant. When the restaurant closed at night, I had to mop the floor of the dining room. In winter, I had to shovel snow. Yorkie paid $60 a month, out of which I sent $40 to my parents, but he taught me his culinary skills.

In 1962, the Diefenbaker government introduced the Chinese Adjustment Statement Program that offered amnesty to illegal immigrants who were not engaged in illegal immigration activities.[330] Cameron went to the immigration office to declare his false identity and replace it with his own name and age. By then his family had left their village and moved to Hong Kong, where his father worked in a restaurant. His parents then asked him to leave school and get a full-time job so that he could send more money to help support the family. After he had completed grade 6, he left school and became the chef in the restaurant.

Cameron remained in Castlegar where he met his sweetheart, Jayne Jay Bow Chin (谢宝珍), through his landlady. Jayne had immigrated to Canada in 1954 from Hoiping (开平县). Her father had come to BC much earlier. Cameron and Jayne were married in 1966. When their first child was on the way, they moved to Nelson, where his parents-in-law and family were residing. Their daughter, Ginger, was born in 1967. Jayne worked for what was then BC Tel and he worked at the Ken's Café restaurant in Nelson. His reputation for culinary skill had preceded him, and several restaurants offered him work. In 1970, he and five of his friends began to think about starting their own restaurant. When the word got out, he was fired from Ken's Café.[331] Then they established the KC (Kootenay Centre) Restaurant. It was a smashing success! The restaurant was exceptionally busy in the summer, when the population in Nelson was often boosted from 8,000 people to 30,000 by tourists visiting the city.

In 1973, Cameron sponsored his second and third brothers to come to Nelson, and they helped out in the restaurant. In 1975, he sent for his parents and the rest of his siblings. When the family arrived, he went to Vancouver to meet them. As his parents had been corresponding with Faye Leung, his grand-aunt in Vancouver, they introduced Leung to him.

The restaurant business, however, had kept him fully occupied, giving him little time to do whatever he wished to do. "I wanted to visit Faye Leung, my grand-aunt in Vancouver, more often," he said. "She is dear to my heart. She was the one who showed me the photograph of my grandfather, Mah Fong, and took me to visit his grave at Mountain View Cemetery in Vancouver." He paused, then continued,

> Restaurant people spend most of the time in their business. They work and eat in their restaurant day and night, and have hardly any time to see their kids, as their work schedule is from 4 o'clock in the afternoon to 12 midnight! The restaurant is their home. When I was in the business, I hardly had the time to see my kids growing up, I missed them! I liked to get involved with them. For instance, I wanted to watch my daughter play volleyball and my son play soccer and baseball in school but I never had the chance then!"[332]

When his brother Russel could shoulder a big load of the restaurant business work, he volunteered to help in the community, and at times, worked as an interpreter in the citizenship court. He shared an amusing interpretation between the citizenship judge and a Chinese woman during the declaration for citizenship in court:

> Once I was helping twenty-five Chinese women to declare in a citizenship court. None of these women could speak a word of English. The judge said to one of them: "You don't speak English and you don't work. What are you good for in Canada?" The woman asked me to tell the judge that she was raising the future prime minister of Canada!

The citizenship judge almost fell from his chair when he heard the answer. Immediately, he granted her Canadian citizenship.

Cameron was a gentle and soft-spoken person, friendly and kind, very well liked in the community. He and Jayne raised four children. After working tirelessly as a chef for many years, he finally retired in 2001, although he still enjoyed cooking for his family and friends. He volunteered much of his free time to the Fraternal Order of Eagles, Lodge 641. In his leisure time, he went fishing, did carpentry work, played poker and socialized with his friends over coffee at the food court of the Chahko Mika Mall in Nelson. On June 8, 2019, he had a heart attack and passed away at the age of 72. He was predeceased by his parents, Yew Mah and Tsui Ying Mah, and survived by his wife, Jayne, four children, one granddaughter, four brothers and one sister, and a few nephews and nieces. He was buried in the Nelson Memorial Park Cemetery.

The Nelson Memorial Park Cemetery

This cemetery is located in a peaceful setting in the 2300 block of Fall Street. It is maintained by the City of Nelson, which would charge a one-time fee when a lot was sold at the time of a burial. The city has a good crew that looks after the cemetery. Whenever the caretakers notice any sunken tombstones, they cut the grass around them, straighten them, fill the sunken areas with soil, and reseed them with grass. In about 1996, the late Henry and Audrey Stevenson[333] volunteered to survey the cemetery for the BC Genealogy Society, which needed the information to compile the data in a book and compact disc for easy reference. They found seven thousand tombstones in the cemetery; of these, fifty-three marked the graves of Chinese individuals in plot number 23, a drier area with almost no sunken tombstones. The Stevensons made rubbings of some markers so they could read the writing on them. There were also many unmarked tombstones, although the names of the deceased could be found in the city records. At the beginning of their survey, the Stevensons had a few other people to help them. Gradually, these helpers left the project, so it took the husband-and-wife team four years to complete the survey.

The Stevensons felt that the cemetery would be an important place for future generations to find their ancestors as well as to learn about their roots and cultures.[334] They are correct. Many of the old Chinese markers are inscribed with the full name of the deceased, the dates of his or her birth and death, and the Chinese province, county and village from which they had arrived in Canada. But on some of the old markers, the full name of a Chinese woman was not included; only her last name followed by the word *Shee* (氏), which indicated that the deceased was a married woman.

It was unfortunate, said the Stevensons, that vandalism, including knocked-down tombstones, had occurred in the cemetery. Such vandalism not only disturbed the peaceful environment but also inflated the price of a burial plot, since the city had to finance the costs of maintaining the cemetery.

Shawn Lamb, the former curator and archivist at Touchstones Nelson: Museum of Art and History, provided a list of 178 Chinese people who had been interred in the Nelson cemetery between 1923 and 1999.[335] Whether some of the deceased Chinese were exhumed is yet to be investigated.

Deceased Chinese Interred in the Nelson Memorial Park Cemetery

Name	Date of Death	Name	Date of Death
Bing, Jimmie	1943-07-29	Chow, Cher	1909-01-15
Bing, Soo Quan	1969-02-07	Chow, Chim	1919-08-28
Bing, William	1996-07-07	Chow, Hip	1913-04-15
Bing, Yee Shee	1986-02-12	Chow, Kong	1938-05-08
Boo, Chung Tin	1969-06-02	Chow, Mah	1947-04-06
Car, Gin	1915-06-10	Chow, Ping On	Unknown
Chan, King Chun	1995-12-05	Chow, Wah	1954-01-12
Chan, Solan	Unknown	Chow, Yam	1961-03-28
Chan, Wong Kong	1911-05-09	Choy, Jay Wan	1959-08-19
Chee, Mah	1968-12-13	Chuck Wong Ming	1918-11-08
Chee Wong Chong	1951-11-07	Dan Lung	1943-10-16
Chew, Charlie	1965-10-08	Deaney, Dease	1908-11-13
Chew, Yip	1918-11-05	Der, Wo Lok	1951-05-14
Chin, Go	1919-08-28	Doo, Lee Pan	1958-06-02
Chin, Lui Sak	1984-02-22	Fok, Seto	1952-07-22
Chong, Chan Mon	1956-12-29	Fong, Chong	1959-03-16
Chong, Gee	1942-11-15	Fong Wong	1945-01-15
Chong, Kim	1913-07-02	Gee, Chow Jey	1970-06-30
Chong, Mah	1925-12-30	Gee, Day	1930-11-26
Chong, Quen She	1918-11-01	Gee Sun	1975-04-18
Chong, Quong	1949-05-02	Gim, Lee	1915-02-25
Chong, Tar Hong	1905-11-30	Gooey, Wee	1916-07-11
Chong, Wing	1918-11-19	Him, Henry De	1972-12-11
Chong, Wing Hoy	1973-12-10	Him, Mary	unknown
Chong, Wong	1932-04-04	Hong, Chow	1927-12-06
Chong Wong Wing	1969-09-21	Hong, Lee One	1970-09-18
Chong, Lim	1953-07-22	Hong Woo	1963-11-30
Chou, Bing Ken	1962-08-12	How Fung Gim	1978-11-14

Name	Date of Death	Name	Date of Death
How, Seto	1965-12-31	Loey, Hock Ing	1956-02-06
Hoy, Mah	1954-06-24	Louie, Hoo	Unknown
Hung, Der	1911-06-25	Louie, Joyce	1960-07-06
Hung, So Hue	1906-06-14	Louie, Mar	1911-01-19
Hung, Wo	1904-06-24	Low Chow	1934-04-12
Jack, Der Fong	1954-08-30	Low, Lim Chun	1978-01-09
Jay, Wing Tong	1983-01-17	Lung, Der	1942-08-21
Jay, Po Kwan	1988-04-03	Lung, Son	1913-03-19
Jay, Sam	1971-08-14	Mah, Lung	1957-12-24
Jem, Lee Soy	1961-07-04	Mah, Shung Hing	1980-10-22
Jig, Quan	1952-09-30	Mah, Jung Kong	1960-11-11
Jill, Lew M.	1916-02-15	Man, Dor	1909-10-29
Jing, Gee Kwong	1931-06-24	Mar, Shee Tong	1947-05-21
John, Mar Lee	1945-01-22	Mok, Gee Sing	1926-12-28
Jong, Mong	1922-04-12	Mong, Gee	1911-05-21
Jung, Soo Kak	1916-10-14	Nam, Song Chin	1968-11-04
Kaw, Wong Fong	1962-02-09	Ning, Der	1913-01-04
Kee, Cew Leon	1913-03-17	Ning, Mar	1906-06-19
Kee, Chown	1913-07-29	Quai Wong Shung	1969-03-05
Kee, Der Bing	1951-11-26	Quan, Jay You	1962-02-21
Kee, Wah	1912-03-19	Quan, Ma Sa	1964-01-19
Kog, Jay Song	1966-03-07	Quan, Moy	1947-04-15
Kong, Yun	1927-09-06	Quen, Leong	1928-02-21
Kop, Am	1917-01-29	Quong, Mong	1947-04-07
Kron, Tong	1904-02-01	Quong Wong Tor	1947-08-13
Kung, Wong	1917-02-22	Sang, Dong Mark	1969-01-11
Kwoon, Wong	1949-02-09	See, Mah King	1958-08-11
Lay, Mah Hung	1963-09-20	See, Toy	1924-01-26
Lee, Eng Jung	1963-07-04	Seng, Der	1955-08-30
Lee, Hong	1939-03-14	Shee, Jay	1973-10-11
Lee Wo	1922-05-09	Shee, Mah	1965-12-02
Leong, Der	1936-05-28	Sin, Han	1956-10-18
Leong, Eng Tai	1966-04-12	Sin, Der Jer	1919-11-01
Leong, Lou	1937-12-20	Sing, Der	1966-11-08
Leong, Woo	1922-10-17	Sing, Der Wing	1935-04-11
Leong, Yip Fong	1916-05-15	Sing Hum	1918-02-06
Ling, Seto	1948-09-04	Sing, Kong	1932-09-22
Lo, Joseph, C.K.	Unknown	Sing, Ng Man	1972-07-29
Lo, Ying Way	1991-07-20	Sing, Woo	1918-04-09

Name	Date of Death	Name	Date of Death
Soon, Der	1949-06-06	Yee Yon	1929-01-05
Soy, Chu	1919-05-20	Yet, Chin	1956-08-21
Sun, Wong	1947-04-09	Yet, Lee	1926-01-30
Tei, Wong Sun	1943-01-20	Yew, Charles	1921-02-02
Ting, Wong	1940-12-12	Yew, Loo Lee	1919-12-05
Toy, Lew (Lau)	1946-07-23	Yim, Harry	1918-04-22
Wah, Der Ying	1974-08-30	Yin, Gee Kong	1962-09-09
Wey, Ho Ham	1917-04-26	Yip, Mah Bark	1974-05-23
Wing Chin	1916-05-04	Yip San	1947-04-01
Wing Dong	1947-05-05	Yoke, Mar	1904-01-08
Wing, Gee Kau	1953-09-23	You, Dar	1926-12-07
Wing Louie	1973-01-07	You Mar Lee	1951-12-14
Wing Pon	1954-07-29	Yu, Zhong	1996-12-11
Wing, Wong Chuan	1936-06-03	Yuen, Ho Jin	1907-03-25
Wong, Chun Soon	1961-01-30		
Wong, Louie	1907-05-23		
Wong, Kwok Yuen	1978-11-14		
Wong, Nagn Hong	1992-03-29		
Wong On	1978-11-24		
Wong, Ping	1962-08-04		
Wong, Shee Kew	1952-11-21		
Wong, Sing-Kee	1981-03-15		
Wong, Tom Kong	1952-03-19		
Wong, Tsun-Shan	1984-04-08		
Wong, Wing Fung	1931-01-08		
Wong, Wing Poo	1984-08-14		
Woo, Jung	1963-01-04		
Woy, Dar	1923-12-27		
Yam, Kong	1961-12-07		
Yee, Gee	1974-10-24		

Source: Touchstones Nelson: Museum of Art and History, Shawn Lamb Archives.

The Vestiges of Chinatown

Chinatown has become a memory of the past but some of the Chinese buildings still exist in the area bounded by Vernon Street in the south, Front Street in the north, Ward Street in the west and Hall Street in the east. Many buildings within the corridors of Chinatown had fallen apart or been torn down, although some of them were converted to other usages or businesses. To cite a few examples, the building at 606 Lake Street, erected in 1901, had a tailor shop on the ground floor and a rooming house on the upper floor. Around 1920, Hym Syng, Gee Wing and Gee Kay got together to open the LD (Little Davonport) Café, which they operated until 1947. From 1948 to 2001, the ownership of this restaurant changed hands quite a few times, and bore various names, such as the New Star Café, the Commodore Café, Ken's Café, the Seven Seas Restaurant, Amanda's, and the Redfish Grill. On July 29, 2010, this building was damaged by fire. On October 4, 2019, its new owners announced that this heritage build-ing would be reopened as a craft beer/whiskey bar.[336]

Similarly, the Sing Chung laundry located at 312 Hall Street was the workshop of Jim Sawada into the 1960s. Currently, it is the home of Kootenay Co-op Radio. The KC Restaurant at 546 Baker Street opened in 1970 and is the oldest restaurant in Nelson. At the time of Mah's interview, it was owned and operated by Russel Mah, the brother of the late Cameron Mah, the previous owner.

The building at 601 Lake Street was a brothel. After going out of business in the 1950s, it became a Chinese rooming house. In the 1980s, it was redevel-oped into a hair salon.

Recognition of the Chinese in Nelson

The late Claus Lao Schunke, a Kootenay Co-op Radio broadcaster, initiated the erection of a memorial rock to commemorate Chinatown and the Chinese contributions to Nelson. Together with the support and efforts of the late Cam-eron Mah, Lawrence Mar and other key members of the Chinese community, the proposal for erecting this memorial was approved by Nelson's city council. The rock was donated, and the City of Nelson and the Columbia Basin Trust funded its creation. The Nelson Development Services developed the concept and the design for this commemorative rock, which was inscribed with both an English and a Chinese dedication. On June 12, 2011, Mayor John Dooley dedicated its installation at the corner of Hall and Vernon Streets, where Chi-natown once was. Members of the council, many Chinese Canadians in Nelson, and other citizens from the mainstream community attended the dedication of the commemorative rock.

The Chinese dedication includes an excerpt from a poem by Li Bai (李白), a famous poet of the Tang dynasty (618–906 ACE) in China. The poem comple-ments the road taken by the Chinese people to this land very well, as it has declared that the road was rocky, yet the travellers arrived at their destinations peacefully.

The unveiling of the commemorative monument in 2011. Photo courtesy the *Nelson Star*

In 2015, the Legacy Initiatives Advisory Council of the Ministry of International Trades and Multiculturalism and the BC Heritage Branch of the Ministry of Forests, Lands and Natural Resource Operations recognized and acknowledged the Chinatown and the Sung Chong Laundry in Nelson as heritage sites of British Columbia.

Conclusion

All the early Chinese immigrants who settled in Nelson originally came from Guangdong, China, and travelled to British Columbia via Hong Kong. They worked hard and made life possible for themselves. Many of them were able to support their families, who remained in their home villages in China. However, the arrival of the Chinese was not welcomed by the dominant settler society, especially in BC. Immediately after the Canadian Pacific Railway was completed in November 1885, the infamous Head Tax was imposed on every Chinese arrival. And on July 1, 1923, the Chinese Exclusion Act was passed to stop Chinese immigration entirely, although clergy men and women as well as students were allowed to land in BC. These unfair and unjust laws affected the lives of the Chinese living in Nelson and in many towns and cities in BC and other provinces. The Chinese were single men living by themselves without their parents and family members. However, many of them were resourceful, capable of making life possible for themselves and supporting family members in their home villages in Guangdong, China. Despite the prejudice and discrimination they experienced, they attempted to reach out to the mainstream community. For example, in 1894, Mar Sam, the laundry man, participated in a race on Dominion Day. On February 10, 1899, the Chinese community celebrated Chinese New Year and many Chinese invited people from the mainstream community into their homes for tea and offered them gifts to take home.

As an ethnic group, the Chinese formed organizations to assist and support one another. The Chee Kung Tong in Nelson offered accommodation to its members and new arrivals and assisted them to find employment and remain connected with their families in the villages and towns of Guangdong. The existence of the Chinese Empire Reform Association and the Guomindang (Chinese Nationalist League) indicates their care and concern for political movements in China, their home country. After World War II and the repeal of the Chinese Exclusion Act, many of the single men could sponsor their family members to immigrate and to be reunited with them in Nelson. Many of these families had teenagers. These resourceful young people formed the Nelson Chinese Youth Association and made an effort to reach out to both the Chinese and the mainstream communities. They formed a basketball team to compete with other teams in high schools, and a band to provide music for the Chinese community to celebrate Chinese New Year and other festivals. They also produced yearbooks for at least three years. This youth association was dissolved because many young people left town and continued their education in colleges and universities in the Lower Mainland as well as in other provinces. Elderly Chinese residents left town because their children had left Nelson and taken up professions and work elsewhere. And the warmer weather and the greater variety of Chinese food attracted them to the Lower Mainland.

However, quite a few Chinese citizens in Nelson and its vicinity deserve to be remembered. Charlie Bing was a well-known Chinese cowboy and market gardener who was often called up by people in the mainstream to round up horses that went astray. Kwong Wing Chong, a merchant and entrepreneur, was honoured as the head of the Chinese community in his time. Mah Fong became the first president of the Guomindang in Vancouver. Mah Shu Tong defied the feudal system of arranged marriages. In 1937, he raised funds to support the war efforts of China in the second Sino-Japanese War. Jean D. Hingwing, a young girl, was elected as the vice-president of the Nelson Chinese Youth Association and was actively involved in the basketball team. The late Cameron Mah volunteered his time and efforts to serve the Chinese-Canadian and the mainstream communities. Due to ill health, he passed away on June 8, 2019, and was hailed as a pillar of the Chinese community in Nelson.

The deeds and contributions, the trials and hardships, and the strength and resilience of these wonderful Chinese immigrants and Chinese Canadians will not be forgotten. It is delightful to learn that many of these Chinese Canadians have become professionals and scholars, and those who have retired are living a pleasant and comfortable life.

The Golden City: Rossland

Rossland is an alpine city situated at the base of Red Mountain in the Monashee Mountain Range. This city is about ten kilometres north of the international boundary between West Kootenay and Washington State. It lies immediately east of the intersection of BC Highways 3B and 22, about halfway between Vancouver and Calgary. It does not have an airport but can be reached by car or bus. The nearest airport is in Trail, the industrial city located about ten kilometres northeast of Rossland. The Trail airport provides shuttle buses to transport tourists and visitors to Rossland.

The Sinixt Nation is the traditional gatekeeper of this mountainous region that encompasses the sources of the Columbia River and the West Kootenay region of southeastern British Columbia.[337] This Indigenous people has been the steward of their land and water, and has preserved their language and rich culture.

Rossland, circa 1900. The city was incorporated just three years earlier, and was considered a very orderly place, "especially for a mining camp." Image B-04861 courtesy of the Royal BC Museum and Archives

In summer, the mountains surrounding Rossland offer cyclists and hikers hundreds of kilometres of trails, all radiating from the centre of town. In winter, the spectacular slopes of Red Mountain covered with snow provide enjoyment and challenges for skiers who love to glide on the sparkling snow under the blue sky and shining sun. This city has been producing ski champions since 1897: the first ski race in Rossland was held on March 6, 1897, and the champion was a Norwegian man, Olaus Jeldness.[338] Later champions include Olympic medallists Nancy Greene (1968) and Kerrin Lee-Gartner (1992). The skiing season in Rossland begins in December every year. The Rossland Ski Bus, which runs between various points in the city and the Red Mountain Resort, takes skiers to the lifts for a reasonable price.

The Discovery of Gold

In 1887, gold was discovered in the Red Mountain region, and a settlement grew up there. In July 1890, two miners, Joe Bourgeois and Joe Morris, staked five claims on Red Mountain. They registered four of these claims for themselves and gave one to Eugene Sayre Topping, the Deputy Recorder of Mines, in exchange for the $12.50 in recording fees they would have had to pay. Topping registered his claim under the name Le Roi. It turned out that Le Roi was the richest of the five claims. Leaving government service, Topping joined a Spokane syndicate, which purchased 53 per cent of the property for sixteen thousand dollars that November. The following spring, several tons of ore were transported by horse-drawn wagon down the mountain and along the Dewdney Trail to Trail Creek Landing. Many Chinese labourers were hired to maintain the roads in good condition for $1.50 per day.[339] The ore was then sent by boat to Little Dalles in Washington State where the Spokane Falls and Northern Railway transferred the ore to the Colorado Smelting and Mining Company at Bute, Montana. The strikes of rich gold and copper ores attracted thousands of miners to the area, and the whole area was staked off into hundreds of claims.[340]

In 1892, Ross Thompson pre-empted 160 acres of land at Red Mountain and had them surveyed in order to establish a town, which he called Thompson. In 1894, it was renamed Rossland. The townsite was surveyed, a sewage system installed, streets were opened up and graded, and wide sidewalks were laid where formerly pedestrian trails led to a maze of shacks and cabins. A water works system and an electric light plant with fire protection were installed and operated by a private company. An electric power plant, to be used principally for mining, had been installed at Boddington Falls on the Kootenay River, about five hundred kilometres away. There were sawmills, breweries, a telegraph service, money order post offices, a telephone exchange and trunk line connections with Trail,

The Le Roi Mine, showing the entrance of a tunnel. Le Roi was quickly revealed to be the richest of the five claims registered by Joe Bourgeois and Joe Morris on Red Mountain in 1890. Image D-08404 courtesy of the Royal BC Museum and Archives

Nelson and Spokane. The head offices of a large number of mining companies operating throughout the Kootenays were located in the town. The city had five chartered banks, wholesale and retail stores of every description, carrying a splendid variety of goods—all doing good business—and an opera house with a seating capacity of 1,300. A hospital erected by the Sisters of Peace took care of the poor and the needy as well as afflicted people. All major religious denominations were well represented, having good churches and settled pastors.

On March 18, 1897, Rossland was incorporated as a city. One year later, Mayor Robert Scott of Rossland told a journalist from the *British Colonist* that

> Rossland is a very orderly and law-abiding place especially for a mining camp. The British law for which all have a high respect, is impartially and fearlessly administered, owing no doubt to the excellent police force established by the city. The consensus of opinion is that the future of Rossland is assured.[341]

The population had increased rapidly. By 1897, the number of people—including some Chinese men—living in Rossland was about 7,000.[342] After this year, the population fluctuated, and gradually began to decline as the years went by.

The Red Mountain Railway

The large amounts of gold-copper ore extracted from the Rossland mines led to railway-building. Originally, the ore was carted by horse and wagon down a wagon road to shipping routes that led to smelters in the United States. Daniel Chase Corbin, a mining and railroad magnate who had already built the Spokane and Northern Railway just below the Canadian boundary, realized the potential of the Rossland mines, so he proposed to the Canadian Pacific Railway that he build a railway that would connect Rossland to the American smelters. His proposal was accepted.

In 1893, Corbin gained a charter for the line. In 1896, he added a nineteen-mile (thirty-kilometre) extension to his Spokane Falls and Northern Railroad from Northport, Washington, to Rossland. This extension was known as the Red Mountain Railway in Rossland. It carried some ore from American-owned mines to smelters south of the border, as well as freight and passengers travelling between Spokane and Rossland. Corbin did not record whether he had employed any Chinese labourers in building the extension railroad. However, the *West Kootenay Chinese Heritage Society, Summary Report, 1995* states that many of the Chinese men in Rossland were labourers on the railway construction, and that they were paid a dollar per day.[343] The use of Chinese workers has been estimated to have reduced the cost of building the Canadian Pacific Railway by between three and five million dollars. The Chinese cut a path for the railway, tearing down trees and clearing undergrowth. They removed rubble from tunnels in the mountains and cut away hills. To build up roadbeds, they dug ditches for drainage on both sides of the path and then built mounds of crushed rock and gravel. The tracks and ties were laid on top of this path.[344]

Migration of Chinese Immigrants

When gold and copper ore were discovered in the Kootenay, many Chinese prospectors, miners, labourers and merchants ventured to the gold-mining towns there. The Chinese labourers who arrived in Rossland were hoping they would be able to get employment in the gold mines. Unfortunately, they could not find work in the mines there because these mines used lode mining techniques to extract the ore. In lode mining, the ore is extracted through shafts and tunnels dug deep underground. The gold ore was found in a complex form that required special treatment in smelters.[345] Many gold miners and mining companies felt that the Chinese men were not competent in this kind of mining operation. As well, British Columbia legislation barred the Chinese from employment in underground mining.[346]

On March 2, 1898, the North East Kootenay Mineral Association held a meeting and passed a resolution that excluded the Chinese from all mines.[347] On October 20 of the same year, the Rossland Trade and Labour Council passed a resolution requesting all unions and their members to withhold their support from hotels and restaurants that employed Chinese workers, especially where white labour was obtainable.[348] However, in spite of protests, business owners continued to employ Chinese domestic workers. An article in the pro-union *Industrial World* complained that when "union men [start] requesting them not to patronize these Chinese scum of the Orient, they throw up their hands and tell you that they cannot see how they can possibly get along without the 'Chink'."[349]

Undoubtedly, those resolutions manifested the apprehensions in the white community that the Chinese labourers would take away jobs and reduce their own opportunities for employment. These actions and resolutions certainly prevented the Chinese labourers from employment in lode mining as well as in businesses established by white members of the mainstream community. These responses demonstrate that prejudice and discrimination against the Chinese immigrants existed in this fledging frontier town. Therefore, the Chinese arrivals became isolated in a ghetto—the enclave known as Chinatown.[350]

Before 1918, buildings were heated by burning wood. With the exception of two placer miners, there were about twenty to thirty Chinese workers who cut wood for Mark Han, a manager and operator of an employment agency. Han found jobs for the Chinese men, and provided wood as fuel to restaurants and private homes. Many individual Chinese men would go with their bucksaw, seeking an opportunity to cut wood for households in the mainstream community as well as for the restaurants in town. Besides this, a good number of Chinese operated laundries to make a living.[351] Some Chinese ploughed land to grow and supply vegetables and fruits for the Chinese and the mainstream communities. Others took up jobs as cooks in sawmills and mining camps, and as houseboys or servants and cooks in private homes.

The 1901 census stated that there were 231 Chinese, all males, in Rossland. The occupations of these Chinese are summarized as follows:

Launderers	97
Gardeners	32
Labourers	29
Cooks	53
Other	29
Total:	240[352]

There is some doubt about the accuracy of these census figures, due in part to a language barrier between the census-takers and the Chinese and also to prejudice manifested in lack of care taken when recording information.[353]

The Chinese Laundries

In 1899, *Henderson's British Columbia Gazetteer and Directory* listed the following Chinese businesses in Rossland:

Chong Lee Laundry, S. Washington St.
Chicago Laundry, S. Washington St.
Hop Lee Laundry, Le Roi Street near Earle Street
Hop Chung, location unknown
Wah Leung Laundry, rear of Imperial Block
Wah Lee Laundry, Kootenay Avenue
Wah Sam Laundry, Le Roi Street near Monita Street
Yuen Lung Laundry, off S. Washington St.
Sam Hop Laundry, location unknown[354]

Many Chinese launderers, like Hop Chung and Sam Hop, did not have an address, and quite a few of them lived in lodging houses provided by Chinese bosses or the Chee Kung Tong (Chinese Freemasons Society) in town. The sleeping quarters for these launderers and other Chinese men were just hard wooden bunks. The launderers picked up dirty items from the homes of their customers, washed the soiled clothing, dried and ironed it, and then delivered the clean items to their clients. The laundries were usually equipped with a large, potbellied stove, with flat irons hanging around the edge of the stove.[355] While they were doing the wash, they hummed, sang, or chanted, and they smoked tobacco with bamboo water pipes during breaks.[356] When they retired to their lodging houses in the evening, many of them smoked opium for relaxation (opium use was legal in Canada until 1908). These Chinese launderers worked seven days a week.

The Chinese Market Gardens

The Chinese market gardens occupied about seventy acres of land on the southeastern side of Rossland. These Chinese gardeners cultivated and supplied root crops, fruits and vegetables to the mainstream community as well as to the merchants and grocery stores in the Chinese community. They carried their produce in two large baskets, one at each end of a pole that was balanced across their shoulders, and sold their produce from door to door to their customers to earn a meagre living.[357]

Some children from the mainstream community teased and made fun of the Chinese peddlers, and they often threw stones at them when they were in town trying to sell their produce. They spun the baskets hanging on the ends of the poles to destabilize the peddlers and throw them off-balance. In winter, they threw snowballs at these Chinese gardeners. One time, they stole peas from a Chinese garden and were chased by the Chinese gardener with a hoe! Way Gunn and Louie were two well-known vegetable pedlars in Rossland. Both of them sold peas, turnips, carrots and potatoes to their customers in town. On the southern hillside above the Chinese market gardens were large fruit orchards managed by Louie.[358]

Black bears often destroyed these Chinese gardens. As a result, the gardeners shot the black bears and used the bear paws and gall bladder for medicinal purposes. They boiled the paws, removed the skin and flesh, soaked the bones in large jars of alcohol, then sealed the mouth of the jar with layers of paper, and waited until the mixture was cured before consuming the liquor. These Chinese believed that such a concoction would help to cure rheumatism.[359]

The census taken in 1901 indicated that forty-seven Chinese men were living on farms, including two chicken ranches. In his article about the Chinese in Rossland, Shearer described the farms as they were at the time:

> Two of the farms were relatively large operations just outside the city limits to the north and the east. The one to the north was fifteen acres [six hectares] on leased land and the farm to the east 20½ acres [eight hectares] reported to be owned by the Chinese head. This was the largest Chinese farm and the only one for which the land was said to be Chinese owned.... The other twelve Chinese farms were on small, leased acreages to the south of the city in the valley of Trail Creek.[360]

These latter gardeners and farmers dug ditches to carry water from the Trail Creek to irrigate their gardens and farmlands.

"The vegetable gardeners lived a hard life," said Ron Mah, a merchant in Rossland. He described how they farmed.

> They found a place in the valley where they built their shacks and grew vegetables. The way they built their abode is very interesting. First, they stacked a pile of rocks against the slope to reinforce the back wall and cemented the crevices with mud, then levelled the ground with straw to form the foundation for their shack. Then they put logs up to form sidewalls and the roof. They

left a large space in front as the entrance without a door. By the side of the entrance, they had a big clay pot to store water that they had obtained from Trail Creek for household use and for cultivating their crops. They supplied a great variety of vegetables to the residents in the city. All of them were single men, lonely and isolated, living in their farmland. They visited the Chinese community in town where they found friendship and companionship, and shared their cultural identity."[361]

Mah continued his reminiscence.

There is a very sad story about two brothers who were vegetable gardeners in Rossland. The younger brother got sick and they did not have the means to go to a doctor. Eventually the sick brother died in the hut. The older brother did not know what to do because he did not speak English. He did not report the death to the RCMP or to the hospital because he could not communicate with the officials and was afraid that the officials would charge him with killing his brother. So, he just kept the dead body in the hut. One day, a group of boys cycled to the area and came upon the older brother who was sitting at the door of the hut looking lost and frightened. When the boys went near him, he turned pale, afraid that the boys might accuse him of murdering his younger brother. Yet he wanted his deceased brother to rest in peace. After contemplating for a while, he plucked up his courage and used sign language to convey to the boys that his brother had died and his body was lying inside the hut. The boys immediately reported the case to the RCMP who came and removed the corpse to the hospital. He was not charged. The authority in the hospital did an autopsy and then buried the deceased. This older brother then left his vegetable garden.

Lui Joe, the last Chinese gardener in Rossland, lived in the Thompson Avenue area. Many old-timers could remember him spending time with a couple of his fellow gardeners at the corner of St. Paul Street and Columbia Avenue, smoking water pipes and chatting before they returned home after selling their produce around town.[362] Currently, the location of the Chinese market gardens is a scene of pastoral lands.[363]

Celebrations of Festivals

Chinese merchants, head men or bosses, laundry men, gardeners, wood choppers, labourers, and cooks and servants in private homes celebrated Christmas
and Chinese New Year. Many of them brought Chinese lilies to celebrations
and offered pickled ginger and lichee nuts to guests who came and greeted them
in their residences. During Chinese New Year, they exploded firecrackers to
scare away evil spirits and to welcome a new beginning to the year.

Between the first day of Chinese New Year and the day of the Lantern Festival, which occurs on the fifteenth day of the new year, the Chinese merchants
and bosses of the Chinese lodging houses as well as Rossland's Chee Kung Tong
(Chinese Freemasons Society) celebrated these days to welcome the new beginning of a season. During these festive days, the Chinese went to the stores in
Chinatown to drink liquor and to gamble, playing fan-tan and dominoes. The
Chinese launderers would not offer services or wash clothing for their customers,
who often wished the vacation for these launderers would be a short one.

The Murder of Mah Lin

Mary Chenoweth hired Mah Lin, a Chinese man aged 19, as a cook and servant
in her home on Third Avenue in Rossland. She had four sons; three of them
were teenagers from her previous marriage, and the youngest child, Ernest, aged
8, was from her second marriage. Her marriage had broken down, and she had
to fend for her family. She worked as a cook in the Allan Hotel in town, but she
had a reputation around town as a prostitute.[364]

In addition to cooking meals and packing lunch boxes for the Chenoweth
family, Mah probably performed some other menial tasks around the house like
cleaning and chopping wood. In late afternoon on May 23, 1900, Mah was preparing dinner for the family, peeling potatoes. Ernest Chenoweth, the youngest
boy, entered the kitchen from the back door. Mah greeted him with a smile and
put the potatoes on the stove. Ernest went to his brothers' room and took down
the rifle they used for target shooting. He went to the kitchen, aimed at Mah
Lin with the rifle and pulled the trigger. Mah fell down on the floor. Ernest took
the rifle back to his brothers' room and went out to the railroad yards to play
with his friends.[365]

Later that evening, a woman visited Chenoweth's home and found Mah
Lin lying dead in a pool of blood on the kitchen floor. The police arrived, examined the kitchen and took the deceased to the hospital, where two physicians
performed an autopsy. No further investigation was carried out by the police at
that point, although British Columbia's attorney general was informed about
the tragic death of Mah.

A rumour then went around town saying that a Chinese person had assassinated Mah. The Chinese community and their organizations rejected this scandalous rumour, and they wanted justice for Mah. The Chinese Benevolent Association in Vancouver hired two lawyers to protect the interests of the Chinese community in Rossland.[366] After waiting for two months, the association had received no report about the murder of Mah from the police and the justice system. So the association contacted Jack Ingram, a police officer in Rossland, about the murder of Mah. Ingram recommended the association hire the Pinkerton Detective Agency to investigate the murder. Immediately, the association contacted Pinkerton's and told the agency that the Chinese Benevolent Association would pay for the investigation. Pinkerton's sent Agent Ahern to investigate.

After he arrived in Rossland, Ahern spent his first day interviewing members of the local police force, examining the Chenoweth house, looking at the railway yards where young Ernest had played, and talking to the doctors who had performed the autopsy on Mah Lin. Ahern discarded any notion that a Chinese tong had wreaked vengeance. He suspected that Ernest Chenoweth, the young child, was the culprit. On July 22, 1900, accompanied by H.J. Raymer, a police officer, he went to the hotel where Mary Chenoweth worked, and asked her permission to interview Ernest. Permission was granted. He and Raymer then went to the Chenoweths' home and took the boy to the basement for his interrogation. Raymer took notes during the interview, whereas Ahern asked questions and showed Ernest the shotgun and the bullet, which the doctors had removed from Mah Lin's head. The sight of this evidence incited Ernest to give a full confession about his dreadful and unforgiving action to Ahern. Ernest was immediately arrested.

On October 23, 1900, Ernest was tried in Nelson. H.A. Maclean conducted the prosecution, and H.A. MacNeill, QC, cross-examined the defence witnesses. The two physicians were called on to provide medical evidence. Mrs. Wright, a friend of Mary Chenoweth's, was called as a crown witness. Charles W. Lairley, a gunsmith from Rossland, was called to give expert evidence as to the shooting.[367] Durney, Simpson and Matheson, the three men who were employed on the Rossland waterworks, also testified in the court proceedings.

Young Ernest Chenoweth was carried in and out of the courtroom by a constable. Throughout the entire hearing, Ernest, sitting in the trial box, was never questioned by the lawyers and he watched indifferently, not showing the slightest interest in the court proceedings. He played with a watch, dropped it on the floor several times, and the guard in the court repeatedly picked it up for him. It looked as though he was playing games with the guard. His behaviour

annoyed the judge, who ordered that the watch be removed from Ernest. Instead, he was given a piece of elastic to amuse himself. Mary Chenoweth sat
beside A.H. MacNeill, QC, who appeared for the defence, in the court.

Wright, one of the crown's witnesses, told the judge that in May Mary's
husband had been approached by two Chinese men who offered him five hundred dollars to bring evidence that would secure the conviction of Ernest Chenoweth. This testimony would have a bearing on the trial because it supported
the contention of the defence that Mah Lin was murdered by his fellow countrymen at the instigation of a secret society.

Lairley examined the bullet and testified that the one that killed the man
had been fired from a smooth bore rifle, and the one used by Ernest would have
left marks to the rifling on the bullet. His inference was that the prisoner could
not have killed the Chinese man.

Durney, Simpson and Matheson all told the judge and jury that young
Chenoweth had said to them that he had shot the man, and that he had never
seen "a man die so quick. He fell like a log." But Judge Walkem ruled that the
alleged confession could not be admitted because the conversation among Ernest and the three men was conducted in a mocking spirit, and thus carried no
weight in the court proceedings.[368]

Constable H.J. Raymer wanted to refer to the confession by Ernest. Mac-
Neill objected to this strenuously, implying that the confession had no bearing on the court hearing. Thus, the jury did not hear the confession that was
obtained by Ahern from Ernest. Finding no real proof that Ernest was guilty,
the jury announced an unanimous verdict of "not guilty." So Ernest was acquitted.[369] The white people in the court room applauded and cheered, and hats
were thrown up in the air when the verdict was announced. Thus, the murder of
Mah Lin remained an unsolved crime in the Chinese community.

Chinatown, the Chinese Settlement

The core of Chinatown was one city block on Kootenay Avenue between St.
Paul and Monte Christo Streets. This was only two blocks down a steep hill
from Columbia Avenue, the city's main commercial street.

At the beginning of the twentieth century, there were about ten to fifteen Chinese stores in Chinatown, including a drug store/herbalist shop. Across
from the Columbia and Western Railway Depot was the Lai Yuen Company, a
general and grocery store. The Wong Kung Company had another similar store
south of Washington Street. Also located in the core of Chinatown were the
Lee Maw Company, the Lee Wai Tang Company, and the Lee Man Company.[370] These stores supplied staple foods, clothing such as blue jeans and denim

jackets, and tools to their fellow Chinese. At Hallowe'en, these stores sold fire-crackers for five cents a package to children from the mainstream community.

Between 1897 and 1942, the Chinese in Rossland had a total of 117 properties located on either side of Trail Creek. The number of Chinese-owned properties peaked between 1916 and 1925, but began to drop off significantly after 1931, as the Chinese dispersed to other parts of the province.

Raids, Thefts and Court Cases

As indicated earlier, all the Chinese residents in town were men; they had no wives or family members to assist and keep them company. With long working hours and no English-language skills to communicate their needs for social support, many of these Chinese men spent their leisure time gambling—hoping they would win enough money to help them return to their homes in Guangdong. Unfortunately, good fortune did not shine on them as expected. Instead, many of them lost money gambling, diminishing their hopes and dreams of a bright future in the gold mountains.

Gambling was often practised in the backrooms of shops, restaurants and laundries in Rossland. The police couldn't care less whether the Chinese gambled, but they reacted quickly when they noticed that white men were also playing fan-tan, dominos and the pigeon lottery in Chinese gambling dens. The police assumed that the Chinese had lured the white men to gamble, which they believed posed a threat to the moral rectitude of the white population.[371] On January 18, 1898, the police raided a gambling den and arrested eleven Chinese men and brought them to the police court. Each Chinese gambler was fined twenty dollars by the police magistrate. The gamblers were then released.[372]

Yes, the Chinese immigrants gambled, but this practice was directly linked to the absence of families, according to the Chinese Benevolent Association in Vancouver. Due to the imposition of the Head Tax in 1885 and the Chinese Exclusion Act in 1923, the Chinese immigrants were unable to send for their wives and family members to join them in Canada.[373] Many of the Chinese were unskilled labourers who could only earn enough to bring meagre meals to their tables. And the white Canadians perceived the Chinese as inferior people and excluded the Chinese from the mainstream communities. It is clear that the early Chinese immigrants living in Rossland were lonely and helpless, so they indulged in gambling with the hope that they might win enough to return to their families in their home villages in China.

Many single Chinese men also consumed opium for relaxation and to numb their feelings of hopelessness and loneliness. Unfortunately, those who consumed opium became addicted to the drug. Chinese merchants sold opium, primarily to other Chinese.[374] However, in 1901, Josie Perkin, a white girl who was an opium addict, moved from Vancouver Island to Rossland in an attempt to forget the death of her baby and to leave her abusive husband. One month after her arrival in Rossland she died from an overdose of opium in a Chinese opium den. Thomas Long, Rossland's police chief, blamed the Chinese opium dealers for her death and declared that he was "determined to break up the [opium] dens as it was known that a number of white men and women have been in the habit of frequenting them."[375] That evening the police force ransacked the opium dens and shops in Chinatown, confiscated the opium smoking apparatus and arrested the smokers. All of the merchants and smokers had to pay fines.

On February 25, 1913, the *Rossland Daily News* reported on a theft tried in the Rossland police court.[376] The paper stated that a Chinese man was charged with stealing seven five-dollar gold coins plus two fifty-cent pieces of Hong Kong currency from the home of Lung Yan Wo, a Chinese merchant in Chinatown. At the beginning of the hearing, the merchant told the police magistrate that he had locked his trunk before leaving his house in the morning, but when he returned home around 2:00 p.m., he found the lock on his trunk broken and the money stolen. His friend, another Chinese man who testified in court, said that he saw the suspect leaving the merchant's house at noon, and pointed at the suspect who was accused of looting the treasure from the house of the merchant. The witness claimed that he was on his way to visit the merchant at that time.

The suspect told the magistrate that he had no money, therefore he could not be the thief. A constable in the police court searched the accused's body and found no money. The magistrate then ordered the constable to search his home. When the constable arrived there, he noticed that a handkerchief was tucked under the mattress. He pulled the handkerchief out and found the coins. Returning to court, the magistrate found the suspect guilty and sentenced him to six months' imprisonment with hard labour. The currency and the coins were returned to the complainant.

On June 9, 1914, Constable H.M. Parry, together with Constable Terry and Constable Garnet, arrived at C. Takahassi's poolroom on First Avenue. They evaded the Chinese doorman stationed at the entrance. In the poolroom, they saw four white men playing blackjack. Cards and dice were found on the table, but any money was quickly picked up by the players. Takahassi and the white men were arrested and kept in the police station for the night. The following morning, Takahassi appeared before Police Magistrate Hamilton, who charged him with operating a gambling house. He was fined fifty dollars plus expenses. The others were released but warned not to gamble again.

The Chee Kung Tong (Chinese Freemasons Society)

Many Chinese immigrants who arrived in Rossland were members of the Chee Kung Tong (Chinese Freemasons Society). With effort and perseverance, they erected the Chee Kung Tong building at the corner of Kootenay Avenue and St. Paul's Street.

This building became an important meeting and gathering place for the Chinese of Rossland. The society held Christmas dinners and celebrated Chinese New Year and the Spring Festival for its members as well as for Chinese immigrants who were not members. The society also provided Chinese newspapers, such as the *Chinese Times,* in the early twentieth century so that its members could obtain news from members in other towns and cities, particularly in Vancouver and Victoria, as well as keeping up to date with the political movements in Guangdong, where their home villages were located.

In 1903, the Chee Kung Tong held a grand celebration marking the opening of new lodge rooms on the top floor of a three-storey building in Chinatown. Important citizens from the town and the general public were invited to the grand opening. In August of the following year, after an extensive renovation of the lodge, the Chee Kung Tong held another elaborate ceremony, including

The majority of Chinese men that came to Rossland were not involved in the mining industry, however, they provided much-needed services to the developing town. 2282.0049 Kee Chinese Variety Store in Rossland, BC 1898, courtesy Rossland Museum & Discovery Centre and the Columbia Basin Institute of Regional History

a parade through Rossland. The *Rossland Miner* reported that it was "probably unparalleled in the province, certainly it was absolutely novel in Rossland." Led by two men on horses and accompanied by three bands playing "barbaric music," the procession of officials in exotic silk robes and their entourage wound through the streets of Rossland. The *Rossland Miner* acknowledged that the display "was well worth witnessing" and that "scores" of Rosslanders visited the finely decorated lodge rooms.[377]

The majority of the Chinese immigrants believed in and worshipped Guan Gong, or Guan Yun Xiang (关云翔), Lord of Justice, one of the heroes in the Three Kingdoms in Chinese history (220–280 AD); Guanyin, Goddess of Mercy; and the deity Shen Nong, Lord of Agriculture. The presence of images of these deities, especially those representing Guan Gong, reflected the role of Chinese culture in Rossland's early history. The worship of these deities offered the Chinese comfort and consolation as they lived alone in the gold mountains, far from home. The presence of these deities alongside the living quarters in the Chee Kung Tong building met both the social and spiritual needs of the men in the Chinese community.

In addition, the board members of the tong took time to celebrate the Chinese festivals for the Chinese men to lessen the feelings of loneliness and isolation they experienced. These celebrations provided the single men with a sense of belonging living in a foreign country.

On October 1, 1914, the *Chinese Times* (大汉公报) published the names of Chinese contacts in British Columbia and Alberta. In Rossland, the proprietor of the general store, Yong An He (Mandarin, 永安和) or Wing On Wo (Cantonese) would be the contacts.

In 1919, the building of the Chee Kung Tong in Rossland was destroyed by fire. On October 16, 1920, election of its officers took place most likely in a Chinese restaurant or another lodging house. Huang Hua Can (黄华璨) was elected as the chairman, Huang San Duo (黄三多) as the Chinese secretary, Chen Ji De (陈齐德) as the English secretary, and Huang Lan Jie (黄兰洁) as the treasurer. The names of the board members were published in the *Chinese Times* in Vancouver.

On October 19 of the same year, the organization announced in the *Chinese Times* that it would hold a commemorative event to honour the five founders of the society and the grand opening of the lodge. This announcement listed the post office box (272), rather than the location of the lodge in Rossland.

The announcement urged all its members to attend and also invited the public to the event. The election was to be held in the private home of an executive member since the lodge of the Chee Kung Tong had yet to be rebuilt after the fire.

In the same month, a key member of the Chee Kung Tong posted an advertisement in the *Chinese Times* directed to his friend, Huang Xi Lan (黄喜兰), inquiring whether he would like to work in vegetable gardening. The duration of the job would be seven months, and the pay would be fifty dollars per month. If Huang was interested in the job, he could apply for the job through the Chee Kung Tong in Rossland. It thus appears that the Chee Kung Tong acted as an employer in Rossland.

In 1929, the building of the Chee Kung Tong was rebuilt, but in 1952 it was pulled down. Although the building is no longer standing, its history remains.

Mr. Lou Crowe, an old-timer, had visited the building of the Chee Kung Tong. He said that this Chinese association had a brass band and that Chinese men practised and played in the building. Inside the building, there were "dragons and lions and different animals with long tails."[378] As well, large turtles were imported for medical purposes by the association. His observations and memories are truly remarkable.

Other Chinese Enterprises

Crowe also said that in the 1930s there were quite a few Chinese restaurants in town. The Empire Café was located near the opera building. The Commodore and Silver Grill owned by Sammy Loo and Seto was located in the vicinity of the Cathleen Apartment block[379] and the Headquarters Café was at the corner of Washington Street and First Avenue. The Kaiwe family operated a café at Rossland's outdoor swimming pool, the first outdoor pool to be built in British Columbia.[380] This swimming pool was located on the south side of Columbia Avenue, at the western edge of the downtown core in Rossland. It is gratifying that Crowe remembered the Chinese people who lived in Rossland. The information he shared is important as it may stimulate students and scholars to carry out research that documents Chinese-Canadian history in Rossland in more detail.

The Deceased Chinese in Rossland

The Chinese population declined after 1931. Many of the Chinese old-timers aged and passed on. Some of the Chinese immigrants, however, died young or in their prime. The old-timers lived in shared lodgings where they took turns sleeping on the same beds.[381] White people in the mainstream community condemned these living quarters, considering them dirty and therefore unhygienic. Yes, the conditions of the living quarters were not ideal or hygienic but this was the accommodation these men could afford. They earned considerably lower wages than white people. Imagine, they could only earn $1.00 or $1.50 per day maintaining good roads leading to the mines! They were poor and destitute, lonely and depressed! Consequently, many of them consumed liquor and alcohol to numb their feelings and emotions, and that might have led to heart failure, stroke, stomach and intestinal problems and lung diseases. Here is the list of illnesses related to the Chinese deceased:

Date	Age	Occupation	Cause
May 23, 1900	19	Cook	shot dead
December 1, 1901	45	Launderer	unknown
March 23, 1902	35	Gardener	tuberculosis
October 10, 1902	27	Unknown	tuberculosis
June 27, 1904	23	Unknown	opium poisoning
March 3, 1905	45	Farmer	tuberculosis
July 3, 1908	61	Unknown	stroke
December 25, 1909	40	Farmer	tuberculosis
January 29, 1910	62	Gardener	stroke
June 16, 1916	28	Launderer	heart failure
June 19, 1918	51	Farmer	heart failure
November 19, 1918	50	Clerk	pneumonia
March 31, 1921	47	Cook	scarring of liver
May 10, 1929	59	Gardener	stomach bleeding
February 22, 1935	58	Rancher	pneumonia
February 28, 1945	82	Merchant	heart failure
May 3, 1958	86	Cook	cerebral hemorrhage

Source: Ronald A. Shearer, "The Chinese and Chinatown of Rossland: Fragments from Their Early History," 2nd ed., 2018, rosslandmuseum.ca, 11.

Some of the deceased Chinese were buried in Mountain View Cemetery but their ages and the dates of their burials were not recorded.

Cemetery Data, Mountain View Cemetery, Rossland

Name	Section	Plot
Ching Chung	6	114
Chong Hong	15	102
Chow John	15	180
Chow Sue	8	160
Chow Yuen F.	1	448
Eng Jim	4	114a
Kai Chun	8	178
Kee Chong	6	307
Kim Hugh	n/a	588
Lee Chang Kai	6	311
Lee Hong	2	161
Lee Kee Tun	19	105
Lee Kwock Kee	7 Ext.	287
Lee Lim	3	31
Lee Pui Lan	7 Ext	286
Lee Yim Nam	3	30
Lem C.C.	n/a	467
Look, Lee	8	199
Lu, Hong	8	28
Mah Kee	3	33
Mah Ling	3	10
Mah Sing	3	10
Mah Sing	3	38
May Maw Gaw	3	88
Paw Morris	4	27D
Quong Chong	3	32
Sam N.B.	3	15
Tai Mah	2	148
Wing Yin Mah	3	62
Wong Joe	9	157
Wong Harry P.	4	90C
Wong Haw	3	87
Wong How Taw	15	179
Wong Kee	3	14
Yaw Sing Yue	9	111

Source: Kutenai West Heritage Consulting, *West Kootenay Chinese Heritage Society, Summary Report, 1995.*[382]

Recognition

In 2013, the Red Mountain Railway bed was recognized as a heritage site. The construction of this railway took place between 1895 and 1896. The Statement of Significance claims that:

> The Red Mountain Railway bed is a testament to both the significant American involvement in the development of the mines of Rossland and the richness of the ore deposits. Large capital dollars were spent in the late 1890's to construct the rail line and the bridge over the Columbia River at Northport to take the ore to American smelters. The owner of the rail line, D.C. Corbin, received large land grants from the provincial government in return for building the line which totalled 510 acres within the City of Rossland.... The line carried some ore from American owned mines to smelters south of the border, but mostly freight and passengers between Spokane and Rossland. In 1898 the American owned LeRoi Mining Company cancelled its contract with the Trail Smelter and built its own smelter at Northport with the Red Mountain Railway becoming the major ore carrier. The Smelter in Northport was used for only a short time as the LeRoi Mine was taken over by the British North America Company and its ore again went down to the Trail Smelter. Ultimately absorbed into the Great Northern Railway Company, the Red Mountain Railway continued to link Rossland with Spokane on a daily basis until the line was abandoned in 1922. The ties, trestle structures and rails were removed shortly thereafter. The bed today is not continuous as parts have been taken over by Highway 22 that connects Rossland with the Paterson border crossing.

In 2014, the Rossland Heritage Commission officially recognized the Chinese gardens, established in 1898, as a heritage site. The Chinese Gardens Statement of Significance described the importance of this site.

> The Chinese Gardens, covering over 70 acres of land in lower Rossland, are culturally and historically significant to Rossland. For over 50 years, until the 1950's, fresh fruit and vegetables were grown here and sold to the people of Rossland by the Chinese farmers who peddled their produce, door to door, from large baskets hanging from a yoke worn across their shoulders. The small farms were worked by hand and each farmer had his own tiny

shack and garden plot, and water was obtained from Trail Creek. Some land was owned by the Chinese but most was leased. While playing an important role in the community in term of food production, the Chinese were not accepted socially by the white population. Today, this area is identified mostly by open grassland, around Trail Creek as it flows down the Trail Creek Valley to the Columbia River. There is little evidence of the Chinese farms and their owners—some fruit trees, a rock wall, rock piles, trenches and depressions where there were once root cellars.

In 2015, the Legacy Initiative Advisory Council (LIAC), British Columbia, also recognized the Chinese market gardens, as well as the building of the Chee Kung Tong (Chinese Freemasons Society), as heritage sites.[383] The report of LIAC stated that

> the market gardens are important as a representation of the importance of Chinese Canadian in agriculture industry. While the Masonic Hall or the building of Chee Kung Tong, though no longer existing, was the site of Rossland's Chinese Canadian neighbourhood. These two sites have left a page of important history in west Kootenay.

Conclusion

This chapter documents the many occupations and endeavours of early Chinese immigrants to Rossland. Many were self-employed, operating laundries and establishing general and grocery stores and restaurants; others owned or leased land where they established market gardens. The laundries provided services to the mainstream community, which only offered them token acceptance. The Chinese general and grocery stores supplied goods, clothing and merchandise to their fellow Chinese. The restaurants catered Chinese food and the market gardeners cultivated land to produce vegetables and fruits for all in town.

Quite a few Chinese immigrants took jobs as cooks, domestic servants or wood choppers. None of these occupations paid well, enabling them only to earn a meagre living. In truth, the work of domestic servants was not appreciated. The murder of Mah Lin, a young cook in the Chenoweth household, the trials in court and the verdict announced by the jury demonstrated classic intolerance and rejection of the Chinese at that time.

The roles and functions of the Chee Kung Tong, also known as the Chinese Freemasons Society, illustrated the mutual assistance and supports members of the Chinese community provided for one another. The association's lodge offered accommodation and provided recreational activities to members and non-members, and helped retain and share Chinese culture by hosting Chinese festivals and taking care of the sick and dying, and organizing funerals for the deceased. It also attempted to find employment for Chinese immigrants, and to provide links to their home villages in the districts of the Zhujiang Delta in Guangdong Province, China.

Afterword

This book describes the efforts and endeavours of the early Chinese immigrants who settled in one town and four major cities in the Kootenay—Fisherville, Cranbrook, Nelson, Revelstoke and Rossland. It was the mineral wealth—mainly the discovery of gold—that attracted the first Chinese immigrants to the Kootenay region. These metropolises, overland trails and roads, and much of the early infrastructure were built to support the mining activities. Without the desire for wealth and comforts in life, the Chinese immigrants would not have ventured overseas, risking their lives in foreign countries.

In 1863, gold was discovered at Wild Horse Creek that brought gold seekers, including Chinese prospectors and miners, from the Cariboo to Fisherville, a fledgling town established near where gold had been found. These Chinese gold seekers settled in the Wild Horse area and established Chinatown adjacent to Fisherville. An existing image of the Chinese altar at Fisherville showed that the Chinese had arrived in the gold-mining town; many of them were members of the Chee Kung Tong (Chinese Freemasons Society). When gold was depleted in the area by 1865, some of these Chinese left and ventured to the Big Bend on the Columbia River where gold had been found. Those who remained in the Wild Horse area cultivated food crops and vegetables to support themselves. In addition to placer mining, images of Chinese miners operating hydraulic mining equipment to obtain gold can be found in the Royal British Columbia Museum in Victoria and other museums and archives in the Kootenay. Some of the early Chinese prospectors and miners established mining companies in Fort Steele, now a heritage park in the East Kootenay. Many of the gold companies were later dissolved and their management left the area, except for the Ban Quan and International Placer Companies, and the Gold Hill Stinger Resource Enterprises. Jack Lee was the only Chinese miner who remained in the Wild Horse district; he stayed until his death on May 29, 1929. The mineral wealth and the construction of the Dewdney Trail enabled the founding of Fort Steele and later the establishment of Cranbrook.

In addition to gold and other minerals, coal and oil were found in the neighbourhood of Cranbrook. Many Chinese immigrants migrated to Cranbrook hoping they could find employment in the coal mines. Unfortunately, many mining companies refused to hire Chinese labourers. However, a few ranches employed the Chinese to irrigate their fields. Some families in the mainstream community also employed Chinese cooks and servants in their households. Unable to find employment in the mining industry, some of the Chinese immigrants established grocery stores and laundry shops, while others cut wood and carried water for merchants and owners of private homes to make a living.

Many of the early Chinese immigrants were peasants who came from villages in the districts at the Zhujiang Delta. They had little knowledge of European standards of hygiene, and were not accepted by the mainstream white community. Without employment and acceptance, they lived together in boarding houses to keep each other company. Many of them smoked opium and drank alcohol to numb their feelings of loneliness and isolation. Their living conditions and habits, and their inability to communicate with the white residents created misconceptions of their needs physically and mentally. Consequently, the *Cranbrook Herald*, the English newspaper looked upon the Chinese establishments "as a menace to the city."[384]

The office of this newspaper was located next to the Chinatown in the city of Cranbrook. The Chinese people in its neighbourhood greeted one another with loud voices. Their greetings and talking were so loud that they irritated the editor, who said that he had to use a megaphone to communicate with his staff. The loud calling of the Chinese immigrants reflected the culture of Chinese farmers. Many of these Chinese immigrants had been farmers in their home villages, cultivating rice and other food crops on their farmlands, each farm separated from the others by a fair distance. Whenever they wanted to speak to one another, they had to call out loudly. When meals were brought to the fields, the person who brought the food to them had to shout so that the farmers in the fields could hear him or her and come to the area where food was served. An individual who heard the calling usually echoed it, with the intention of gathering all the farmers in the neighbouring fields to get together to enjoy their meals as a group.

In addition, there were two Chinese organizations in Cranbrook—the Chee Kung Tong (also known as the Chinese Freemasons Society) and the Guomindang (also known as the Chinese Nationalist League). These two Chinese organizations did not always see eye to eye with one another. So-called "tong wars" occasionally occurred between them. The Chee Kung Tong collected funds from its members and the Chinese merchants in town to establish a joss house to honour the five historical ancestors of the association. This undertaking manifested the members' respect for the founders of their organization.

It also created a reading room in its building for its members and Chinese immigrants to read the *Chinese Times* and magazines so that they could learn about the economic situation and political movements in their homeland. This kind provision demonstrates that the Chinese immigrants were not illiterate. They were not ignorant—only unable to express themselves in English or French.

The Guomindang was a republication political party led by Dr. Sun Yat-sen in China. On the occasion of his visit to British Columbia to gain support for the republican revolution, Sun encouraged the Chinese immigrants in various communities to join the Guomindang to demonstrate their care and compassion for China, their home country. It was the hope and dream of the Chinese immigrants that they would be able to return home one day to enjoy their sunset years with their families and people living in their villages.

Unfortunately, in 1929, civil war broke out between the Guomindang and the Chinese Communist Party. The civil war stopped when the Japanese invaded China in 1937 but resumed in ~1941. The Guomindang was defeated and forced to leave mainland China, relocating itself to Taiwan, where it remains today. When the Chinese Communist Party established the People's Republic of China in 1949, membership in the Guomindang diminished in British Columbia and other provinces in Canada.

The Chee Kung Tong, however, remained active in Cranbrook and other cities in Canada. John Lee, a prominent Chinese merchant in Cranbrook, was a key member of the organization. On May 6, 1926, Lee passed away, but he had spent his entire adult life in Cranbrook. The Chee Kung Tong had offered accommodation in its building for its members, who arrived without wives and family members in Cranbrook and its vicinity. This society helped its members find jobs and provided recreational activities for their leisure, usually in the form of gambling such as betting in fan-tan, dominoes, blackjack and other games. Unfortunately, the building of the Chee Kung Tong building in Cranbrook was destroyed by fire in 1952, although it was rebuilt in later years.

Chu Ban Quan, a prospector and miner, was another Chinese man who succeeded in trades and acquired wealth in the East Kootenay region. He spent his early days in the Wild Horse district and later years in Cranbrook, where he built the Tamarack Mall. On May 13, 1947, he passed away and was buried in the Westlawn Cemetery in Cranbrook.

In 1947, the infamous Chinese Exclusion Act was repealed. The repeal of the act allowed many of the Chinese to send for their wives and any children under the age of 18 to join them in Cranbrook. Many of these Chinese arrivals came from Hong Kong and Guangdong Province. Some of them obtained employment in sawmills or the lumber or forestry industries, and in restaurants or grocery stores, while others established and operated their own businesses, or attended schools, colleges and universities to learn English.

It is interesting to note that the foundation of Revelstoke began with a dispute between Arthur Stanhope Farwell, a surveyor, and the Canadian Pacific Railway. It ended in a court case that took a few years to resolve. Finally, the town created by Farwell and the area surrounding the railway station, the property of the Canadian Pacific Railway (CPR), were amalgamated into one city, known as Revelstoke.

Although many of the early Chinese immigrants who migrated to various towns and cities in the Kootenay aimed to find gold, it was the blazing of a trail from the coast and the building of the CPR that brought a large number of Chinese immigrants to Revelstoke. In 1861, Edgar Dewdney, a civil engineer and contractor, employed a large number of Chinese labourers to construct a trail from Hope and through the Similkameen to Wild Horse Creek. This trail is known as the Dewdney Trail. Between 1880 and 1885, the CPR hired about 17,000 Chinese labourers to build the railway in British Columbia.[385] It was the construction of this railway that mainly brought the Chinese labourers to Revelstoke. Many of the Chinese labourers who were dismissed when the railway construction was completed arrived in the vicinity of Revelstoke; some of them were retained by the CPR to do maintenance work for the railway.

On November 7, the last spike of the CPR was nailed at Craigellachie, a place located several kilometres west of Eagle Pass; this marked the completion of the transcontinental railway in Canada. No Chinese labourer was invited to bear witness to this historical event, although Wing Chung, a dismissed labourer, said that he was standing behind the large crowd of people at this event.

Many of the dismissed Chinese labourers settled in Revelstoke and searched for employment there. Quite a few of these individuals found work as casual labourers. They carried water and chopped wood for some families and the hotels in the city as well as operating small businesses such as laundries and grocery stores. Wing Chung was one of the Chinese merchants who established and operated a small business. Similarly, Wah Chung, another dismissed labourer, owned and operated a general store and had two more houses in block 10, and one more building in block 11 located on Front Street.

Hong Chung had a general store on block 8 of Front Street. The Lun Ching Laundry was located on the riverside of block 3, Front Street, and the Shing Kee Laundry was situated between Benson and Hanson Streets. Eventually, the site of Farwell town and the area surrounding the CPR station were owned by Chinese merchants, and these two Chinese settlements were referred to as Chinatowns.

Obvious discrimination against the Chinese immigrants was manifested in the community. In 1891, for example, a town hall meeting was called in the mainstream community. The people who attended voted against the employment of Chinese workers on public works. However, the Chinese immigrants lived their own lives, and observed and celebrated their festivities in the city. In the winter of 1894, for example, the Chinese community celebrated Chinese New Year for fifteen days, and both the Wah Chung store and the Lun Ching Laundry invited all white callers to suppers and gave them presents.

It was not always pleasant and joyful for the Chinese immigrants living in Revelstoke. In the fall of 1895, a Chinese cook who worked in the CPR Hotel mysteriously disappeared. Later a skeleton with no skull was found on a mountain near Revelstoke. Whether these bones were the remains of the cook, a doctor and police were unable to ascertain. In September 1899 Dr. Cross inspected some Chinese shacks north of the city and ordered them to be destroyed by fire. A journalist who accompanied Dr. Cross and the police on their inspection of the Chinatowns labelled them "Dirt, Disease, and Death." Since they had discovered the poverty and unhealthy conditions in Chinatowns, why didn't they offer some solutions instead?!

Almost all the Chinese immigrants were single men who might be married but could not afford to bring their wives and families with them due to the Head Tax. In 1885, the first Head Tax of $50 Canadian per person was implemented. In 1901, the Head Tax was increased to $100, and in 1903, to $500. The imposition of these levies were aimed at discouraging the Chinese to immigrate to Canada; the tax effectively created a bachelor society in the Chinese settlements throughout the country.

Many of the Chinese single men were living in houses owned and operated by the Chee Kung Tong in Revelstoke. One of the buildings, known as the joss house, had two floors. On the ground floor, there was an altar for honouring several Chinese deities. In addition, there was a reading room for the members and guests to read Chinese newspaper and magazines. The upper floor with two large rooms contained rows of beds for the single Chinese men and guests. This organization celebrated Chinese New Year and other Chinese festivals such as Duan Wu Jie (the Dragon Boat Festival) in the fifth moon of the Chinese lunar calendar and Zongqui Jie (the Mid-autumn Moon Festival) on the fifteenth day of the eighth month. It also observed Qing Ming (Tomb-sweeping Day) around Easter, and Yu Lan Jie, on the fifteenth day of the seventh moon, and assisted with burying and organizing funerals for its deceased members. In an attempt to reach out to the mainstream community, this organization collected and donated money to the Revelstoke hospital to help it purchase an X-ray machine.

In addition, there was Guomindang (the Chinese Nationalist League) in Revelstoke. Wong Kwong, who recruited Chinese labourers for the construction of the Dewdney Trail in 1914, was the chairman of the Guomindang. Kwong and his wife, Yee Von, established and operated the Kwong Lee Laundry in Revelstoke. Together, they raised five girls and four boys in their home. Kwong also erected a rooming house near his home for Chinese labourers. He was the strength and blessing in the Chinese Canadian community in his time.

In 1932, while driving a team of horses, Kwong stopped to look at one of the horses. That mare kicked him on his head and killed him, leaving his wife to raise and nurture their children. All their children assisted Yee Von to operate the family's laundry shop, yet all of them attended and graduated from high school. A few of them attended colleges and university in Vancouver. All Yee Von's children had good careers and a few of them became professionals. This family has left a beautiful legacy in Revelstoke.

The history of the Chinese in Nelson began in the spring of 1890, when the construction crews of the Columbia and Kootenay Railway arrived in the neighbourhood. The crews included 175 Chinese labourers. After this railway was completed, some of the Chinese labourers settled on Vernon Street and in its vicinity. This Chinese settlement was referred to as Chinatown. In 1897, Nelson was incorporated as a city. By 1899, three Chinese general and grocery stores were found in Chinatown and the names of Kwong Wing Chong, Wo Kee and Yick Sang Lung appeared in the *British Columbia Directory*. The *Nelson Miner* reported on a Chinese New Year celebration, and commented that "the Chinese colony is by no means a small one."[386] The 1901 census recorded that 325 Chinese individuals lived in Chinatown. This number included 50 cooks and domestic servants, 20 workers in four laundries, plus 40 who cut wood, 50 who worked in 12 market gardens, 10 merchants, and another 150 unemployed people. These numbers were supplied by merchant Kwong Wing Chong when he testified at the Royal Commission on Chinese and Japanese Immigration, held from 1900-02.[387]

Around 1905, Mar Juck returned to his home village in Guangdong, where he married. He and his wife had a son, Shu Tong. Later, his wife and son joined him in Nelson. In 1910, another son, Shu Ling, was born, and in the following year, a daughter, Hon Wan, was added to the family. All the Mar children attended school in Nelson. In 1922, Mar Shu Tong graduated from the local high school, and continued his studies at the University of Washington. He defied the tradition of an arranged marriage. He returned to Nelson shortly after the Japanese invasion of China, and raised funds for the Chinese republican government to help the fight against the Japanese invasion. He joined and supported the Guomindang—the Chinese Nationalist League—by raising funds for the party in Vancouver. In 1941, he suffered from pneumonia and passed away at the age of only 36.

When the Chinese Exclusion Act was repealed in 1947 and the Chinese in Canada could send for their family members to be reunited with them in Canada, Shu Ling immediately sent for his wife, Kung, and his son, Lawrence, who immigrated to Nelson. In an interview, Lawrence said that his father told him that there were a few Chinese organizations, namely the Chinese Freemasons Society, the Chinese Empire Reform Association and the Chinese Nationalist League in Nelson's Chinatown. Lawrence and other young Chinese arrivals, including some Chinese Canadians, formed the Chinese Youth Association. They played basketball and learned to play musical instruments, produced newsletters, and raised funds for the association to carry out its activities. During Christmas season and Chinese New Year, the association's band entertained the Chinese people in the city. After two years, members of the executive and board members graduated from high school, left town and continued their education at colleges and universities in the Lower Mainland, ending this association.

In 1959, Cameron Mah arrived in Vancouver, and then migrated to Castlegar to work as a dishwasher in a Chinese restaurant owned and operated by Yorkie Mah. He went to school in the morning, and worked in the restaurant after school. He remained in Castlegar where he met Jayne Jay Bow Chin through his landlady. In 1966, they married and moved to Nelson where his parents-in-law and family lived. His reputation for culinary skill had preceded him, and several restaurants offered him work. In 1970, he and five of his friends established the KC (Kootenay Centre) Restaurant. It was a smashing success!

In 1973, Cameron sponsored his second and third brothers to come to Nelson, and they helped out in the restaurant. Two years later, he sent for his parents and the rest of his siblings to immigrate to Nelson. When his brothers could manage and operate the restaurant, Cameron volunteered his time serving the Chinese community and interpreting for Chinese immigrants in citizenship court in the West Kootenay region. He was hailed as a pillar of the Chinese community. On June 8, 2019, he had a heart attack and passed away at the age of 72. He was buried in the Nelson Memorial Park Cemetery.

Again, it was the mineral wealth—mainly gold, coal and oil—that attracted Chinese prospectors and miners in the Cariboo and Chinese merchants to migrate to and settle in Rossland. They hoped to find employment in the mining camps, but their hopes could not be realized, due to anti-Chinese legislation. Instead, they cut wood and carried water for merchants and private homes. Some of them established grocery stores, restaurants and laundry shops to earn a living. Quite a few of the Chinese immigrants served as houseboys, servants and cooks in the households of the mainstream community. They were single men who lived in boarding houses and in the building of the Chee Kung Tong. After work in the evenings, they enjoyed each other's company.

Unfortunately, on May 23, 1900, a Chinese cook, Mah Lin, was shot dead in the kitchen of the Chenoweth's house. A young boy, Ernest Chenoweth, confessed his guilt to three workers at the waterworks in town. Young Chenoweth was arrested and tried in a trial that lasted many days. Surprisingly, despite his confession, he was acquitted. The murder of Mah Lin remained a mystery in Chinese-Canadian history in Rossland.

Ronald Mah, a Chinese merchant and a leader in the Chinese community of Rossland shared stories about two Chinese brothers who cultivated a vegetable garden in the vicinity of Rossland. The stories were sad and depressing, indicating that it was not easy for many Chinese immigrants to flourish in a foreign land. It is comforting to learn that Louie Joe, the last Chinese vegetable gardener in Rossland, made life work well in Rossland. His story was recorded by the Rossland Museum and Discovery Centre, which has a photograph of him carrying his baskets of produce from 1940. It was wonderful to have the opportunity to interview Lindsay Wong, a Chinese-Canadian woman who was elected to Rossland's City Council in 2001. It was also great that the West Kootenay Chinese Heritage Society kept delightful stories about the lives and achievements of the early Chinese immigrants who made their home in Rossland.

The research and writing of this book required time and energy, but finally, I have completed it. I sincerely hope my readers have enjoyed reading it, and gained some understanding of the efforts and endeavours of the Chinese immigrants and Chinese Canadians who resided in the Kootenay.

Lily Chow Siewsan
Fall 2022

Notes

Introduction

1   Ronald Mah, interview with the author, Rossland, August 14, 2001.

The Wild Horse Creek Gold Rush: Fisherville

2   First Peoples' Cultural Council, "About the Ktunaxa People," https://www. firstvoices.com/explore/FV/sections/Data/Ktunaxa/Ktunaxa/Ktunaxa.

3   Derryll White, "Fort Steele," *Canadian Encyclopedia*, February 7, 2006, thecanadianencyclopedia.ca; "Wild Horse Creek Historic Site," *Canada's Historic Places*, historicplaces.ca.

4   "Millions in Gold Taken from Wild Horse Creek," *Fort Steele Prospector*, November 9, 1895, 2.

5   The forty-eight tons (forty-four tonnes) in gold would be worth about $2 billion today, according to Stinger Resources, https://stingerresources. com/?page_id=122.

6   "Millions in Gold," *Fort Steele Prospector*, November 9, 1895, 2.

7   "Millions in Gold," *Fort Steele Prospector*, November 9, 1895, 2.

8   *Cariboo Sentinel*, July 22, 1865, 2.

9   According to David Griffith, a miner at Wild Horse Creek, quoted in the *Cranbrook Herald*, December 18, 1902, 8.

10   *Cranbrook Herald*, December 18, 1902, 8.

11   *East Kootenay Miner*, December 16, 1898, 1.

12   *Fort Steele Prospector*, November 11, 1895, 2; *Fort Steele Prospector*, November 30, 1895, 3.

13   *Cariboo Sentinel*, September 30, 1865, 1.

14   E. Brian Titley, "Dewdney, Edgar," in *Dictionary of Canadian Biography*, vol. 14, University of Toronto/Université Laval, 2003, http://www.biographi.ca/en/bio/dewdney_edgar_14E.html.

15   Informational poster developed by the Fort Steele Heritage Town, posted at the entrance of the Wild Horse Creek historic site.

16   Laura J. Pasacreta, "White Tigers and Azure Dragons: Overseas Chinese Burial Practices in the Canadian and American West (1850s to 1910s)" (MA

thesis, Simon Fraser University, 2005), 74–75.

17   *Cariboo Sentinel*, July 22, 1865, 2.

18   *Walla Walla Statesman*, June 1, 1866.

19   August 18, 1866, Government Record (hereafter GR) 318, BC Archives.

20   "Early Days in Wild Horse Creek," *Cranbrook Herald*, December 18, 1902, 8.

21   *Cariboo Sentinel*, September 2, 1865, 3.

22   "Millions in Gold," *Fort Steele Prospector*, November 9, 1895, 2.

23   *Cariboo Sentinel*, July 29, 1865, 2.

24   *Cariboo Sentinel*, August 26, 1865, 5.

25   *Cariboo Sentinel*, August 26, 1865, 5.

26   *Evening Telegraph*, July 22, 1866, 3.

27   *Cranbrook Herald*, December 18, 1902, 8.

28   "Birth of Fort Steele," *Cranbrook Herald*, December 20, 1900, 3.

29   "Early Days in Wild Horse Creek," *Cranbrook Herald*, December 18, 1902, 8.

30   "Top Ten Gold Rushes of BC—Part 1," https://www.westcoastplacer.com/tag/wild-horse/; "Birth of Fort Steele," *Cranbrook Herald*, December 20, 1900, 3.

31   "Top Ten Gold Rushes"; Gerry Burnie, "Shootout at Fortier's Café," *In Praise of Canadian History*, July 11, 2013, https://interestingcanadianhistory.word-press.com/2013/07/11/125/.

32   The poster at Fisherville is quoted in full by Hammerson Peters, "Wild Horse Creek—Canada's Forgotten Gold Rush," 2019, mysteriesofcanada.com.

33   "The Columbia River Diggings," *Cariboo Sentinel*, June 24, 1865, 5.

34   "The Galbraiths: First on the Block," *Cranbrook Daily Townsman*, May 15, 2015, www.cranbrooktownsman.com/our-town/the-galbraiths-first-on-the-block/.

35   "Birth of Fort Steele," *Cranbrook Herald*, December 20, 1900, 3.

36   John Ostler, *Geomorphological and Geological Surveys of the Spillway Property*, BC Geological Assessment Report 36622, 2017.

37   "Wild Horse Creek: An Old Time Creek—Constant Producer of the Yellow Metal," *Fort Steele Prospector*, December 28, 1901, 2.

38   "Wild Horse Creek," *Fort Steele Prospector*, December 28, 1901, 2.

39   Pasacreta, "White Tigers and Azure Dragons," 87–88.

40   *Fort Steele Prospector*, August 22, 1896, 1.

41   *Cranbrook Herald*, July 27, 1899, 1.

42   *Cranbrook Herald*, September 7, 1905, 6; *East Kootenay Miner*, August 12, 1897, 4.

43   *Cranbrook Herald*, February 9, 1922, 5.

44   Naomi Miller, "Chinese in the East Kootenays," *British Columbia History* 21, no. 2 (Spring 1988): 16–18.

45   *Fort Steele Prospector*, February 15, 1896, 3.

46   *New Westminster Pacific Canadian*, October 28, 1893, 5.

47   *Golden Era*, December 15, 1894, 2.

48   *Fort Steele Prospector*, January 22, 1898, 2.

49   *Golden Era*, October 17, 1901, 2.

50   *Cranbrook Herald*, December 18, 1902, 8.

51   Naomi Miller, "The Lum and Ban Quan Families," *BC Historical News* 21, no. 2 (1988), 19.

52   Miller, "The Lum and Ban Quan Families," 19.

53   Miller, "The Lum and Ban Quan Families," 19–20.

54   Miller, "The Lum and Ban Quan Families," 20.

55   *Fort Steele Prospector*, April 25, 1896, 2.

56   Miller, "The Lum and Ban Quan Families," 20.

57   Miller, "The Lum and Ban Quan Families," 20.

58   *East Kootenay Miner*, May 31, 1898, 1.

59   Naomi Miller, "Chinese in the East Kootenays," *BC Historical News* 21, no. 2 (Spring 1988), 17.

60   Pasacreta, "White Tigers and Azure Dragons," 84.

61   "Reburial: Exhuming the Dead and Returning Them to China 塵土歸路: 先友回唐 – 墓地 葬仪 过程," Chinese in Northwest America Research Committee (CINARC), http://www.cinarc.org/Death-2.html.

62   Miller, "Chinese in the East Kootenays," 17.

63   BC Heritage Branch, Ministry of Forests, Lands and Natural Resource Operations; historicplaces.ca. The ceremony for this recognition was hosted by Parks Canada.

The Key City: Cranbrook

64   "Cranbrook," *Encyclopedia Britannica*, www.britannica.com/place/Cranbrook-British-Columbia.

65   William A. Sloan, "Cranbrook," *Canadian Encyclopedia*, Historica Canada, last edited March 4, 2015, www.thecanadianencyclopedia.ca/en/article/cranbrook.

66   Cranbrook Community Album, Columbia Basin Institute, 3; Jim Cameron, "The Galbraiths: First on the Block," *Cranbrook Daily Townsman*, May 15, 2015.

67   "Cranbrook Community Album: Introduction," Columbia Basin Institute, basininstitute.org/exhibit-cranbrook/1.html.

68   "Cranbrook Community Album: Joseph's Prairie," Columbia Basin Institute, 3, basininstitute.org/exhibit-cranbrook/3.html.

69   "Crowsnest Pass: Transportation," *Wikipedia, the Free Encyclopedia*, https://en.wikipedia.org/wiki/Crowsnest_Pass.

70   Colonel James Baker served as an MLA from 1886 to 1890, the East Koote-

nay MLA from 1890 to 1898, and East Kootenay South from 1898 to 1900. He also served in the provincial cabinet as provincial secretary and minister of Education, Immigration and Mines. In 1900, he retired to England.

71   "James Baker (Canadian politician)," *Wikipedia, the Free Encyclopedia*, last revision April 28, 2022, https://en.wikipedia.org/w/index.php?title=James_Baker_(Canadian_politician)&oldid=1085051870.

72   "The Town of Cranbrook: Future Capital of S.E. Kootenay," *East Kootenay Miner*, August 5, 1897, 3.

73   *Cranbrook Herald*, October 11, 1900, 1.

74   *East Kootenay Miner*, August 5, 1897, 3.

75   *Cranbrook Herald*, March 22, 1898, 1.

76   *Cranbrook Herald*, April 26, 1898, 3.

77   *Cranbrook Herald*, April 26, 1898, 2.

78   *Cranbrook Herald*, August 11, 1898, 4.

79   "Mining Notes," *Cranbrook Herald*, August 3, 1899, 4; "Chinamen Can Work Under Ground," *Cranbrook Herald*, August 17, 1899, 1.

80   Lily Chow, *Sojourners in the North* (Halfmoon Bay, BC: Caitlin Press, 1996), 173.

81   *Cranbrook Herald*, May 23, 1901, 2.

82   "Cheap Labor Means Cheap People," *Cranbrook Herald*, November 9, 1899, 2.

83   "Local Notes," *Cranbrook Herald*, March 9, 1911, 5.

84   *Cranbrook Herald*, October 12, 1911, 1.

85   *Cranbrook Herald*, June 21, 1898, 1.

86   "Accident to Chinaman," *Cranbrook Herald*, October 16, 1902, 1.

87   *Cranbrook Herald*, April 19, 1900, 1.

88   *Cranbrook Prospector*, June 1, 1907, 6.

89   *Chinese Times*, August 4, 1914, 4.

90   *Cranbrook Prospector*, March 28, 1914, 1.

91   "Enduring Hardship—Chinese Hand Laundry," Canadian Museum of History, historymuseum.ca.

92   *Cranbrook Herald*, October 4, 1900, 2.

93   *Cranbrook Herald*, May 11, 1899, 4.

94   *Cranbrook Herald*, May 31, 1906, 5.

95   *Cranbrook Herald*, December 7, 1899, 1.

96   "Editorial Notes," *Cranbrook Herald*, October 25, 1900, 2.

97   *Cranbrook Herald*, January 31, 1901, 4.

98   *Cranbrook Herald*, November 9, 1911, 1.

99   Jim Cameron, "Chinatown," *Cranbrook Daily Townsman*, March 12, 2015, www.cranbrooktownsman.com/our-town/chinatown.

100   *Cranbrook Herald*, June 8, 1911, 7; June 15, 1911, 2.

101   Jim Cameron, "Chinatown," *Cranbrook Daily Townsman*, March 12, 2015, cranbrooktownsman.com.

102   "Local Notes," *Cranbrook Herald*, May 3, 1906, 5.

103   "Cranbrook Chinese Celebrate," *Cranbrook Herald*, February 29, 1912, 1.

104   *Cranbrook Herald*, January 25, 1900, 1.

105   Chinese New Year's celebrations were described by the *Cranbrook Herald* in numerous years. The quotations here were published in the *Cranbrook Herald*, February 1, 1900, 1.

106   "Local Notes," *Cranbrook Herald*, February 8, 1900, 4.

107   *Cranbrook Herald*, February 13, 1902, 1.

108   *Cranbrook Herald*, October 20, 1898, 3.

109   "Pretty Bit of Superstition," *Cranbrook Herald*, November 8, 1900, 3.

110   *Cranbrook Prospector*, June 1, 1907, 1.

111   *Cranbrook Herald*, November 2, 1899, 3.

112   "Uprising in Chinatown," *Cranbrook Herald*, October 4, 1900, 4.

113   "A Cry of Help," *Cranbrook Prospector*, December 14, 1912, 5.

114   "City Officials Visit Chinatown," *Cranbrook Herald*, April 9, 1914, 1.

115   "Chinaman Is Convicted," *Nelson Daily News*, September 19, 1908, 2.

116   *Cranbrook Herald*, October 5, 1911, 4.

117   *Cranbrook Prospector*, July 29, 1911, 4.

118   "A Chinese Suicide?," *Cranbrook Herald*, August 1, 1912.

119   *Nelson Daily News*, September 13, 1912, 1.

120   *Cranbrook Herald*, August 24, 1905, 2.

121   *Cranbrook Herald*, April 7, 1921, 6.

122   "Police Raid in Chinatown," *Cranbrook Herald*, April 2, 1914, 1.

123   "Mah Sing, Chinaman Again in Toils; Secures Six Months Berth in City Jail for Selling and Smoking Opium," *Cranbrook Herald*, June 11, 1914, 1.

124   *Cranbrook Herald*, July 9, 1914, 1.

125   "Republic of China (1912–1949)," *Wikipedia, the Free Encyclopedia*, https://en.wikipedia.org/wiki/Republic_of_China_(1912%E2%80%931949).

126   "Cranbrook Chinamen Will Celebrate," *Cranbrook Prospector*, February 24, 1912, 1.

127   "Cranbrook Chinese Celebrate," *Cranbrook Herald*, February 29, 1912, 1.

128   This passage is an excerpt from *The Week*, reproduced by the *Cranbrook Herald* on February 29, 1912, 1.

129   "Song Jiaoren: Chinese Politician," *Encyclopedia Britannica*, www.britannica.com/biography/Song-Jiaoren.

130   "Inaugural Meeting of Local Chinese National League," *Cranbrook Herald*, January 6, 1921, 2.

131   "Local Chinese Memorialize US Govt. as to Conference," *Cranbrook Herald*, October 6, 1921, 2.

132   "Chinese Celebration Tenth Anniversary of New Republic," *Cranbrook Herald*, October 13, 1921, 1.

133   *Cranbrook Herald*, October 20, 1921, 6.

134   *Cranbrook Herald*, November 17, 1921, 1.

135   Chow, *Sojourners in the North*, 13.

136   Chow, *Sojourners in the North*, 175.

137   Lily Chow, *Blossoms in the Gold Mountains* (Halfmoon Bay, BC: Caitlin Press, 2018), 93.

138   This translation is an extract/summary of the denunciation published in the *Chinese Times* on July 22, 1921, 3.

139   *Cranbrook Herald*, February 2, 1922, 6.

140   *Cranbrook Herald*, February 23, 1922, 6.

141   "Local News," *Cranbrook Herald*, February 9, 1922, 6.

142   "Chinese Assault Case Up for Trial by Judge Thompson," *Cranbrook Herald*, May 18, 1922, 1.

143   *Cranbrook Herald*, May 18, 1922, 1; May 25, 1922, 1.

144   *Chinese Times*, August 24, 1922, 3.

145   *Chinese Times*, December 10, 1923, 6. Only the executive members were listed and translated, not the names of the other board members.

146   *Chinese Times*, December 17, 1923, 1.

147   *Chinese Times*, January 14, 1924, 3.

148   Chow, *Sojourners in the North*, 173.

149   *Cranbrook Herald*, March 21, 1924, 6.

150   "Local Happenings," *Cranbrook Herald*, August 8, 1924, 4.

151   *Cranbrook Herald*, March 4, 1926, 5.

152   "Obsequies of Chinese Merchant Are Very Largely Attended," *Cranbrook Herald*, May 14, 1925.

153   "Chinese Building Damaged," *Cranbrook Herald*, June 3, 1926, 1.

154   *Chinese Times*, November 8, 1928, 2.

155   *Cranbrook Courier*, February 21, 1952, 1.

156   "Chinese Masons Rebuild," *Cranbrook Herald*, May 29, 1952; Columbia Basin Institute (0051.0261), 1.

157   Jim and Helen Chiu, interview with the author, Cranbrook, August 2001.

158   Eva Kwong, interview with the author at the Golden Star Restaurant, Cranbrook, August 20, 2001.

159   Mrs. Cai Zhong Lan Ma, interview with the author at the Champion House Restaurant, Cranbrook, August 12, 2001.

160   Peter Mar, interview with the author, Cranbrook, August 20, 2001.

161   Mrs. Mar, interview with the author, Cranbrook, August 20, 2001.

Once the Farwell Town: Revelstoke

162   B.R. Whalen and Mary Kline, *Revelstoke Diversity Action Plan*, updated March 2015 by Laura Stovel (Revelstoke, BC: n.p., 2015), 2.

163   Cathy English, *Brown Bag History*. Vol. 1. *Revelstoke Origins* (Revelstoke, BC: Revelstoke Museum & Archives, 2015), 2.

164   *Daily Colonist*, January 17, 1884, 1.

165   "How the Station Was Built a Mile and a Half Away," *Revelstoke Kootenay Star*, February 6, 1892, 1.

166   *Daily Colonist*, January 17, 1884, 3.

167   "Provincial Prerogatives," *Daily Colonist*, October 27, 1893, 6.

168   "Provincial Prerogatives," *Daily Colonist*, October 27, 1893, 6.

169   "From Farwell to Revelstoke," Revelstoke Museum, revelstokemuseum.ca.

170   *Daily Colonist*, January 17, 1884.

171   *Daily Colonist*, June 5, 1885, 3.

172   *Daily Colonist*, March 26, 1886, 3.

173   *Kootenay Star*, February 6, 1892, 1.

174   Margaret McMahon, *Pioneers of Revelstoke, British Columbia* (Revelstoke, BC: Revelstoke Senior Citizen Association, 1986), 152.

175   *Daily Colonist*, March 14, 1893, 1.

176   "The History of Revelstoke," Revelstoke Museum & Archives, revelstokemuseum.ca.

177   Pierre Berton, *The Great Railway: The National Dream/The Last Spike* (Toronto: McClelland & Stewart, 1974), 295–96.

178   Lily Siewsan Chow, *Blood and Sweat over the Railway Tracks* (Vancouver: Chinese Canadian Historical Society of British Columbia, Initiative for Student Teaching and Research in Chinese Canadian Studies at UBC, 2014), 31–32.

179   "Wing Chung," Revelstoke Museum & Archives, revelstokemuseum.ca.

180   *Kootenay Star*, September 27, 1890, 4.

181   *Revelstoke Kootenay Star*, September 27, 1890, 4; November 1, 1890, 4.

182   *Vancouver Sun*, Centennial edition, July 4, 1938, 38.

183   *Kootenay Star*, June 28, 1890, 3.

184   "Our Member's Visit," *Kootenay Star*, February 21, 1891, 4.

185   *Kootenay Star*, February 21, 1891, 4.

186   *Kootenay Star*, November 21, 1891, 3.

187   *Kootenay Star*, February 10, 1894, 1.

188   "He Never Came Back," *Kootenay Mail*, November 23, 1895, 1.

189   "Seeking a Skeleton," *Kootenay Mail*, April 30, 1898, 1.

190   "The Mysterious Skeleton," *Revelstoke Herald*, May 4, 1898, 1, 4.

191   This report from Revelstoke was published in the *Golden Era*, a newspaper published in Golden, BC. "A Chinese Funeral," *Golden Era*, January 16, 1897, 2.

192   This description of the funeral rite was also reprinted in the *Golden Era* newspaper, accessed via the Revelstoke Museum & Archives, revelstokemuseum.ca.

193   *Revelstoke Mail*, January 16, 1897, 4.

194   *Revelstoke Herald*, January 18, 1897.

195   *Revelstoke Herald*, May 7, 1898, 5.

196   "Rogers' Pass Tragedy," *Revelstoke Herald*, February 4, 1899, 1; "Rogers Pass Station Snowslide, 1899," Revelstoke Museum & Archives, revelstokemuseum.ca.

197   *Kootenay Mail*, September 2, 1905, 4.

198   *Kootenay Mail*, July 16, 1913.

199   "Fearful Filth," *Kootenay Mail*, September 30, 1899, 1.

200   *Kootenay Mail*, September 30, 1899, 1.

201   *Kootenay Mail*, September 30, 1899, 1.

202   "Chinatown As It Is," *Kootenay Mail*, October 14, 1899, 1.

203   *Revelstoke Herald*, October 30, 1901, 2.

204   *Revelstoke Herald*, November 22, 1901, 2.

205   *Revelstoke Herald*, November 20, 1901, 1.

206   *Chinese Times*, March 29, 1911.

207   *Revelstoke Review*, January 22, 1920, 3.

208   *Revelstoke Review*, June 3, 1920, 1.

209   *Revelstoke Review*, March 31, 1921, 3.

210   Information obtained from the property locations file at the Revelstoke Museum & Archives.

211   *Revelstoke Mail Herald*, September 12, 1914, 3; November 28, 1914, 8.

212   *Revelstoke Herald*, November 2, 1901, 2.

213   *Revelstoke Herald*, January 29, 1903, 8; originally printed in the *Nelson News*.

214   *Revelstoke Mail Herald*, February 1, 1913, 7.

215   *Revelstoke Mail Herald*, September 12, 1914, 3.

216   *Revelstoke Mail Herald*, September 16, 1914, 1.

217   *Revelstoke Mail Herald*, November 28, 1914, 8.

218   *Revelstoke Review*, September 8, 1933, 1.

219   Lisa Smedman, *Vancouver Courier*, August 5, 2004.

220   *Revelstoke Review*, February 19, 1932, 5.

221   M. Gale Smith, "Chinese Market Gardening in BC," British Columbia

Food History Network, 2017, bcfoodhistory.ca.

222 "Chinese Vegetables," *Revelstoke Herald*, April 3, 1901, 1.

223 "Chinese Vegetables," *Revelstoke Herald*, April 3, 1901, 1.

224 "Yes Wee Can: Study Gives Green Light to Use Urine as Crop Fertilizer," *The Guardian*, January 22, 2020, theguardian.com.

225 Canada 150 Timeline, https://www.revelstokemountaineer.com/canada-150-timeline-cool-facts-about-revelstoke-you-probably-didnt-know/.

226 *Revelstoke Review*, February 12, 1920, 1; February 26, 1920, 1.

227 *Revelstoke Review*, April 15, 1920, 1.

228 *Revelstoke Review*, February 17, 1921, 1.

229 *Revelstoke Review*, February 24, 1921, 1.

230 *Revelstoke Review*, January 13, 1921, 1.

231 *Revelstoke Review*, December 13, 1922, 6.

232 *Kootenay Star*, September 27, 1890, 4.

233 *Kootenay Mail*, February 2, 1895, 4.

234 *Nelson Miner*, October 25, 1898, 1, 2.

235 *Kootenay Mail*, November 4, 1905, 3.

236 *Revelstoke Herald*, April 19, 1899, 4.

237 *Revelstoke Herald*, October 23, 1901, 4.

238 *Kootenay Mail*, November 4, 1905, 4.

239 Sham Lai Mee, Donald and Georgina Mee, eds., *as given and remembered, Revelstoke Review: History & Heritage,* September 19, 1990.

240 *Revelstoke Review*, January 20, 1921.

241 Chow, *Blossoms in the Gold Mountains*, 94.

242 *Revelstoke Review*, January 5, 1956, 4.

243 Chow, *Blossoms in the Gold Mountains*, 103.

244 Ron Kwong, interview with the author, Revelstoke, June 30, 2020.

245 Lisa Smedman, *Vancouver Courier*, August 5, 2004.

246 *Revelstoke Review*, March 11, 1925.

247 *Revelstoke Review*, April 11, 1923, 1.

248 All the deaths from 1925 to 1945 were recorded in Vital Events at the Revelstoke Museum & Archives.

249 Information gathered from the Mountain View Cemetery Directory, Revelstoke in 2002. The ages of many deceased were not specified.

The Queen City: Nelson

250 Dick Dar, *Nelson: The Queen City of the Kootenays* (Nelson, BC: Chinese Youth Association, July 1, 1954), 18.

251 *Nelson Miner*, June 21, 1890, 3.

252   *Nelson Tribune,* June 21, 1890.

253   Art Joyce, *Nelson Daily News,* Heritage Beat Section, December 17, 1999.

254   Shawn Lamb, *A Brief History of Nelson,* Touchstones Nelson: Museum of Art and History, 2000.

255   *Nelson Miner,* September 6, 1890, 1.

256   *Nelson Miner,* August 16, 1890, 8; both Chinese and First Nations people were disenfranchised in 1872.

257   *Nelson Miner,* August 22, 1891, 12.

258   "To Their Credit Be It Said," *Ainsworth Hot Spring News,* February 10, 1892, 1; *Nelson Daily News,* July 5, 1904, 2.

259   *British Columbia Directory,* 1892.

260   *Nelson Miner,* July 7, 1894, 4.

261   Appendix 1, *BC Directory,* 1892, lists the Chinese businesses and organizations in Nelson's Chinatown.

262   Shawn Lamb's reference card in the Touchstones Nelson Museum. Actually, in 1895, there was a Samuel Mar laundry listed in Nelson without a mailing address in the *British Columbia Directory,* 130.

263   *Nelson Tribune,* April 2, 1898, 3.

264   Art Joyce, "The Chinese in the West Kootenay," Part 4: "A Neglected History: The Chinese Laundry Controversy," *Nelson Daily News,* January 7, 2000.

265   "Laundry By-law Upheld," *Nelson Daily News,* June 11, 1905, 3.

266   *Wrigley's British Columbia Directory, 1922,* 446.

267   Greg Nesteroff, "Chinese Canadian Pioneers of West Kootenay: Mar Sam," *The Kütne Reader,* March 4, 2018, https://gregnesteroff.wixsite.com/kutne-reader/post/pioneer-chinese-canadians-of-west-kootenay-mar-sam.

268   *Wrigley's British Columbia Directory* lists this address in the 1923 and 1924 editions, among others.

269   *Nelson Daily Miner,* December 2, 1898, 3.

270   *Nelson Tribune,* January 20, 1984, 1.

271   *Nelson Daily Miner,* December 2, 1898, 3; Greg Nesteroff, "An Anonymous Woman also Began Offering English Classes."

272   *Nelson Daily Miner,* December 6, 1898, 2, 3.

273   *Nelson Miner,* November 1, 1898, 2.

274   "A Funny Burial Service: How John Chinaman Is Laid to His Long Last Rest," *Nelson Daily Miner,* April 29, 1899, 3.

275   *Nelson Daily Miner,* April 29, 1899, 2.

276   *Nelson Daily News,* November 29, 1910, 4.

277   Shawn Lamb, archivist, Touchstones Nelson: Museum of Art and History.

278   *Nelson Daily Miner,* March 17, 1899, 2.

279   *Nelson Economist,* May 4, 1898, 3.

280   See Chinese businesses in Nelson's Chinatown in Appendix I, *BC Directory*, 1892.

281   "Their New Year: Chinamen Are Celebrating in Royal Style," *Nelson Daily Miner*, February 10, 1899, 3.

282   *Nelson Tribune*, May 7, 1898, 1.

283   *Nelson Tribune*, May 19, 1900, 1.

284   The quotation from the *Nelson Tribune* was included in Art Joyce, "Hidden in Plain Sight," Heritage Beat, *Nelson Daily News*, ~2016.

285   Information supplied by Greg Nesteroff and Shawn Lamb.

286   *Nelson Daily Miner*, May 31, 1901, 1.

287   *Nelson Economist*, 1901.

288   Shawn Lamb, Touchstones Nelson: Museum of Art and History, memorandum, 2001.

289   *Nelson Daily Miner*, September 4, 1911, 1.

290   "Firebug Makes Another Attempt," *Nelson Daily News*, August 21, 1911, 1.

291   *Wrigley's British Columbia Directory, 1922*; this is not a comprehensive list of Chinese businesses, but a representative one.

292   "Another Tax for Chinese," *Nelson Daily News*, April 29, 1902, 1.

293   Bing's immigration certificate number is 8999.

294   Greg Nesteroff, "Chinese-Canadian Pioneers of Western Kootenay: Charlie Bing," February 3, 2019, updated July 12, https://gregnesteroff.wixsite.com/kutnereader/post/chinese-canadian-pioneers-of-west-kootenay-boundary-charlie-bing.

295   "Chinese Charlie Rode 'Em!", *Vancouver Province*, August 28, 1948.

296   *The Ledger*, July 4, 1912, 4.

297   "Horse Riding Days of Charlie Bing Recalled," *Nelson Daily News*, September 1, 1948, 2.

298   Eva Wrangle (née Bing), interview by Brenda Hornley, 1999; transcript received from Nelson Touchstones: Museum of Art and History.

299   *Nelson Daily News*, March 14, 1944.

300   "Chinese Graduate from Local High School to Leave for Coast Shortly," *Nelson Daily News*, October 21, 1922, 3; "Shu Tong Mar Escapes from the Old Folks," *Nelson Daily News*, November 28, 1922, 3.

301   Art Joyce, "The Two Threads Finally Meet Again," *Nelson Daily News*, March 10, 2000, 13.

302   Lawrence Mar, interview with the author, Nelson, August 14, 2001.

303   Chow, *Blossoms in the Gold Mountains*, 47, 61.

304   The earlier address is noted in a memorandum at Touchstones Nelson and the later address was supplied by Greg Nesteroff. The information has been verified with *Wrigley's British Columbia Directory*.

305   Cameron Mah, interview with the author at Mr. Mah's residence, Nelson, August 14, 2001. Mr. Mah passed away on June 8, 2019.

306   *Chinese Times*, July 22, 1921, 3.

307   This interviewee requested anonymity.

308   *Nelson Daily News*, March 23, 1904, 4.

309   *Nelson Daily News*, October 6, 1905; "Awakening of China," *Nelson Daily News*, October 11, 1905, 1.

310   Zhang Lei, *Kang Youwei, Liang Qichao and The Reform Movement* (China: Guangdong, Nanhai, and Xinhui Museums, June 12, 1998), 21–30.

311   *Nelson Daily News*, November 1, 1911, 5.

312   *Nelson Daily News*, November 1, 1911, 5.

313   "Yuan Shikai," *Wikipedia, the Free Encyclopedia*, https://en.wikipedia.org/wiki/Yuan_Shikai.

314   *Nelson Daily News*, August 15 and 27, 1917.

315   Chow, *Sojourners in the North*, 183.

316   Kutenai West Heritage Consulting, *West Kootenay Chinese Heritage Society, Summary Report, 1995* (Trail, BC: Kutenai West Heritage Consulting, 1995), 64.

317   *Chinese Times*, March 12, 1920, 3.

318   *Chinese Times*, sixteenth day of the eleventh moon of the ninth year of the Chinese republic, 3.

319   Art Joyce, "Nelson's Chinatown: A Tale of Two Families," *Nelson Daily News*, February 18, 2000, 13.

320   Chinese immigrants had the right to vote in the early days, but they were disenfranchised in 1872.

321   Soong Mei Ling was the wife of Chiang Kai-Shek, and Soong Qing Ling was the second wife of Sun Yat-sen.

322   "Chinese Community Fetes the New Year," *Nelson Daily News*, January 7, 1952; January 9, 1952.

323   "New Officers of the Nelson Chinese Nationalist League," *Nelson Daily News*, January 8, 1952.

324   "China Clippers Newest Cage Threat," *Nelson Daily News*, March 18, 1952.

325   Lawrence Mar, interview with the author, Nelson, August 14, 2001.

326   All the information about the Nelson Chinese Youth Association was obtained from the 1954 yearbook.

327   Lawrence Mar and Mrs. Mar, interview with the author, August 14, 2001.

328   "Pillar of Nelson's Chinese Community dies at 72," *Nelson Star*, June 12, 2019, https://www.nelsonstar.com/news/a-pillar-of-nelsons-chinese-community/.

329   Cameron Mah, interview with the author, August 14, 2001.

330   Chow, *Sojourners in the North*, 146.

331   Greg Nesteroff, "Following in his Grandparents' Footsteps," *Nelson Star*, January 22, 2012, https://www.nelsonstar.com/news/following-in-his-grandparents-footsteps/.

332   Cameron Mah, interview with the author, August 14, 2001.

333   Henry Stevenson passed away at the age of 99 on June 1, 2015, and Audrey Stevenson passed away at the age of 92 on November 18, 2018.

334   Henry and Audrey Stevenson, interview with the author, Nelson, August 17, 2001.

335   This list does not include the late Cameron Mah, who died in Nelson on June 8, 2019.

336   Greg Nesteroff, "Nelson Heritage Building Rises from the Ashes," *Nelson Star*, October 4, 2019, https://www.nelsonstar.com/business/nelson-heritage-building-rises-from-the-ashes/.

The Golden City: Rossland

337   "Rossland, British Columbia," *Wikipedia: The Free Encyclopedia*, https://en.wikipedia.org/wiki/Rossland,_British_Columbia.

338   Chic Scott, *Powder Pioneers: Ski Stories from the Canadian Rockies and Columbia Mountains* (Vancouver: Rocky Mountain Books, 2005), 20.

339   Rosa Jordan and Derek Choukalos, *Rossland: The First 100 Years* (Rossland, BC: Rossland Museum Association, 1995), 2.

340   *Sunshine Coast News*, September 7, 1976, 10.

341   *British Colonist*, January 16, 1898, 5.

342   *British Colonist*, January 16, 1898, 5; Michael R. Ripmeester, "Placed on the Margins: The Idea of Chinatown in Rossland, British Columbia, 1890–1902," *Mining History Journal* 4 (1997); *Henderson's British Columbia Gazetteer and Directory and Mining Companies for 1899-1900*, vol. 6 (Victoria and Vancouver: Henderson Publishing Company, 1899).

343   *West Kootenay Chinese Heritage Society, Summary Report, 1995*, 192.

344   Lily Siewsan Chow, *Blood and Sweat over the Railway Tracks* (Vancouver: Chinese Canadian Historical Society of British Columbia, Initiative for Student Teaching and Research in Chinese Canadian Studies, and UBC, 2014), 37–39.

345   Chow, *Blood and Sweat*, 2.

346   Michael R. Ripmeester, "Everyday Life in the Golden City: Historical Geography of Rossland" (MA thesis, University of British Columbia, September 1990), 143.

347   *East Kootenay Miner*, March 3, 1898, 1.

348   *Cranbrook Herald*, October 20, 1898, 1.

349   Ripmeester, "Placed on the Margins," 32.

350   Ronald A. Shearer, "The Chinese and Chinatown of Rossland: Fragments from Their Early History," 2nd ed., 1.

351   *West Kootenay Chinese Heritage Society, Summary Report, 1995*, 196.

352   *West Kootenay Chinese Heritage Society, Summary Report, 1995*, 196.

353   Shearer, "The Chinese and Chinatown of Rossland," 4–5.

354   The list from *Henderson's British Columbia Gazetteer and Directory and Mining Companies for 1899–1900* was included in *West Kootenay Chinese Heritage Society, Summary Report, 1995*, 192.

355   *West Kootenay Chinese Heritage Society, Summary Report, 1995*, 192.

356   *West Kootenay Chinese Heritage Society, Summary Report, 1995*, 207.

357   Rossland Historical Museum Association, *Historical Guide Map and Story of the City of Rossland, British Columbia* (Rossland, BC: Rossland Historical Museum Association, 1958); Legacy Initiatives Advisory Council, *Recognizing Chinese Canadian History in British Columbia: Historic Places Nomination Report*, July 28, 2015, 15.

358   *West Kootenay Chinese Heritage Society Summary Report*, 207.

359   *West Kootenay Chinese Heritage Society Summary Report*, 192.

360   Shearer, "The Chinese and Chinatown of Rossland," 17.

361   Ronald Mah, interview with the author, Rossland, August 14, 2001.

362   Allyson Kenning, "Joe Lui: Uncovering Rossland's Chinese History," *Rossland Telegraph*, November 23, 2010, https://rosslandtelegraph.com/news/lui-joe-uncovering-rosslands-chinese-history-8400#.YalktfHMJuU.

363   *Rossland Miner*, May 2, 1903.

364   Allyson Kenning, "Legends and Tales of the Mountain Kingdom: Rossland's Most Infamous Murderer… an Eight-year-old Boy?," *Rossland Telegraph*, April 24, 2012, https://rosslandtelegraph.com/news/legends-and-tales-mountain-kingdom-rossland%E2%80%99s-most-infamous-murderer-an-eight-year-old-boy-18691#.Yalm5PHMJuU.

365   Kenning, "Legends and Tales of the Mountain Kingdom."

366   Kenning, "Legends and Tales of the Mountain Kingdom."

367   *Nelson Daily Miner*, October 23, 1900, 1.

368   *Nelson Tribune*, October 24, 1900, 1.

369   *Nelson Tribune*, October 24, 1900, 1.

370   Legacy Initiatives Advisory Council, *Recognizing Chinese Canadian History in BC: Historic Places Nomination Report*, July 28, 2015, 13.

371   James R.Q. Bliss, " 'A Criminal in One Place, a Gentleman in Another': Regulating Early Canadian Gambling Venues" (LL.M thesis, University of British Columbia, 2000).

372   *Nelson Economist*, January 19, 1898, 2.

373   Suzanne Morton, *At Odds: Gambling and Canadians, 1919–1969* (Toronto: University of Toronto Press, 2003), 142.

374   Shearer, "The Chinese and Chinatown of Rossland," 12.

375   Jamie Bliss, *Kootenay Mountain Culture Magazine*, 6.

376   *Rossland Daily News*, February 25, 1913, 8.

377   Shearer, "The Chinese and Chinatown of Rossland," 1.

378   Presumably, Crowe was referring to the costumes used to represent these animals, certainly not the live ones.

379   This area was known as the Cathleen Apartment until 1960s. *West Kootenay Chinese Heritage Society, Summary Report, 1995*, 207.

380   Lou Crowe was the interviewee. This interview was conducted by Kutenai West Heritage Consulting and published in the *West Kootenay Chinese Heritage Society Summary Report, 1995*, 207.

381   The late Cameron Mah, the brother of Ron Mah, shared this information.

382   *West Kootenay Chinese Heritage Society, Summary Report, 1995*, 198.

383   Legacy Initiatives Advisory Council British Columbia: Historic Places Nominations Report 13, July 28, 2015.

Afterword

384   *Cranbrook Herald*, May 31, 1906, 5.

385   Chow, *Blood and Sweat*.

386   "Their New Year: Chinamen Are Celebrating in Royal Style," *Nelson Daily Miner*, February 10, 1899, 3.

387   *Nelson Daily Miner*, May 31, 1901, 1.

Bibliography

Books

Berton, Pierre. *The Great Railway: The National Dream and the Last Spike.* Toronto: McClelland & Stewart, 1974.

Chow, Lily. *Sojourners in the North.* Halfmoon Bay, BC: Caitlin Press, 1996.

———. *Blood and Sweat over the Railway Tracks.* Vancouver: Chinese Canadian Historical Society of British Columbia, Initiative for Student Teaching and Research in Chinese Canadian Studies at UBC, 2014.

———. *Blossoms in the Gold Mountains.* Halfmoon Bay, BC: Caitlin Press, 2018.

English, Cathy. *Revelstoke—Creating a Community. Brown Bag History*, 2 vols. Revelstoke, BC: Revelstoke Museum and Archives, 2018.

Jordan, Rosa, and Derek Choukalos. *Rossland: First 100 Years.* Rossland, BC: Rossland Museum Association, 1955.

McMahon, Margaret. *Pioneers of Revelstoke, British Columbia.* Revelstoke, BC. Revelstoke Senior Citizens Association, 1986.

Rossland Historical Museum Association. *Historical Guide Map and Story of the City of Rossland, British Columbia.* Rossland: Rossland Historical Museum Association, 1958.

Smith, Charleen P., Jonathan Swainger, and Constance Backhouse, eds. *People and Place: Historical Influence on Legal Culture.* Vancouver: UBC Press 2003.

Williams, R. David. *Call in Pinkerton's: American Detectives at Work for Canada.* Toronto: Dundurn Press, 1998.

Articles

Burnie, Gerry. "In Praise of Canadian History: Shooting at Fortier's Café." In Praise of Canadian History, interestingcanadianhistory.wordpress.com, July 11, 2013.

Kenning, Allyson. "Legends and Tales of the Mountain Kingdom: Rossland's Most Infamous Murderer... an Eight-year-old Boy?" *Rossland Telegraph*, April 24, 2012.

Miller, Naomi. "Chinese in the East Kootenay." *British Columbia Historical News* 21, no. 2 (1988).

———. "The Lum and Ban Quan Families." *British Columbia Historical News* 21, no. 2 (1988).

Ripmeester, Michael R. "Placed on the Margins: The Idea of Chinatown in Rossland, British Columbia, 1890–1902." *Mining History Journal* (1997): 31–44.

Ross, Edward Douglas. "Barkerville in Context: Archaeology of the Chinese in British Columbia." *BC Studies* 185 (Spring 2015): 161–92.

Shearer, Ronald A. "The Chinese and Chinatown of Rossland: Fragments from Their Early History." Rossland, BC: Rossland Museum, August 14, 2018, rosslandmuseum.ca.

Theses

Bilsland, W. William. "A History of Revelstoke and the Big Bend." MA thesis, University of British Columbia, 1955.

Bliss, James R.Q. " 'A Criminal in One place, A Gentleman in Another': Regulating Early Canadian Gambling Venues." LL.M thesis, University of British Columbia, 2000.

Pasacreta, Laura J. "White Tigers and Azure Dragons: Overseas Chinese Burial Practices in the Canadian and American West (1850s to 1910s)." MA thesis, Simon Fraser University, 2005.

Ripmeester, Michael R. "Everyday Life in the Golden City: A Historical Geography of Rossland, British Columbia." MA thesis, University of British Columbia, 1990.

Smith, Charleen, P. "Regulating Prostitution in British Columbia, 1895–1930." MA thesis, University of Calgary, 2001.

Government Records

GR 318, 1866

GR 0429 –1903: Attorney General, inward correspondence.

Events and Reports

Recognition of Wild Horse Creek as a Provincial Heritage Site, BC Heritage Branch, Ministry of Forests, Lands and Natural Resource Operations. The ceremony for this recognition was assisted by Parks Canada.

Minister of Mines, 1874, 1900.

Kutenai West Heritage Consulting, *West Kootenay Chinese Heritage Society, Summary Report, 1995*. Trail, BC: Kutenai West Heritage Consulting, 1995.

Legacy Initiative Advisory Council: Recognizing Chinese Canadian History in British Columbia, Historic Places Nomination Report, July 28, 2015.

Ministry of Energy, Mining Division: Fort Steele, BC Geological Survey, 2017.

Newspapers

Boundary Creek Times, 1896
British Colonist, 1898
Cariboo Sentinel, 1862–72
Chinese Times (in Chinese), 1914, 1920, 1923
Columbia Basin Institute, 1952
Cranbrook Herald, 1865, 1898–1902, 1905–06, 1908, 1911–12, 1914, 1921–22, 1940
Cranbrook Daily Townsman, 2015
Cranbrook Prospector, 1912–1914
Daily Colonist, 1884, 1893
East Kootenay Miner, 1897–99
Evening Telegraph, 1866
Fort Steele Prospector, 1895–1896
Golden Era, 1894, 1901
Kootenay Star, 1890, 1891
Kootenay Mail
Kootenay Review
Nelson Daily Miner, 1900
Nelson Daily News, 1908–1912
Nelson Miner, 1898
Pacific Canadian, 1894
Revelstoke Herald, 1901
Revelstoke Review, 1920, 1921
Rossland Telegraph
Vancouver Courier, August 5, 2004
Vancouver Sun, 1938

Interviews

Cai Yi Hai, Cranbrook, August 12, 2001.
Chui, Jim and Helen, Cranbrook, August 2001.
Kwong, Eva, Cranbrook, August 20, 2001.
Ma Zhong Lan, Cranbrook, August 12, 2001.
Mah, Cameron, Nelson, August 14, 2001.
Mah, Ronald, Rossland, August 14, 2001.
Mar, Lawrence, Nelson, August 14, 2001.
Mar, Peter, Cranbrook, August 20, 2001.
Mar, Mrs. Peter, Cranbrook, August 20, 2001.

Stevenson, Henry and Audrey, Nelson, August 17, 2001.

Wong, Lindsay, Rossland, August 15, 2001.

Wrangle, Eva (nee Bing), interview by Brenda Hornley, Nelson, 1999.

Websites

Britannica, https://www.britannica.com

Canadian Museum of History, historymuseum.ca

Cranbrook Daily Townsman, https://www.cranbrooktownsman.com

Columbia Basin Institute, https://basininstitute.org

Dictionary of Canadian Biography, http://www.biographi.ca

First Voices, https://www.firstvoices.com

Stinger Resources, "Gold Hill," https://stingerresources.com/?page_id=122

West Coast Placer, https://www.westcoastplacer.com/tag/wild-horse/

Wikipedia, the Free Encyclopedia, https://en.wikipedia.org

Directories

British Columbia Directory, various years.

Henderson's British Columbia Gazetteer and Directory and Mining Companies for 1899–1900, vol. 6. Victoria and Vancouver: Henderson Publishing Company, 1899.

Wrigley's British Columbia Directory, vol. 5. Vancouver: Wrigley Directories, Ltd., 1922.

Acknowledgements

Many kind and wonderful individuals, institutions and organizations in the Kootenay provided support and assistance to me while I was searching for historical information about Chinese immigration and settlements in this region. When I began exploring the history of the Chinese in the Kootenay, it was necessary for me to visit local museums and archives, and ask the curators and archivists at these institutions for guidance and assistance. Many of them allowed me to go through the files in which historical information about the livelihood of early Chinese immigrants were kept. Some of the managers at these museums introduced me to local historians, journalists and well-known Chinese Canadians in their communities. These wonderful citizens shared their findings with me—stories that reflected the endeavours and great efforts made by the early Chinese immigrants to make their lives possible and comfortable living in these new areas.

This book would not have been published without the blessing of and encouragement from Vici Johnstone, the publisher at Caitlin Press, to whom I offer my sincere thanks. To this end, I am also grateful to Catherine Edwards, the editor who has fine-tuned my writing; to Sarah Corsie, the editorial and production manager, who worked on compilation and design as well as locating illustrations; and to Malaika Aleba, the marketing director, who has promoted and publicized this book.

In fall 2001, I visited the Rossland Museum & Discovery Centre to carry out research. Joyce Austin, the curator and manager of the centre, allowed me to go through the files that contained information about the first Chinese immigrants in Rossland and the early Chinatown. While I was in Rossland, I met and interviewed Ronald Mah, a merchant, who took me to the deserted Chinese vegetable gardens and told me the history of the Chinese immigrants and settlements in Rossland. In 2018, Dr. Ronald A. Shearer, an emeritus professor of economics at the University of British Columbia, published an essay entitled "The Chinese and Chinatown of Rossland: Fragments from Their Early History." In his essay, he included a list of the registered deaths of Chinese men in Rossland from 1900 to 1986. I asked him to allow me to include this data in my book, and he graciously gave me his permission to do so. I acknowledge the contributions of this wonderful lady and these gentlemen to my research.

Following my visit to Rossland, I visited the Revelstoke Museum & Archives. Cathy English, the curator at the archives there, gave me permission to go through all the collections, and to copy the necessary information about Chinese immigrants and settlements in Revelstoke. In the museum, Margaret McMahon, the author of *Pioneers of Revelstoke, British Columbia*, gave me a copy of her publication. In this book, McMahon documented the history of Wong Kwong and Yee Von, who established and operated a laundry and other businesses in Revelstoke, and who took care of the aged and sick Chinese immigrants in the city. In later years, English sent me copies of early twentieth-century issues of the *Revelstoke Review*, a newspaper that reported on the Chinese-Canadian history in the East Kootenay, including the activities in Revelstoke's Chinatown. She also introduced me to Barry Kwong, a grandson of Wong Kwong and Yee Von. This gentleman shared with me the history of his grandparents. As well, he gave me contact information for his cousin, Ron Kwong. The two cousins shared with me their perspectives about living in Revelstoke. To these two ladies and the Kwong descendants, I extend my heartfelt thanks.

I met Derryll White, the former curator of the Fort Steele Heritage Town and its museum and archives. He allowed me to go through the documents containing historical information about the Chinese miners and immigrants who made their living at Wild Horse Creek. He gave me an image of the Chinese altar that was in the Chinatown at Wild Horse Creek, near the location of Fisherville, once a prosperous town in the gold-mining area. The staff of the historic town accompanied me to the deserted site of Chinatown on Wild Horse Creek. While I was at the Fort Steele Heritage Town, I had the opportunity to meet Naomi Miller, a historian who generously shared with me her contacts with the Lum and Chu families in the area. As a result, I had the opportunity to meet Pete Lum and his grand-niece, Ingrid Lum. In the past year, Susanna Ng, the Head of Interpretation and Content Development at Vancouver's Chinatown Storytelling Centre, sent me links related to Jack Lee, a famous Chinese miner at Wild Horse Creek. I acknowledge these historians and the staff of the Fort Steele Heritage Town, as well as the Lum family members.

In Cranbrook, I interviewed the late James Chiu, a Rotary governor, and his wife, Helen Chiu, as well as Eva Kwong, Cai Yi Hai, Ma Zhong Lan, and Peter Mar and his wife, who immigrated to Canada after the repeal of the infamous Chinese Exclusion Act in 1947. They all shared with me their stories of immigration and their experiences living in an adopted country. Through an introduction made by John Haugen, a member of the Nlaka'pamux Nation

Tribal Council in the village of Lytton, I was able to contact Margaret Teneese, a Ktunaxa Nation Council member and the head of the Cranbrook Museum. Teneese introduced me to David Humphrey, the curator of the museum. Humphrey is a kind and generous person who sent me an image of the Chinese Chee Kung Tong building and some documents about the early Chinese immigrants and Chinatown in Cranbrook. To all these wonderful and helpful people, I offer my appreciation.

In Nelson, I interviewed the late Cameron Mah, who was hailed as a pillar of the Chinese community, and Lawrence Mar, who had been the chair of the Guomindang in the city. Mah told me that there had been a Chinatown, and he gave me a copy of a magazine written in both Chinese and English that was published by a Chinese Youth Organization in Nelson. In addition, Mah introduced Shawn Lamb to me. Lamb was the archivist and curator at the Touchstones Nelson: Museum of Art and History, and she shared with me the records of the Chinese merchants and Chinese immigration and settlements in the city. She also introduced me to Art Joyce, an author and journalist at the *Nelson Daily News*. Art gave me the articles about the history of Chinatown in Nelson that he had published in the newspapers. In 2019, I had the opportunity to meet Greg Nesteroff, a historian and journalist in Nelson. Later on, he bought a piece of paper written in Chinese characters from eBay. It was an announcement from the Nelson chapter of the Chinese Nationalist League. He gave it to me so that I could use it to illustrate the activities of that political party in Nelson. To all these wonderful people, I extend my grateful thanks.

Warren Chow, my son, assisted me in finding information about the Chinese immigrants who lived in Nelson and Cranbrook. And all my children supported me and offered me assistance whenever I needed it in my research and writing. Bing Chow, my husband, gave me the freedom to leave home whenever I needed, which gave me the opportunity to visit and find out about the Chinese settlements in the various cities in the Kootenay. Indeed, I am blessed and very fortunate to have a wonderful and understanding family. Now I want to say "Thank you very much" to every member in my family.

I also want to acknowledge the management, curators and staff at the Royal British Columbia Museum and Archives who assisted me in my research and gave me permission to use the facilities in the archives. As well, the BC Historical Newspapers digital archive available through the UBC Library Open Collections site was of great value in researching newspaper coverage of the Chinese in the Kootenay communities.

If anyone has been missed out in these acknowledgements, it is not intentional, and I apologize for any oversights.

About the Author

Lily Chow, a researcher and writer, immigrated to Canada in 1967. She possesses a master's degree of Education and has taught high school in Prince George and Mandarin at the University of Northern British Columbia. Her book publications include *Blossoms in the Gold Mountains* (2018), *Blood and Sweat over the Railway Tracks* (2014), *Chasing Their Dreams* (2000), and *Sojourners in the North* (1996). She also has written articles for *Ricepaper Magazine* and the *Prince George Citizen*. In her twenty-five years of writing, she has won the Jeanne Clarke Memorial Award (1996) and certificates of merit from the BC Historical Federation in 2014 and 2019. Her volunteer services have been awarded with two Queen Elizabeth II's Jubilee Medals (2002 & 2012). In October 2022 she was appointed to the order of Canada. Currently, she resides in Victoria, BC.